Yuendumu Everyday

To my mothers —
Heidi, Kay, Linda, Lucy, Maggie, Ruth and Salwa

Yuendumu Everyday

Contemporary life in remote Aboriginal Australia

Yasmine Musharbash

Aboriginal
Studies
Press

First published in 2008 by Aboriginal Studies Press
Reprinted 2009

© Yasmine Musharbash, 2008

Aboriginal Studies Press
is the publishing arm of the
Australian Institute of Aboriginal and Torres Strait Islander
Studies.
GPO Box 553, Canberra, ACT 2601
Phone: (61 2) 6246 1183
Fax: (61 2) 6261 4288
Email: asp@aiatsis.gov.au
Web: www.aiatsis.gov.au/aboriginal_studies_press

National Library of Australia
Cataloguing-In-Publication data:

Author: Musharbash, Yasmine.
Title: Yuendumu everyday : contemporary life in a remote
Aboriginal settlement / Yasmine Musharbash.
ISBN: 9780855756611 (pbk.)
Notes: Includes index. Bibliography.
Subjects: Aboriginal Australians — Northern Territory
— Yuendumu. Warlpiri (Australian people) — Northern
Territory — Yuendumu. Warlpiri (Australian people) —
Social life and customs. Yuendumu (NT) — Social life and
customs.
Dewey Number: 305.89915

Printed by Blue Star Print Group, Australia

Cover image: © Liam Campbell

CONTENTS

ILLUSTRATIONS

FIGURES

TABLES

ACKNOWLEDGMENTS

I am lucky to be have been taught by three exceptional teachers, who kindled and fuelled my passion for anthropology: Lukas Werth (at Freie Universität Berlin) made me fall in love with ideas, the late Dawn Ryan (at Monash University) made me appreciate that anthropology is about people, and Nic Peterson (at the Australian National University) made me see the exciting in the real. Their mantra (ideas, people, data) sustained and guided me through my fieldwork and the writing of this book. It led to my focus on the everyday: the ideas encapsulated in and expressed through it, the mechanics of it, and the people living it.

My most heartfelt thank-yous go out to the people I lived with, who tolerated my presence and incessant questioning with good humour, who drew me into their life, let me participate and taught me so much, who made fieldwork such an enjoyable experience and through their friendships turned Yuendumu into a true home for me. Special thanks go to Kumunjayi Jakamarra Ross, Kumunjayi Napaljarri Ross, Yuurltu, Kumunayi, Gurtley, Kieran, ENR, Keith, Kumunjayi Napangardi, Eugene, Nana, Shane, NO, RO, Ruth Napaljarri Oldfield, Warungka, Jorna, Lizzie, Serita, Rosie, Jeannie, Jangala, Dadu, Victor, Cecily, Uni, Andrea, Warren, Watson, Sera, Regina, Valery, Kumunjayi Napurrurla Wilson, Kumunjayi Nampijinpa Daniels, and Kumunjayi Japanangka Granites.

I thank Yuendumu Council and the Central Land Council for issuing the necessary permits and always being of assistance. For being supportive, generous and helpful in many small and some larger emergencies, I thank Mt Theo Substance Misuse Programme and Jaru Pirrjirdi, Yuendumu Women's Centre, Warlukurlangu Artists Aboriginal Association, Warlpiri Media Association, Yuendumu Mining Co., and

Yuendumu Clinic. At Yuendumu and Alice Springs I am especially grateful to Megan Hoy and Tristan Ray, Charlie and Clancy, Sue Morrish and John Boffa, Ronnie and Leonnie Reinhardt, David Raftery, Liam Campbell, the Little Sisters, Frank and Wendy Baarda, Mamata Lewis, Pam Malden, Andrew Stojanowski (Yakajirri), Olaf Geerken, Tara Lackey, Rita Cattoni and Brett Badger, for thousands of cups of tea, fabulous conversation, encouragement, and once in while a quiet place to stay.

This book grew out of my PhD thesis, and I am deeply grateful for the financial assistance I received from the Australian National University during my PhD degree and from the University of Western Australia during my postdoctoral fellowship. At both institutions I found wonderful friends and colleagues, who in one way or another helped me along with this book, through critical engagement, passionate debate, helpful advice, thoughtful insights, most welcome help with the fiddly things, and more cups of tea. I would like to especially mention Jon Altman, Sallie Anderson, Marcus Barber, Emily Buckland, Victoria Burbank, Paul Burke, John Carty, Georgia Curran, Richard Davis, Derek Elias, Sue Fraser, Don Gardner, Katie Glaskin, Chris Gregory, Nick Harney, Melinda Hinkson, Ian Keen, Alex Leonard, David McGregor, Andrew McWilliam, Erik Meijaard, Francesca Merlan, Howard Morphy, David Nash, Damon Parker, Michael Pinches, Greg Rawlings, Tim Rowse, Alan Rumsey, Will Sanders, Dionisio Soares, John Taylor, Bob and Myrna Tonkinson, Allon Uhlmann, Andrew Walker, Jill Woodman and Michael Young.

Extra special thanks go to Debbie McDougall, Kevin Murphy and Raelene Wilding for their generosity with red ink. More extra special thanks to Françoise Dussart and Lee Sackett, for their fine comments on my thesis and their friendship. Heartfelt thanks also to the anonymous reviewer who made such insightful comments on an earlier draft of this book, to Caroline Williamson for her considerate editing, and to Rhonda Black and the Aboriginal Studies Press team.

As always, I am deeply grateful to Heidi, Nazih, Dina and Yassin for accepting my choices, visiting me as often as they can, and looking after me from afar.

More than anybody else, 'that Jampijinpa', Nicolas Peterson, deserves my gratitude. Without him, this book would have never been written. He first suggested a PhD to me, he assisted me in coming to ANU and acquiring my scholarships, was the best supervisor a student could wish for and continues to be a wonderful friend. He helped me through every crisis, no matter whether at Yuendumu or Canberra, pushed me and my work when pushing was needed, always welcomed me in his office, even if it was three times in a day that I bothered him, and to this day most generously splashes red ink over everything I give him to read. Thank you very, very much for looking after me proper.

NOTE ON SPELLING AND ORTHOGRAPHY

I follow the Warlpiri spelling as taught by the Institute for Aboriginal Development, Alice Springs, and at Yuendumu School, based on the orthography developed by Kenneth Hale (for more information see Hale 1990). Warlpiri words are italicised on the first occasion that they are used.

All Warlpiri words used in this book are listed and translated in the glossary at the end of the book. I have relied extensively on an electronic copy of the manuscript of the Warlpiri dictionary made available by Robert Hoogenraad. Next to the anthropological literature, the Warlpiri dictionary was the most used source in this book. As it is unedited, unpaginated and comes in a number of files, I have not been able to reference it properly. All elaborations on Warlpiri words in the book were made in accordance with it, and if I found a different use than those listed in the dictionary, it has been noted.

A number of Aboriginal English terms are also used, and are typeset in italics to distinguish them from different meanings they might hold in standard English (e.g. camp and *camp*).

Kinship terms are sometimes presented in tables and figures using the standard abbreviations: M = mother; F = father; D = daughter; S = son; Z = sister; B = brother; C = child; W = wife; H= husband.

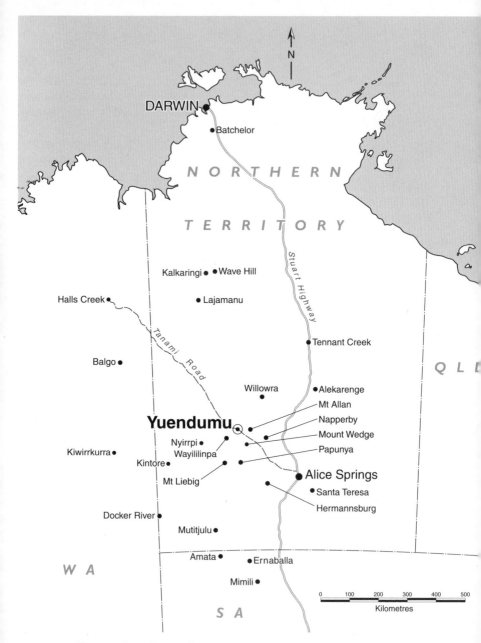

Figure 1: Central Australia

CHAPTER 1

Everyday life in a remote Aboriginal settlement

The starry night sky above us, we had arranged piles of blankets and pillows so that we could lounge comfortably on top of our mattresses, a fire crackling cheerfully on the side, and a television set on a long extension cord in front of us. We were watching *Who Wants To Be A Millionaire*, a game show popular in Yuendumu. Tamsin, a seventeen-year-old Warlpiri girl, came to join our row of bedding, nestling down between her mother Celeste and myself. 'Who wants to be a millionaire?' the game master asked on the television. 'Me', 'me', 'me', the residents of the *camp* shouted in reply, Tamsin loudest of them all. 'What would you do with a million dollars?' I asked her.

Tamsin: I would build a house.
Yasmine: Where?
Tamsin: In Yuendumu.
Yasmine: And what will it look like?
Tamsin: It's really, really big, with lots of rooms, and every room has furniture in it. Sofas, and beds, new blankets, and tables and chairs. And every room has a stereo in it, and a television, and a video player and a playstation.
Yasmine: And who will live in that house?
Tamsin: Me.
Yasmine: And who else?
Tamsin: Nobody else. Just me!
Yasmine: Won't you be lonely?
Tamsin: No, I'll have peace and quiet. And I'll keep the door locked. I won't let anybody in.

The fantasy of winning a million dollars provides a license to dream about what one desires most. Since ever having access to so much money is utterly unrealistic for most Warlpiri people, the dream might as well be about something one will never get, acquire or achieve. In Tamsin's case this was her own new house filled with large numbers of desirable items such as new blankets, video recorders and playstations. This is understandable enough, given the impoverished material circumstances in which people at Yuendumu live and the long waiting lists for council-provided housing. Her desire for material goods is identical to that of many other Warlpiri people.

But there was more to the fantasy. As I lay on those swags, cosy not only because of the warmth of the fire, the blankets and pillows, but also in the presence of the people around me, my body comfortably snuggled close to those of my friends, curled around Tamsin on one side and with Greta behind me, her arm slung over my waist, Tamsin's desire to be alone in that dream house struck me as extraordinary. Living in the *camps* of Yuendumu, I had taken quite some time to get used to being constantly surrounded by and involved with other people all day and every day. Whenever I sat down with a book in the shade of a tree, people immediately joined me and started conversations, assuming I was sad or lonely. Once I went to get firewood on my own, only to get into trouble afterwards. I could have been bitten by a snake! Gotten lost! Been assaulted by strangers or spooky beings! And had I forgotten the people who were *looking after* me, those who were responsible for me? Imagine the trouble they would get into if something happened to me!

No, being alone was never an option in Yuendumu. And after a while I came to appreciate the constant company, and even to depend on it. Once I stayed in a friend's guestroom in Alice Springs, and woke up panic-stricken in the middle of the night, because I couldn't hear anybody else breathing!

Of course, relations weren't always as smooth as they were on that evening we were watching *Who Wants To Be A Millionaire*. Fights broke out frequently and then people left the company of those they were fighting with, but only to join others, never to be alone.

Yet here was Tamsin yearning for a space that was hers and hers alone. While her desire for material goods can be understood literally, the space inside the house requires, I believe, more interpretive work, and can be better 'read' in ways suggested by the French philosopher Gaston Bachelard. His *The Poetics of Space* (1994, first published in 1958) is a psycho-philosophical treatise on the house as a primary metaphor in thoughts, memories, and dreams. He describes how it is 'reasonable to say we "read a house," or "read a room," since both room and house are psychological diagrams that guide writers and poets in their analysis of intimacy' (1994: 38). This is not only true of poets and writers. Tamsin's fantasy house strikes me as an excellent if puzzling 'diagram of her analysis of intimacy'. The house in her fantasy is a space she can only dream about. It is a space where she is independent: the house contains quantities of everything she needs. It is a space filled with peace and quiet, where she is happy. It is a space where she is in control; she holds the keys to the doors.

Why would a seventeen-year-old Warlpiri girl living in Yuendumu formulate such a curious desire? The answer lies, I believe, in considering more deeply the issue of intimacy. What does Bachelard mean by 'intimacy' when he calls the house a diagram of an analysis of intimacy? As I understand him, he conceptualises intimacy as a kind of innermost protected idea of selfhood, a way of being and seeing oneself. If we are to truly understand what Tamsin expresses in her fantasy, we need to understand not only the wished-for intimacy, but how and why this differs from more common Warlpiri forms of intimacy. These find expression in the ways in which Warlpiri people define their personhood in everyday social practice by relating to each other. Exploration of such Warlpiri expressions of intimacy opens paths towards understanding the contradiction inherent in Tamsin's wish for a house of her own, with keys to lock the doors so she can exclude others, while at the same time defining herself through relating to others. This contradiction arises, I contend, out of the dynamics between the social practices of contemporary everyday life in a remote Aboriginal settlement and the realities of living in a First World nation state.[1] Exploring these dynamics and the meanings encapsulated within them is the central aim of this book.

My way of approaching this aim is to further problematise, question, and unpack the metaphor which encapsulates the space of intimacy of Tamsin's fantasy: the notion of the house. Bachelard (1994: 6) aims to 'show that the house is one of the greatest powers of integration for the thoughts, memories and dreams of mankind'. I do not wish to diminish what he says about the house; in fact, I believe its metaphoric potency cannot be emphasised strongly enough. However, I take issue with extending this metaphoric potency to all of 'mankind' in a unified way.

While Bachelard shows *how* the house has great metaphoric potency, I find that the essay 'Building Dwelling Thinking' (1993, first published in 1951) by the German philosopher Martin Heidegger best explains *why* this should be so. He identifies the ways these three practices are related to each other. In order to dwell, one has to build; and the way one builds mirrors the way one thinks: which in turn is inspired by the way one dwells, creating a processual cycle. This goes beyond Bachelard, who asks: 'if the house is the first universe for its young children, the first cosmos, how does its space shape all subsequent knowledge of other space, of any larger cosmos?' (Bachelard 1994: viii).[2] In Heidegger's idea there is no unidirectionality; instead he demonstrates how the three practices are interdependent and how, as a series, they encapsulate ideology; and by that I mean nothing more or less than a socio-culturally specific way of looking at the world and being in the world. The ideology, or the multidirectional connectivity between the physical structures in which people live (building), their social practices (exemplified through their practices of dwelling) and their world views (thinking), can be expressed – and here Bachelard again is useful – in metaphors of great potency. In the Western context, this ideology can be symbolised by a stereotypical house:

In his essay, Heidegger commences his theory on building–dwelling–thinking with the assertion that the verbs 'to build', 'to dwell' and 'to think' stem from the same etymological root in Germanic languages. From this alone we can infer that Heidegger is concerned with a socio-culturally and historically particular series of building–dwelling–thinking, valid in Germanic or, more contemporarily, Western contexts. The etymological link in his particular example is interesting but dispensable; significant are the meanings he attaches to the series, meanings which substantially transcend the linguistic level. My point (not necessarily Heidegger's) is that it is more than likely that the same series may exist with different implications but equal potency in other (non-Western) contexts, independent of the presence or absence of etymological links. If this is true, then such ideologies, or the interconnectivity between the physical structures in which people dwell, their social practices and their world views, can be metaphorically encapsulated in symbols for different physical structures of domestic space. Such symbols representing the physical structures express the 'integration for the thoughts, memories and dreams' of the people who live in them. In short, each such symbol can be taken as a metaphor embodying the socio-cultural series of building–dwelling–thinking and encapsulating a particular way of looking at and being in the world.

I propose that in the Warlpiri context the term that encapsulates the parallel metaphoric load to the house in the Western context is *ngurra* — a conceptual term of profound depth, encompassing multiple levels of meaning ranging from the mundane to the ontological. Most immediately, ngurra can be translated as camp, burrow, or nest; but this meaning of 'shelter' expands to include place, land, country, and fatherland. On an emotional plane ngurra means home, as well as the place with which a person is associated by conception, birth, ancestry, or ritual obligation. Socially its meanings encompass the people living in one *camp*, being one family, being from the same place. Temporally, ngurra is a label for the period of twenty-four hours, and is used to designate numbers of days or nights. Lastly, it is used for socio-spatial designations during ritual. Warlpiri people have two iconographic representations for ngurra:

concentric circles which may serve to represent the entire range of meanings listed above, or any context-specific ones; and

a combination of one horizontal and a number of vertical lines.

The latter iconographic design always denotes a specific *camp* in which particular people have slept, with the horizontal line depicting the windbreak and each vertical line standing for a person.

Following the Warlpiri iconography, throughout this book I use the first design of concentric circles and the Warlpiri term ngurra when I refer to the entire range of meanings, and the Aboriginal English term *camp* and the iconographic depiction using lines when referring to a particular *camp* or when reproducing maps of particular sleeping arrangements. In short, a *camp* is one of many possible manifestations,

.and represents only one of a number of levels of signification contained within the term ngurra. Or, put differently, a *camp* in this regard is the equivalent of an actual house (rather than the house as symbol). In terms of the series of building–dwelling–thinking, a *camp* and an actual house are both manifestations of two aspects, building (the material structure) and dwelling (social practices of relating to domestic space). Ngurra, on the other hand, encapsulates the entire Warlpiri series of building–dwelling–thinking; as a term, concept and metaphor it contains Warlpiri ideology in exactly the same way as the metaphor of the house does in the West. From this it follows that we can say that

represents building–dwelling–thinking in the West, and

represents building–dwelling–thinking Warlpiri way.

Since the creation of the settlement of Yuendumu, sedentisation and the advent of Western-style housing as entailed in the processes of colonialism and post-colonialism, Warlpiri people have been experiencing an intersecting of these two series of building–dwelling–thinking. This intersection shapes the contemporary settlement everyday, those things that people consider normal, routine and mundane; it shapes contemporary Warlpiri ways of being in the world. It also shapes Tamsin's fantasy. Here she is, wishing for a house, her own, just for herself, and smack-bang in the middle of Yuendumu, no less, while cosily snuggled up to her mothers in a *camp*. Taking into account her way of being in the world, her experiences of settlement life, her life history, we must ask ourselves whether she wishes for a house and only a house, or whether the imagery of the house in her fantasy also stands for something else.

Like those pictures used in psychological testing, in which, depending on how one looks at them, one sees either an old woman or a young one but never both, houses at Yuendumu, I contend, also have at least two mutually exclusive meanings. The house, which at Yuendumu materially embodies the intersection of the two series of building–dwelling–thinking, in Tamsin's fantasy is a vehicle for expressing a particular desire; but it can also stand for the expectations which the Australian state has of Warlpiri people.

The framework of the book

If we credit the house with the metaphoric potential which Bachelard ascribed to it, state-provided housing can be viewed as carrying a specific agenda: the imposition of a particular way of 'thinking'.[3] This goes some way to explain why housing, from the onset of the Australian state's engagement with Aboriginal people, has been and continues to be among the biggest items in Australia's annual Aboriginal Affairs portfolio budgets, consistently accounting for between 25 and 35 per cent of the total (Sanders 1990: 41).[4] Viewed from the perspective of the Western series of building–dwelling–thinking, Yuendumu houses stand for the expectations the state has of Indigenous people — that they become like 'us'. The always 'over-crowded', often dysfunctional and partly derelict houses at Yuendumu become an expression of the Warlpiri 'failure' to comply, a failure to be in the world in 'acceptable' ways. Yet Warlpiri people want Western-style houses: council discussions of housing allocation are by far the most heated as well as the best attended meetings; and Tamsin, asked what she would do with a million dollars, answers that she wants a house.

Why do Warlpiri people want those suburban houses so badly, seeing that their practices of dwelling and their ways of thinking about and being in the world conflict so starkly with the values that houses are imbued with in the mainstream? In order to understand more fully the nature of the contradictions between the state's expectations and Warlpiri people's desires, I employ the lens of the intersecting series of building–dwelling–thinking to the ethnographic data presented throughout this book.

The ethnography of this book is based on the dramas of everyday life as they unfolded in the *camps* of Yuendumu during my fieldwork, and particularly revolves around the three values that seemed to shape the everyday as I experienced it: mobility, intimacy and immediacy. I suggest that these values (mobility, immediacy and intimacy) are constitutive of the contemporary settlement everyday because they are manifestations of the Warlpiri series of building–dwelling–thinking. In order to make this case, to convey a sense of the 'feel' of Yuendumu everyday life, to illustrate the interconnectedness between intimacy, immediacy and mobility, and to shed light on the particular socio-cultural forms these take, I provide extensive case studies of significant everyday interactions, situations, conversations, and experiences.

The clues to understanding the ways in which people are in the world and the view(s) they take of the world lie hidden underneath the commonplace, and can be revealed by analysing the everyday. By 'the everyday' I mean those things that people consider 'normal' and often (no matter whether in an Indigenous or non-Indigenous context) not worthy of reflection. The strength of anthropology as I see it, and here I am drawing on *Outline of a Theory of Practice* (1977) by the French sociologist Pierre Bourdieu, lies in understanding and explaining exactly such apparently mundane matters as who sleeps where and next to whom; why people are mobile in the way they are; where the boundaries between public and private lie; how food and other material items are distributed; how people relate to each other; and what we can learn from the ways in which people use their bodies. Kinship, ritual, exchange and so forth all can be formulated in esoteric terms, but ultimately, I believe, they need to be understood as grounded in and arising out of everyday social practice. Primarily focussing on the former, anthropology has largely ignored the contemporary everyday of remote Aboriginal settlements.[5]

The case studies in this book centre around one particular *camp* (a *jilimi* or women's *camp*) at Yuendumu, and I use them to consider Warlpiri people's high residential mobility by examining the flow of people through *camps*. I present examples of Warlpiri sleeping arrangements, which change on a nightly basis, and interpret them as expressions of the current state of social affairs and statements about the person. These discussions are framed with a view of understanding the connections between people and how they are negotiated, reinforced, maintained or broken; or, how Warlpiri ideas of intimacy are lived out in everyday life. I also explore Warlpiri sociality during the day, mapping the movements of people in and out of *camps* and throughout the settlement, to elaborate how the particular feeling of immediacy, that so characterises the contemporary Yuendumu everyday, is created.

The contemporary everyday, however, cannot be understood without relating it to the 'before'. The relationship between 'then' and 'now' entails continuities, changes and ruptures which critically shape the here and now. The most decisive date of rupture in this sense is 1946, the year Yuendumu was set up as a government ration station. Analysis of contemporary everyday social practice at Yuendumu needs to proceed from an understanding of what the situation was before 1946, and what has happened since to affect it. In regard to this crucial date, Warlpiri people themselves distinguish between two types of historical past: [6] the *olden days* and *the early days*. The Aboriginal English term *olden days* is used to label pre-contact and early contact times, characterised by a nomadic lifestyle, a hunting and gathering economy and an elaborate ritual life. *Early days*, on the other hand, is the period of initial settlement and strict institutional control which brought with it, among other things, Christianisation, sedentisation, and a new economy.

Quite a few people still alive today experienced the *olden days*, growing up and living in *the bush* before either coming voluntarily or being brought by force to live at Yuendumu. Others do not remember the *olden days* themselves and grew up during the *early days*. Their children and grandchildren, on the other hand, were born and raised in Yuendumu; to them the *olden days* and the *early days* are known as stories from the past, and their lives and histories are intricately linked with the settlement of Yuendumu as their home.

Throughout the book, I examine some of the key ruptures, continuities and transformations in social everyday practices that have taken place in the last sixty years or so. I focus on the impact sedentisation has had on social practices relating to domestic space, elaborating on past as well as contemporary residential arrangements, and within this specifically the increased significance of women's *camps*, or jilimi.[7] I suggest that jilimi and their older female residents have become central foci of everyday social life generally, in particular for young mothers and their children. Also, I establish how life in the jilimi is intensely social, not least since the great majority of people who pass through them are unemployed and live on social security payments. Inclusion of this historical perspective allows me to illustrate how contemporary forms of intimacy, immediacy and mobility are the result of Warlpiri engagements with both the present and the past.

The arena within which I explore these contemporary forms lies in the interplay between Warlpiri people's social practices and the spatiality of the settlement, which enables me to analyse more precisely the ways in which the two series of building–dwelling–thinking intersect at Yuendumu. The crux of the book, then, is to unveil the meanings contained in Tamsin's fantasy and through this to elucidate how and why the imagery of the house can serve to express the dilemmas of contemporary settlement life.

Fieldwork, ethnography and key protagonists

I began research at Yuendumu in 1994, and I have returned there every year since. The most concentrated research took place between 1999 and 2001, during which time I lived at Yuendumu for eighteen months. The Warlpiri 'everyday' described in this book is different from the everyday of previous decades, and, it can safely be assumed, will be different again from everyday life in the future. I emphasise this temporal dynamic of the 'ethnographic present' by using the past tense and the present tense interchangeably in the descriptive parts. The past tense flags that the period of research for this book is over, and things are already changing. People have passed away, children have been born, new marriages have been made and others have deteriorated, and government policies and incomes have changed, as indeed has the physical appearance of Yuendumu. New houses are being built, others have fallen into disuse, *humpies* (shelters of corrugated iron and bush materials) occur less and less often, there seem to be fewer jilimi and many are smaller than they were in the 1990s, new roads have been sealed, and so forth. The present tense, on the other hand, is used as a literary device to convey the distinct atmosphere of the immediacy of everyday life at Yuendumu.

Fieldwork was conducted in classical participant observation style. Since 1994 I have spent more than three years in total living in *camps* with Warlpiri people, who, fortunately, insisted on my incessant participation in everything they themselves were involved in. My co-residents, neighbours, friends and I experienced the everyday I describe and analyse, and this everyday was created, lived and shaped by all of us, including me.

There is no point even trying to write myself out of the book. While I doubt that I caused major shifts and changes, my presence and participation was certainly responsible for the crystallisation of certain disputes that otherwise may have lain dormant, and for an increase in options for a number of people through access to my resources, in particular my Toyota.[8] The Warlpiri view of Toyotas is that they should run until they die. This meant that as soon as I arrived back in the *camp* from one trip, other people turned up (or were waiting already) requesting a lift, a firewood trip, or just to go *cruising* around the settlement. On average, I drove about 1000 kilometres a week. A substantial part of this mileage was taken up by just driving in and around Yuendumu, but we also frequently went further afield. The Toyota loaded to maximum capacity, we went on hunting trips throughout the Tanami Desert; we drove to settlements all around central Australia to visit people's relatives or to participate in 'Sports Weekends'; we travelled in large convoys for *sorry business* (mortuary rituals), *women's business* (women's ceremonies), and *business* (initiation ceremonies); and of course we often went to Alice Springs (to shop and to visit people in hospital and in jail). Having the Toyota in the field also allowed me to gain a comprehensive insider's view of Warlpiri mobility.

While participation in such extensive mobility was physically exhausting, immediacy was a challenge in other ways. Immediacy shaped my fieldwork every day in multiple ways, and I struggled to come to terms with it (and in the end, came to miss it very much when away from Yuendumu). Immediacy meant that I could not plan ahead. Specific data collection, language lessons, everything happened when it happened, rather then when I wanted it to happen. Big events (such as mortuary rituals in the case of death) overruled any other activity, but even without them, everything had to be slotted in with what was happening in the settlement on that particular day, and coordinated with large numbers of people and their assorted ideas and desires. Appointments simply did not work. Once I let go of my ideas of scheduling and planning (and believe me, this was no easy task!), once my life and my fieldwork agendas fell into sync with whatever it was that happened on any given day in Yuendumu, I discovered a way of being in the world very different from the one I was used to. There is a fundamental difference between waking up in the morning and knowing what lies ahead and waking up in the morning full of curiosity about what the day might bring. It not only meant experiencing time in new ways, but also entailed a fundamental shift in my ways of relating to others. Immediacy meant that rather than seeking to fulfil my own desires (be they a particular interview, a hunting trip, or listening to *olden time* stories), I learned to have them fulfilled by fully participating in the collective push and pull of 'being in the present'.

This, in turn, taught me much about Warlpiri forms of intimacy, of how to know and how to relate to others in Warlpiri ways. Many anthropologists before me have noted the Aboriginal maxim of 'knowing because of doing' (rather than through verbal answers), and this is not only true for ritual but also for everyday life (see amongst others Harris 1987; Morphy 1983; Myers 1986a: 294). Only through living with Warlpiri people, through being in the same space and time with them, sharing activities and stories, and, not unimportantly, through submitting to the wishes of others did I learn what intimacy in this socio-cultural context means: a reciprocal awareness of the other as a person, of their life histories, their desires, their quirks, their habits, and a willingness to let this awareness influence how one acts in the world.

Out of the three values underpinning everyday life at Yuendumu, intimacy is perhaps the hardest to convey in a book. To bring some sense of it to the reader, most of the case studies revolve around a small number of key protagonists, with the aim of familiarising the reader not only with Warlpiri social practices but also with a range of actual Warlpiri people.[9]

Next to Tamsin, these key protagonists of the book are Tamsin's adopted mother Celeste, Celeste's mother Polly, and two classificatory sisters of Polly: Joy and Nora. Joy was my first 'mother', as her husband, Old Jakamarra, had been the one who when I first came to Yuendumu had given me my skinname [subsection term] 'Napurrurla', thus making me his classificatory daughter. This meant that I was henceforth able to work out the ways in which I should relate to all Warlpiri people I met. As I was Old Jakamarra's 'daughter' Napurrurla, Joy Napaljarri became my adopted mother, as did all other Napaljarri women. In the same way, I would now relate to all other women with my own skinname, Napurrurla, as my classificatory sisters, Celeste amongst them.[10] Nora, another Napaljarri and hence 'mother' of mine, was one of my co-residents in the jilimi (and in some other *camps* later on), and instrumental in my education about *olden days* and *early days*. After I had a fight with Joy, Polly adopted me, and to this day in Yuendumu I am known as Polly-*kurlangu*, belonging to Polly. These four women were some of my key informants, and those still alive remain close friends, and indeed adoptive relatives.

In this book I introduce different aspects of these four women: how they relate to each other, how they related to others in the *camp* we were staying at the time, how they presented their selves in the ways in which they positioned their bodies at night, and how they cooperated with some people and fought with others. All of these descriptions are presented by me as author. As the nature of my own personal relationship to each of these women is particular and unique, I here provide sketches in narrative form about the personal ways in which I related to them, recapitulating interactions between these women and myself as they took place around the time we all lived together in the jilimi. These vignettes represent my own portraits of the four women as I experienced them, and hopefully will convey to the reader the nature of our relationships, which, I am sure, has impacted on how I represent them in the case studies throughout this book.

Joy Napaljarri, 'my first mother'

In the evenings, Joy and I often sat around the fire, telling stories. Many were about other white women Joy *grew up*. 'And then I helped that anthropologist, but she left me for that West Camp mob, and that linguist, she left for Leah, and that Women's Centre coordinator, she left, too.' Her stories inevitably ended with: 'And now I got Napurrurla, she is like a real daughter, she'll look after me for a long time, and when I get my house, she'll move in, too.' Joy's name was right at the top of the list at council; the next house to be built in Yuendumu was going to be hers. 'When we move into that house, it won't be like those other houses, our house will have a garden with flowers and an orange tree, and a green lawn. Inside, there'll be curtains, and chairs and sofas, and pictures on the walls. And everybody will have their own room. One for me and Kiara [her grand-daughter], one for Napurrurla and one for Lydia [her daughter].' I liked sitting around that fire, in the evenings and sharing dreams — and often it reconciled us after the clashes we had during the day. It was nice to be compared favourably to 'the other' Kardiya [*Whitefella*] women, those ones that 'left' Joy. Sitting around that fire, we felt snug, warm and content, looking forward to the future, when our dreams would come true.

In the jilimi, every once in a while, somebody, most often Joy, would decide it was time to clean. 'This place is a mess, let's clean up!' Cleaning means a trip to the shop to buy a rake, a broom, and Ajax. The rubbish in the yard would be raked up and burned, and the bathrooms would be sprinkled with Ajax, scrubbed with brooms and hosed down with water. One time, Joy said to me, 'Go back to the shop and get some Pine-O-Clean'. When I came back, she opened the bottle, generously splashed it all over the bathroom and stood in the middle of it, her hands on her hips, looking expectant. After a couple of minutes, her face dropped and she murmured, 'Maybe it only works for *Whitefellas*.'

In the end, Joy and I did not get along, and I, like all the other white women before me, 'left' her. I always felt I disappointed and hurt her gravely. Her biggest dream was having her own house, Kardiya-style, and she knew that on her own she could not create and maintain a suburban dream house in the middle of Yuendumu. Her hope was that my presence, the presence of a Kardiya in her house, would achieve that. We fought a lot, and when she finally got her own house, I decided to stay in the jilimi and did not move in with her. I always felt that for her I was a disappointment in the same way the Pine-O-Clean was. In ads on TV she had seen what it could achieve: clean gleaming bathrooms with tiles in which your face would be reflected. The Pine-O-Clean did not fulfil its promise, that bathroom never sparkled, and I did not move in with her; and thus, although she was so close to achieving her dream of living in a Kardiya-style house, it was always my fault that it did not eventuate.

Celeste Napurrurla, 'my sister'

The first time I saw Celeste, I was living in Old Jakamarra's *camp* and she came over to pick up Joy for a Night Patrol shift. Celeste is small, a head shorter than me at least. There she was, looking fierce in a large black bomber jacket with NIGHT PATROL written in silver letters on the back, swinging a big *nullahnullah* in her left hand, a black beanie on her head. After she left with Joy I said to Old Jakamarra, 'Who was that?' He chuckled. 'Your sister that one.'

Later, Joy and I moved into the jilimi and Joy resumed working full time at the school's Literacy Centre. Because of that and her many other responsibilities, she asked Celeste to keep an eye on me and make me tea and damper in the mornings. In retrospect I think the main reason she asked Celeste and not anybody else was that she never perceived Celeste as a threat in respect to her 'ownership' of me. Celeste is excellent in arranging domestic matters, but nobody thinks she is too bright when it comes to politics; neither is she pushy. And while Celeste's value as an anthropological informant is most limited, as a person to hang out with, to live with, and to be around, she is bliss.

Celeste made sure I had a break once in a while. This is not to say that she didn't have her own agenda. She was working around the jilimi all day long, looking after children and old people there, preparing food and organising firewood and sleeping arrangements, and it was when she insisted I needed a break that she could have one, too. And in the mornings we managed to stay in bed longer because of each other. I kept thinking, 'As long as Celeste is not up, I won't need to get up either'. So I spent contented extra minutes in my swag listening to the clatter in the jilimi, pretending to be still asleep, once in a while peeping out from underneath my blankets to make sure Celeste was still asleep underneath hers. One morning as I emerged for a quick glance, she did the same at the same moment. Having caught each other at it, we laughed and she said, 'Oh, now we have to get up after all'.

One of my favourite memories of Celeste is of a very, very hot summer afternoon when we borrowed a fan and went into her room to have a siesta. There we are lying on the blankets with the fan keeping us moderately cool. Celeste's steady breathing next to me is as always the most soothing sound. I keep drifting in and out of sleep, once in a while opening my eyes for a glance to the outside. Through the half-open door I can see the roof of the verandah, the wall dividing the verandah from the yard and in between them a strip of blue, blue sky. Occasionally there is a cloud in it, sometimes two; sometimes there is none.

Nora Napaljarri, 'another mother'

When finally, after many months, I had my big fight with Joy and the two of us stood on the jilimi's verandah yelling at each other, it was Nora who ended our fight. She was sitting at the other end of the verandah next to a small cooking fire, making tea and damper. In the middle of our yelling, she calmly said, 'Napurrurla, come over, your tea is ready'. I went and sat down with her, accepting a pannikin full of tea and putting chops on the fire for us. Joy stormed off. When the chops were done, I gave one to Nora and one to Polly and ate one myself. Polly nodded towards the door of Joy's room and said, 'Too cheeky, that one. I will be your mother now', and Nora nodded in agreement. Up until that moment I had not been sure whether the fight with Joy was 'a good idea'. Emotionally it was more than overdue; rationally I was unsure about the consequences it would have. What I had not counted on was the presence of somebody like Nora, whose experience in politics and negotiations is considerable.

Nora had 'won' a 'medal from the Queen' for organising Yuendumu Night Patrol, she had been a big *business woman*, a skilful and experienced singer, dancer, and painter. She was cranky a lot when I lived with her, often because she was ageing too quickly. While very much alive and full of ideas, her bones hurt and walking became more and more difficult. To be limited by one's own body is most frustrating, and Nora did not give in easily. To have been powerful once and now to be becoming 'just another old lady' was very hard for her. In turn, I often found her demands on me a challenge, mainly because they were made with an almost royal air. There was no way to refuse a request of Nora's. Thus, I would drive her to the shop, to the clinic, to look for her grandson, or to go hunting, and I would bring her meat, tea, fruit, and soft drinks from the shop whenever she asked. And it must be said that she always reciprocated; she would sing songs or perform love magic for me in the evenings, and sometimes she would slip me a twenty dollar note on pension days.

Two years after I left Yuendumu, I rang up, as I often do. This time, Nora was around and she came to the phone to talk to me. She told me about the house she had moved into in the meantime, about her grandsons, her sons and other gossip. Then she said, 'Napurrurla, I am poor one, your mother has no skirt and no blouse, no shoes and no blankets'. This is the Warlpiri way of asking me to send up some things for her, but as I was broke at the time I had to tell her that I was *dolla-wangu* — without money. 'Oh poor bugger, my daughter,' she said. 'I'll send you one hundred dollar.'

Polly Napaljarri, 'my mother'

The first day of cold time: my sisters and I return home to the jilimi from that day's hunting. In our absence, the others have cleaned up. We join them in the yard, where there are two fires: one smouldering with lots of thick white smoke in which the rubbish burns, and one on which Nangala is making fresh damper. The white smoke of the rubbish fire against the crisp blue sky reminds me of the potato fires that are lit in my German village in autumn. For the first time in years I feel homesick. One of my grandmothers asks, 'What's wrong, Napurrurla?' and passes my answer on to the others. 'Napurrurla is thinking of home, little bit sad one, poor bugger.' Polly, without replying, gets up. She takes a rake lying in the yard and starts to dance with it around the rubbish fire. She dances, first the way Warlpiri women dance in ceremonies, with quivering, slightly bent legs and abrupt movements. Then she starts mimicking the movements of the young girls at disco nights: circling her hips, faster and faster. Her dance becomes more and more lewd. Everybody claps and sings and laughs. At night, when my sisters and I are lying in our swags next to each other, we are still laughing. 'That Polly, she's clown woman, that one.'

Some months later. I am in the Big Shop and have just heard the *bad news*. One of Polly's nieces has passed away. As I leave the shop, I can hear wailing coming from all directions. I hurry to the jilimi and start hugging and wailing with the women who are sitting lined up on the verandah. As I turn around I see Polly. She is sitting alone, crouched in the cold ashes of last night's fire. She has already shaved off her hair, and her head and body are covered in grey ash. The only visible parts of her warm, brown skin are the tracks on her cheeks made by the flood of tears. Her wail pierces the afternoon air.

One day in summer, as I hang up my laundry on the barbed wire in the yard strung between poles as a clothes line, Polly comes over. There are wet blankets on either side of us and it is like standing in a tunnel. Polly is not lively, demanding, noisy or intimate, like most of the other women. She is quieter, and she mainly watches, mostly from a distance that she herself determines. Sometimes she looks like a young girl and sometimes she looks as old as she must be. She has had two husbands and eight children of whom four have passed away. She has twenty-two grandchildren and nineteen great-grandchildren. In the tunnel of blankets, she comes towards me, touches my head, says 'My daughter', and then she is gone.

Yuendumu

Having introduced the key themes and the main protagonists of this book, what remains is to set the scene by introducing the settlement of Yuendumu.[11] Located in central Australia, Yuendumu is situated about 300 kilometres north-west of the town of Alice Springs, in the south-eastern corner of the Tanami Desert that stretches from the Northern Territory towards Western Australia. Before sedentisation, Warlpiri people lived throughout the Tanami Desert, in an area roughly extending 500 kilometres to the north-west, about 250 kilometres to the north and

200 kilometres to the south of Yuendumu, and bordered in the east by Anmatyerre country. Warlpiri people had some previous experiences of engagement with non-Indigenous people from intermittently living and working at the early gold mines in the Tanami, the Wolfram mine at Mission Creek, and Mt Doreen pastoral station, and from the horrific 1928 Coniston Massacre (see Michaels 1987; Hinkson et al. 1997).

The first step in the government's effort to institutionalise sedentisation of Warlpiri people in the area was the setting up of three Warlpiri government ration depots by the Native Affairs Branch: Yuendumu, Warrabri (now called Alekarenge) and Hooker Creek (now called Lajamanu). Thus was the settlement of Yuendumu born in 1946. Long describes the development of such postwar settlements as aiming to

> control the shift of Aborigines to towns; to develop the potential of the reserves; to train the Aborigines in order that they might contribute to the development of the reserves in particular and of the country generally; and to provide health services to the Aborigines. (Long 1970: 199)

During the 1950s, a Baptist Mission was established at Yuendumu, and for a period of a few years this mission had charge of the management of the settlement. The mission ran a store, a school and a clinic, and later a kitchen was added for communal meals. In the mid-1950s a government supervisor took over the administration and operation of the settlement. Also around that time, the Yuendumu Cattle Company came into existence under government ownership and with workers' wages paid by the Department of Aboriginal Affairs (DAA).[12] In 1959 social security legislation was passed to include Aboriginal people, and from 1966 pensions and family payments started flowing to them. However, payment was often made via third parties, and unemployment payments were not generally paid in remote areas. A push to have 'direct' payments was instituted by Social Security and Aboriginal Affairs Minister Bill Wentworth in 1968, a year after the 1967 referendum that led to the Commonwealth Government assuming responsibility for various Aboriginal issues (see Sanders 1986: 115–16). At Yuendumu, direct and full payment of social security entitlements came into effect in 1969; simultaneously communal meals and the issuing of blankets ceased. In 1978 the first elected Yuendumu Council assumed responsibility for settlement administration after the withdrawal of DAA officials.

Of these developments, the direct receipt of social security has been identified by most social scientists as the single most significant factor determining the economic status of Aboriginal people and their relationship to the state.[13] Having carried out research in the late 1970s, Young wrote in relation to Yuendumu:

> the town has virtually no economic rationale. It is neither a market town, a mining centre, nor a centre for communications — functions which have been responsible for the growth of other towns in the [Northern] Territory. It remains dependent on the rest of Australia for almost every cent its community spends, and every article consumed (Young 1981: 56).

During Young's research, 19 per cent of the Indigenous population at Yuendumu received wages; during my research, if CDEP work (Community Development and Employment Program, a federal-government-run 'work for the dole' type program for Indigenous people) is included as wage labour, the number was around 29 per cent, or, put differently, Yuendumu had a 71 per cent unemployment rate. This stands in bleak contrast both to the overall Australian unemployment figures (around 6 per cent at the time of research), as well as to the overall Aboriginal rate, which Sanders estimated to encompass 44 per cent of non-employment income (Sanders, 1994: 1003). At the time of writing, there is much uncertainty about these financial arrangements, which were targeted in the Liberal Federal Government's 'NT Intervention' in the second half of 2007 (see Altman and Hinkson 2007 for descriptions and critiques). While I am here not concerned with the reasons underlying Yuendumu's extremely high rate of unemployment, they do present a significant context for the ethnography. The lack of employment is a distinguishing factor of life at Yuendumu; it is not only expressed through statistics but manifested, as I attempt to show throughout the book, in the ways Warlpiri people live their lives (see also Musharbash 2007).

Today, there are between 500 and 900 Indigenous residents living at Yuendumu, most of them Warlpiri people (and small numbers of Anmatyerre and Pintupi people).[14] An additional 100 residents are non-Indigenous. Socially, culturally, and socio-economically speaking, Aboriginal people, locally called *Yapa*, and non-Indigenous people, locally called *Kardiya*, constitute two distinct populations.[15] (Note that I follow this local terminology throughout the book, and employ the terms 'Kardiya' and 'non-Indigenous people' to refer to local non-Aboriginal people and the terms 'Yapa' or 'Warlpiri people' for local Aboriginal people.) In the main, Kardiya are living and working in Yuendumu as service providers. Except for Yuendumu Council, which always has a Yapa president (but a Kardiya town clerk), all organisations and institutions at Yuendumu are managed by Kardiya staff (see Appendix for descriptions of these organisations and institutions).

During the *early days*, Yuendumu had at its centre a gardened area adjacent to the houses of the Missionary and the Superintendent. Known as the Park, this area became flanked by an increasing number of Kardiya staff residences and buildings for Yuendumu's growing number of institutions (the school, the store, the soup kitchen, the clinic, and so forth). The residential arrangements for Yapa were located at some distance from the Park. Hinkson quotes two Yuendumu men describing early developments of settlement at Yuendumu:

> … in those days, the houses were just a few and only *kardiya* were living in the houses. But us, we used to live out in the camps or *humpies*. We never used to sleep close to the houses or the settlement at that time. We used to be a couple of miles, or at least a fair way from the settlement and the houses. For water, the women used to come and collect water with buckets and billy cans, in the evenings and in the mornings. […]
>
> … *kardiya* doesn't want *yapa* to come in close up because they might steal something. And *yapa* doesn't want to come in (Japanangka and Japangardi quoted in Hinkson 1999: 18).

Stories I was told confirm that in the *early days* there was a mutually maintained separation between Warlpiri people living at a significant distance from the centre of the settlement and non-Indigenous staff living in houses and working in buildings located around the Park. During these times, Yapa used to live in traditional shelters built out of bush materials, sometimes augmented by corrugated iron and sackcloth (so-called *humpies*). Above and beyond the spatial ordering of Kardiya living in centrally located houses and Yapa living in *camps* and *humpies* surrounding the settlement, the locations of Yapa living quarters followed the cardinal directions from which people had originally come 'in' to the settlement. Munn describes this spatial ordering in the mid to late 1950s thus (see also Meggitt 1962: 55):

> Mt. Doreen, Mt. Allan (and Coniston), and Vaughan Springs are areas that represent for the Warlpiri general regions in which different sections of the Yuendumu community based themselves in the recent past [...]. The camps of each segment are oriented accordingly: Mt. Doreen Ngalia camp to the west or north-west, and members of the northern community of Waneiga Warlpiri camp with them; the Mt. Allan Ngalia (also linked with Cockatoo Creek near Coniston) camp on the east or south-east of the other camps; the Vaughan Springs (and Mt. Singleton) people camp in the south-easterly clusters (Munn 1973: 11).

With the advent of the provision of housing for Aboriginal people at Yuendumu, more substantial residential arrangements began to surround the central administrative area, bringing Yapa closer to the settlement from their corresponding quarters and into more permanent structures. These structures (originally crude one- and two-bedroom huts with communal ablution blocks; see Keys 1999 for details of structures and history of housing at Yuendumu) were arranged in clusters, and over time these clusters became named and suburb-like entities. Originally there were four such 'suburbs', named after the cardinal directions as seen from the Park: East Camp, South Camp, West Camp and North Camp. (I spell Camp with a capital 'C' when referring to one of Yuendumu's 'suburbs', and with a lower case 'c' and in italics when referring to individual residences, *camps*.) Much has been made of this socio-geographical patterning of Yuendumu's four Camps, and more recent ethnographies have perpetuated the earlier observations by Munn and Meggitt (see amongst others Michaels 1986, 1994; Rowse 1998; Young and Doohan 1989). Jackson for example, obviously picking up on earlier reports by Meggitt and Munn, discusses location as an index of social identity and claims that 'in Yuendumu, for instance, people from different parts of the country live in different quarters' (1995: 19).

By claiming that orientation to traditional country determines residency, the four Camps have effectively been presented as not only residential units but as social units based on shared country affiliations. If this was the case originally, it is not true today. Life histories reveal that most Yuendumu residents have lived in different Camps at different times of their lives, with their residential choices motivated by a multiplicity of reasons, most of which do not have anything to do with country affiliation.[16] Looking at the composition of any one Camp today makes clear that its residents originally came from a number of areas. Moreover, the residential compositions of Yuendumu's Camps are in constant flux. The two interrelated issues of slow encroachment towards the Park and the splitting and growth of further new Camps compound this.[17]

Nowadays, Warlpiri people live in and name six Camps at Yuendumu: North Camp, South Camp, East Camp, West Camp, Inner West Camp, and Kulkurru Camp (see Figure 2). West Camp and Inner West Camp are separated by a football oval and have both independently grown so much that they are now considered to be two separate 'suburbs', or Camps. However, Kulkurru Camp is particularly pertinent, as it is the most recent. *Kulkurru* is the Warlpiri word for 'inside'; and this Camp is right next to the Park. Houses in what is now called Kulkurru Camp used to be exclusively occupied by non-Indigenous residents, but over the last decade or so Warlpiri people have moved into some of these houses, showing that the encroachment on the Park is continuing. Significantly, it was around the time that Warlpiri people moved into this part of Yuendumu that it acquired its Warlpiri name.

An inverted development is currently taking place in Yuendumu's south-west, in an area nicknamed Kardiyaville by some of the non-Indigenous population, because it has by now the largest concentration of non-Indigenous people and also experiences the greatest growth of new houses designated for non-Indigenous use.[18] Kardiyaville is a cluster of staff houses owned by the Department of Education and the Yuendumu Council, and more recently also by Warlpiri Media, the Mt Theo Substance Misuse and Youth Program, and the Clinic. Kardiyaville is located between Yuendumu's South Camp and Inner West Camp.

So what is Yuendumu like today? Except during the big summer rains, the drive from Alice Springs to Yuendumu takes three to four hours. The Tanami Road (which connects Alice Springs in the Northern Territory and Halls Creek in Western Australia, crossing the Tanami Desert) is not the rough track it once was; the first half between Alice Springs and Yuendumu is bituminised, and the rest is wider and is graded more regularly than before. More Yapa have cars than even a short time ago, and bigger cars as well, and there is a regular flow of traffic between Yuendumu and Alice Springs. The Yuendumu turn-off from the Tanami

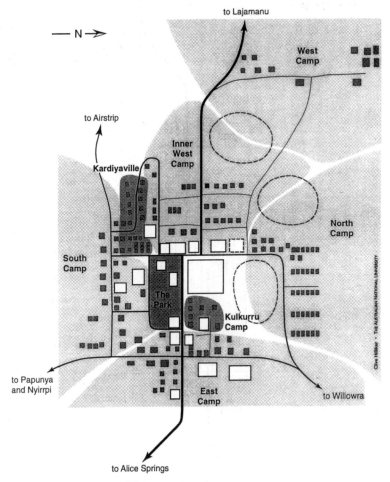

Figure 2: Spatial Camp divisions at Yuendumu

Road leads down two kilometres of partially sealed road, now flanked by small African mahogany trees planted by local CDEP workers, past the Police Station, and some occasional humpies, into Yuendumu's East Camp, and continues towards the Park. There the corrugated tin ruins of the old soup kitchen still stand, but are surrounded by an ever-growing number of newer buildings: the Old People's program, the new Council building, the new clinic (see Figure 3). On weekdays this area is bustling. People walk along the four streets flanking the Park, on

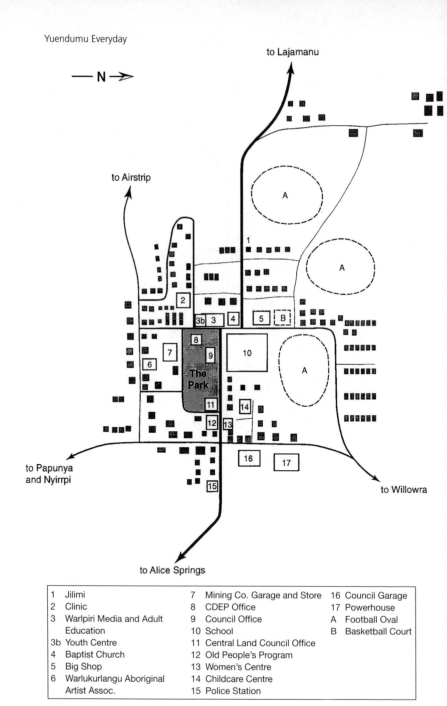

Figure 3: Yuendumu settlement (see Appendix, p. 158 for description of main organisations listed here).

their way to one organisation or another, to the shop, or the post office. Government and Yapa Toyotas drive around, picking up and dropping off people. Beyond the Park, in the Camps, the red Tanami sand is more prominent, a reminder that Yuendumu is indeed a desert settlement. Around the Yapa houses there are the obligatory packs of camp dogs, people sitting in groups in the shade or around their fires, and little kids running around playing. Music, both Yapa and Western, echoes from many of the houses, as well as from cars driving past. If it is windy, a small whirlwind might sweep through, carrying with it more red sand, empty chips packets, and perhaps someone's laundry. Kardiya houses are quieter and have higher fences, and some have gardens, religiously watered by their owners in an attempt at defying the desert.

All in all, Yuendumu is very much a typical central Australian remote Aboriginal settlement. It is bigger than most — some say it is the biggest in central Australia. And, of course, having started as a government ration station rather than a mission has its own implications, as does the fact that it accommodates a Baptist mission rather than some other denomination. A crucial difference between Yuendumu and most other settlements is that most of its organisations and institutions are independent of the council, meaning that many are more dynamic than their counterparts elsewhere, and also that Yuendumu has a much higher Kardiya population than most other settlements (both in total numbers and in proportion to the Yapa population). In the *camps* however, these differences are hardly noticeable. Accordingly, much of what is presented in this book did take place at Yuendumu, but could have happened in any one of many other remote communities.

CHAPTER 2

Camps, houses and ngurra

The realities of everyday life at Yuendumu are characterised by the intersection of the Warlpiri and the Western series of building–dwelling–thinking, a highly complex, ongoing and multidirectional social process. A first step towards understanding this process, and hence, the meanings contained in, expressed by and created through the contemporary everyday, lies in analytically disentangling different strands of the intersection.

I begin this work of disentangling by drawing on some anthropological analyses of the relationship between meaning and domestic space. These originate from the vast anthropological literature on the socio-cultural significance of structures of dwellings, beginning perhaps, with LH Morgan (1965, first published in 1881).[1] However, this literature has two shortcomings in regards to conceptualising how Warlpiri people interact with Western-style state-provided houses, which need to be acknowledged.

First, this literature has generally taken the 'house' as a key symbol expressing world views. Put differently, anthropologists have displayed an overwhelming tendency to focus on 'the house', while other forms of domestic structures, such as camps, igloos, caves, caravans and so forth, have largely been ignored. That is to say, anthropologists working with people who have domestic structures resembling a Western house (dwellings possessing walls, doors and ceilings) have undertaken studies in this vein, whereas anthropologists working with people living in differently structured dwellings have rarely focussed on issues relating to domestic space. Some might argue that dwellings that are unlike houses do not lend themselves to such analyses, but my own view is that this trend relates anthropologists' own inclinations. This can partly be explained by reference to the work of Heidegger and Bachelard, both of whom give good reasons why the Western mind (and hence, most anthropologists) favour the house. This book is an attempt to show that other types of dwellings, in this case the Warlpiri *camp*, carry as much meaning and in similar ways.

My second misgiving about the anthropological literature about domestic space is that much of it favours structure over social practice. Most studies identify the way in which a house represents the cosmos, for example, and pay little or no attention to the ways in which people live in these dwellings. Or in regards to Heidegger's series of building–dwelling–thinking, many anthropologists draw connections between building (the physical structures) and thinking (the ways of being in and conceptualising the world), but they ignore dwelling, the ways in which people relate to domestic space in everyday life through their social practices.

The first anthropologist to pay serious attention to the centrality of social practice and bodily movement to the structuring processes was Bourdieu, in his landmark essay 'The Kabyle House or the World Reversed' (1990, first published in 1970). His approach generated a new tradition of anthropological analyses of social practices, emphasising social engagement with domestic space. Two works within this tradition have been particularly influential on my own methods of analysis. The first is Henrietta Moore's *Space, Text, and Gender* (1986). Based on her Kenyan ethnography, she aims to shift the conventional focus of deciphering the meanings encoded in space and their relations to social structure, to a perspective focussed on the creation and maintenance of such meaning. The question she asks is: 'How does the organisation of space come to have meaning and how are those meanings maintained through social interaction?' (Moore 1986: 74). To answer this, she approaches domestic space as a text which is continually read and interpreted by those who live in it — and also by her as the ethnographer. This allows her to analyse change as situated in a web of new readings of new and old practices (rather than simply emphasising new developments, such as, in the case of her ethnography, the introduction of square rather than round houses). Further, she examines how social practice (beyond mere 'readings') produces and reproduces meanings of structured space. Her multilevelled and stimulatingly complex interpretation of domestic space is particularly relevant to the analysis of contemporary Warlpiri engagements with domestic space.

The second is Robben's analysis of the relationship between social practice and spatial ordering in the houses of canoe fishermen and boat fishermen in a Brazilian town (1989). Although these canoe fishermen and boat fishermen live in architecturally identical houses, they read and employ the spatiality of their houses in divergent ways, pointing towards the incessant appropriation of meaning through social practice:

> People have to dwell in a house in order to reproduce the habitus objectified by it. How they dwell is influenced by their early childhood socialization, the architectural structure of their present living quarters, and the nature of their activities and social interaction outside the domestic world. House and society are not only produced and reproduced in domestic and societal practices through a process of structuration, but they also continually generate and regenerate one another in a structurating dynamic (Robben 1989: 583).

His point is pertinent in regard to contemporary Warlpiri uses of and ways of relating to domestic space. Today many Warlpiri people live in houses which architecturally are the same as houses found throughout suburban Australia, yet Warlpiri people dwell in them in quite different ways than do suburban Australians. Robben's approach suggests how to conceptualise the meanings behind different practices in similar dwellings.

Following Robben's and Moore's cues, I first examine the structural, the spatial and some of the conceptual properties of *camps* and houses, as well as their interplay at Yuendumu from the *olden days* to the present. I begin this process of untangling with a description of the structural properties of *olden days camps,* which leads to a discussion of the values underpinning the Warlpiri series of building–dwelling–thinking. I contrast this with the values inherent in the Western series and through this lens of values examine the introduction of housing at Yuendumu and its effect on contemporary Warlpiri practices of relating to domestic space.

Olden days' camps

Before sedentisation Warlpiri people lived a highly mobile hunting and gathering lifestyle, travelling across the Tanami in bands of ever-changing composition.² Before nightfall, the people who formed a band at any one time arranged their sleeping quarters. While the position of these *camps* changed depending on where a band was at a particular time, the shape these *camps* took was always the same, and highly structured. People did not lie down at random, but every night they reproduced the same structure, or building in Heidegger's sense. This was made up of windbreaks, rows of sleepers, and fires. Figure 4 uses Warlpiri iconography to depict a typical *olden days' camp*, and delineates the named spaces within it.

Yunta

In its most restricted sense, the term *yunta* is used to denote a windbreak (see also Keys 1999: 44–6; 165–71). A windbreak is constructed out of leafy branches, either piled on top of each other to create a low, thick wall, or (especially when also used during the day for shade or when

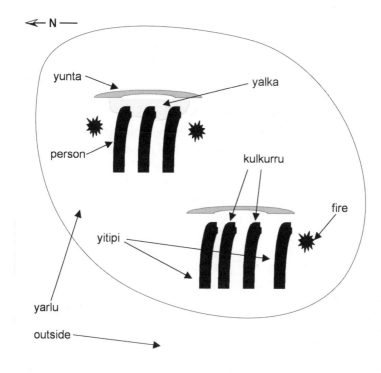

Figure 4: The spatial terminology of *camps*

particularly windy) dug into the earth so they stand upright and are interwoven with further horizontal branches. The windbreak is oriented to the east of the sleepers' heads, stretching from north to south. That is, if at all spatially possible, people sleep with their head to the east and their feet to the west. Often this arrangement shelters people from the prevailing winds, and it keeps sleepers' heads in the shade at sunrise; yet environmental factors alone seem inadequate to explain the practice. While Warlpiri people were not forthcoming with explanations as to why it was so, all were adamant that this is the ideal way to sleep.[3]

In a more expansive sense, the term 'yunta' also means 'open living and sleeping area protected from wind by erected barrier on appropriate side'. A yunta is the spatial manifestation of a row of sleepers, and in this book the term is used to refer to the combination of a windbreak, the places for people to sleep sheltered by it, the people sleeping in it, and, if present, fires. In the past, the sleeping places were indicated through moulds in the sand, one for each person, and in winter people kept warm through huddling together and being close to the fires. A *camp* may be made up of a single yunta, or a number of them. A *camp*, however, is not only made up of yunta, but also incorporates some of the space surrounding the yunta.

Yarlu

The space surrounding one or a number of clustered yunta is called *yarlu*, which according to the Warlpiri dictionary means 'place with nothing on it or over it'. It is thus similar to a yard or a garden in a suburban-style Western house, open space between the public (the street) and the private (the interior of the house). One crucial difference between a yard or garden and yarlu is that the former do not shift their positions (or existence), whereas a yarlu is only there when the yunta and the people sleeping in it are present, meaning it appears with the creation of yunta and it disappears as meaningful and named space when a specific *camp* is deserted. It is this yarlu space, or rather the boundaries around it, which clarify the distinction between yunta and *camp*. A single yunta with a bounded yarlu space is a *camp*; more often however, a *camp* is made up of a conglomerate of yunta surrounded by one yarlu space.

In pre-contact times yarlu space was often marked by a low mound of earth around the yunta where people had scraped the ground free of spinifex grass and similar plant matter. While there is no other visible boundary marking the extent of yarlu space, people are nonetheless aware of it. It is this often invisible boundary that constitutes the threshold between public space outside the *camp* and private space inside it. In the absence of walls, doors, doorbells, porches, halls and other similar physical markers of the threshold between public and private, social rules of behaviour structure its crossing.[4] One never walks straight to the location of an actual yunta but waits at the outer boundary of the yarlu, at an appropriate distance, anything between 5 and 30 metres away from the closest yunta, to be noticed and then invited 'in'.

Yalka

Within the yunta, there is a further delineation of space between the windbreak and the heads of the sleepers, called *yalka* (translated as 'close to windbreak' in the Warlpiri dictionary). Although yalka is a long strip of space between the sleepers' heads and the windbreak, this space is divided up into individual personal spaces. Thus each sleeper in a row has his or her own yalka space, positioned just above his or her own head. These spaces are not physically separated from each other, but there are strong invisible boundaries separating individual portions of yalka. Within the space of a *camp*, the yalka space 'belonging' to a particular person is their most private space, to keep their personal belongings.

Kulkurru and yitipi

Within the yunta, the positions of sleepers are further distinguished in terms of 'inside' and 'outside'. *Kulkurru* means 'between, on the way, amid, in the middle, midway, halfway' and is used to describe the position of sleepers in the middle of a row. '*Kulkurru ngunaka!*' means 'Lie down in the middle!'. *Yitipi* means 'edge, margin, side, outside, on the outer, periphery', and is the term denoting the positions of the sleepers on the outside of a row, the ones who sleep between the fire on the one side and the kulkurru sleepers on the other. '*Yitipi karna ngunami*' means 'I am sleeping on the (out)side'.

Whether a person is a yitipi or a kulkurru sleeper depends on a number of factors. The kulkurru position is considered safer for a number of reasons. It is further away from the fires, which can cause serious harm. It is also believed that if snakes do enter the yunta, one is safer in the middle. Most importantly, there is an emotional element to such positioning, relating to fear of the dark and 'spooky' things. At night when it is dark, one does not quite know what is out there, both in terms of animals and people, and in regards to the potential presence of 'spooky' beings. Accordingly, the kulkurru position quite simply feels safer, and therefore it is the most socially senior people within a yunta who take up the yitipi positions on the outside — sheltering and protecting the sleepers inside. However, other factors contribute to this choice, such as personal disposition, generational status, one's relations to others in the same yunta, and so forth.

The number of yunta on any given night in a particular *camp* depends on how many people are present and the nature of relations between them. The minimum is one yunta, with an open-ended maximum, depending on occasion and location. Generally, even if relations are amicable, yunta considered 'too long' will be broken up. This may happen by placing a number of fires in between sleepers, effectively creating more yitipi positions and thereby more yunta. Alternatively, a potential long row may be broken up into a number of separate yunta arranged parallel to each other, depending on the physical features of the terrain, e.g. when camping in a creek bed.

Gendered camps

Camps are further differentiated by the gender and the marital status of their residents. Married people sleep in *yupukarra,* married people's *camps*; unmarried people sleep in *camps* distinguished by gender, women in jilimi, women's *camps*, and men in *jangkayi,* men's *camps*. Children sleep in either yupukarra or jilimi, never in jangkayi (for detailed ethno-architectural discussion of the three types of *camps*, see Keys 1999, 2000).

In the *olden days*, when a large number of people camped together and all three types of *camps* where present, their order was prescribed in the following way. The married people's *camps*, the yupukarra, were situated in the middle, separated into individual yunta. Located to the west of them was the single women's *camp*, the jilimi. Note that a polite way of referring to women is '*karlarra-wardingki*', 'those belonging to the west', and the spatial association between the cardinal direction west and women, and the east and men, features in much of Warlpiri thought as well as ritual organisation. Accordingly, the single men's *camp*, the jangkayi, used to be to the east of the married people's *camps*.

If within the same area, the jilimi and the jangkayi should be located as far from each other as possible (Keys 2000: 126; Meggitt 1962: 76). The iconographic depiction of an aggregation of all three types of *camps* in one place would look something like the drawing in Figure 5.

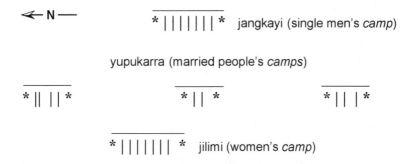

Figure 5: The spatiality of gendered *camps*

Ngurra

In Heidegger's series of building–dwelling–thinking, the three practices relate in a processual cycle. In order to dwell, one has to build; and the way one builds mirrors the way one thinks, which in turn is inspired by the way one dwells. So far, I have focused on aspects of the first two practices, building and dwelling: we may take the *camp* to represent the actual structure of Warlpiri dwellings (building) as well as the physical manifestations of practices of dwelling. *Camp* is the Aboriginal English translation of the term ngurra, which, however, holds meanings surpassing those captured by the term *camp*. If *camp* stand for the aspects of building and dwelling of Heidegger's series, then ngurra stands for the aspect of thinking, encapsulating the values underlying the world views arising out of (and feeding back into) such structures and practices. Ngurra radiates multiple levels of meaning which afford an incipient understanding of how ngurra is a core concept in Warlpiri language and cosmology, and why an analysis of the interconnection between Warlpiri residential patterns and sociality needs to be conceptually anchored around this term.

1) Generic idea of shelter   Ngurra is something every person and every animal has. It designates the place where one sleeps at night. For people ngurra takes the structure of the *camp*; for animals *ngurra* takes the form of whatever physical structure an animal dwells in, e.g. nest, lair, burrow and so forth. For example, when hunting for honey ants, one first looks for the presence of working honey ants on the ground, follows them to the entries of their ngurra and then digs down to find it. Or in cold time, when goannas hibernate, they are most often caught by digging up their ngurra, their burrow.

2) Place where one habitually sleeps   Ngurra in this sense is the term we used to refer to the jilimi when we were all living there. For example, when Celeste was ready to leave another *camp* we were visiting, she would say to me and the others, '*Ngurra-kurra yanirlipa*' [literally 'let's go camp-wards', meaning, 'let's go home to the jilimi']. A related term is *ngurra-yuntuyuntu*, denoting a place where many people lived for an extended period of time, a large and long-term camp, as for example the original *camp* sites on the outskirts of the settlement, where Yapa lived during the *early days* before houses were built.

3) Home   The emotional bond one can have to one's ngurra becomes more pronounced in the term's added meaning of home, with all the emotional depth that can possibly be attached to it. The phrase *ngurra-ngajuku* (my home) is generally used in this sense, especially in Warlpiri songs, many of which are about homesickness. Ngurra-ngajuku in these songs often stands for Yuendumu (if the song writer is from Yuendumu).

4) Ancestral place   Ngurra also designates the idea of the place with which a person is associated by conception, birth, ancestry, ritual obligation or long-term residence: in short, their country, their land. For example, Mawurritjiyi, a place to the south of Yuendumu, is one of Old Jakamarra's ngurra, a place with which he had profound emotional associations, a place for which he knew the songs and dances, where he had lived in the past, for which he was often pining, and which he consequently often painted in his dot paintings.

5) Family   The term *ngurra-jinta* is used to refer to the people living in one *camp*, typically close kin. It connotes being one family, of one household, from the same place. Ngurra-jinta presupposes either family connection or long-term cohabitation, coupled with emotional affiliation. The Aboriginal English translation of this term is *countryman*.

Related terms are *ngurrarntija* and *ngurra-wardingki*, meaning a person belonging to a certain place, and again, *countryman*.

6) Ritual division The terms *ngurra-kurlarni-nyarra* [literally camp–southside] and *ngurra-yatuju-mparra* [literally camp–northside] are used to designate the two patrimoieties into which all Warlpiri people are divided (these are groupings particularly relevant in the ritual context). The first one is the patrimoiety of all people of the J/Nakamarra, Jupurrurla/Napurrurla, J/Nampijinpa, J/Nangala subsections, and the second one is that of the J/Napanangka, J/Napangardi, J/Nungarrayi, J/Napaljarri subsections. During certain rituals these moieties spatially oppose each other, being positioned on the southern and the northern sides of the ceremony ground respectively.

7) Time Ngurra also stands for the period of twenty-four hours, and is used to designate numbers of days or nights that one would set up *camp*. For example, when I asked Celeste about the distance to a settlement up north, she answered, *'Ngurra-jarra'* [literally 'two camps'], meaning a three-day drive with two overnight stays on the way.

8) Country, the world Finally, *ngurrara* means country, fatherland, place, land, home. On one level it can be used to refer to one's own country, e.g. Mawurritjiyi, or more commonly to the Tanami Desert, to the entire Warlpiri lands. However, ngurrara does not only denote the expanse of physical space but everything within it: the people, the animals, the plants, as well as the ancestral beings and spiritual powers contained within the land, the moving clouds, the winds, the stars, the passing of time and so forth.

As this inventory makes abundantly clear, 'ngurra' as a term encapsulates a great number of meanings, beginning with the most generic idea of shelter to the incorporation of the Warlpiri cosmos into a single term. 'Ngurra' is conceptually extensive and covers the entire spectrum between residential units and cosmological concepts — underpinning my thesis that it is comparable to 'the house' in the terms suggested by Bachelard and Heidegger. Put differently, the way in which the Warlpiri series of building–dwelling–thinking distinguishes between a *camp* and ngurra is parallel to the way in which in the Western series of building–dwelling–thinking an actual house is different from 'the house' as metaphor. This analytical separation between *camp* and ngurra is evident also in Warlpiri iconography, in which two different designs are employed in different contexts and carry different connotations (see also Anderson and Dussart 1988; Munn 1966, 1970, 1973; Peterson 1981).

Yapa employ a set of concentric circles (see Figure 6) in the ritual context, in which it constitutes part of body designs, ground paintings, and decoration on ritual paraphernalia, and which incorporates the full range of meanings of the term 'ngurra'.[5]

Iconography using one horizontal and a number of vertical lines (see Figure 7), depicting actual *camps* is commonly used in sand stories, where during everyday conversation the design is drawn into the sand to depict a specific *camp* in which particular people have slept, with the horizontal line depicting the windbreak and each vertical line standing for a person (see also Munn 1963, Watson 1997). In sand stories, the design is oriented in the same way that the *camp* spoken about is, or was, oriented in real space.[6]

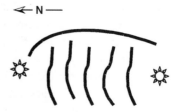

Figure 6: Iconography for *ngurra*   **Figure 7**: Iconography for *camp*

Housing policy and (not so) implicit values

Camps were physical manifestations of people's movements through their country and they accommodated (and created) kin. *Camps* were erected out of bush materials (sand, branches, fire); when people moved on, their *camps* were simply left behind, and new ones were erected whenever the band reached a new place. *Camps* thus embody the core values of mobility, immediacy and intimacy encapsulated in ngurra: core values which clash significantly with those embodied by the house.

Taking an archetypal Western-style house and looking at its conventional uses, those that Westerners consider *normal,* however they actually live themselves, we find that the primary purpose of the house is to shelter the family. An average family is imagined as a nuclear family, as parents and children. The house is removed from the public world by the front lawn (often also a fence and a porch) and accessed through the front door. The inside is expressive of a spatial order in which separate rooms are reserved for specific functions: a lounge room to relax and welcome guests into, a kitchen to cook in, a dining room to eat in, bathrooms for bodily functions, and bedrooms for sleeping. Bedrooms are the most private space within the house; all other rooms are shared, these are not (with the exception of the master bedroom which is shared by the parents). Bedrooms are not only for sleeping, though; they contain each respective person's private possessions, and this is also where these persons spend time on their own (apart from sleeping: presumably to read, to think, to have phone conversations they do not want overheard, to daydream, to play, to cry, and so forth).

Contemporary Western-style living revolves around separate rooms for different people with the ideal of one bedroom per person living in the house and some shared rooms for all, separated from the world outside. Houses both symbolise and enable privacy rather than intimacy. Houses are built of heavy materials (corrugated iron, concrete, bricks, wood) and do not move; they are permanent, at least over significant periods of time. Thus fixed in place, houses in turn fix people in place — they foster stability rather than mobility. In terms of materials needed for building, skills involved in building, as well as in terms of maintenance, houses are costly. Houses in this sense foster and express future-orientation rather than immediacy: generally, one needs to accumulate in order to afford to dwell in a house, either to pay rent, or, preferably, to pay off a mortgage with the ultimate goal of owning one's own house. Similarly, one must budget for household items, furnishings and maintenance.

The values of mobility, immediacy, and intimacy which underpin the Warlpiri series of building–dwelling–thinking thus find their opposites in the values symbolised by the house as metaphor and enabled through the house as actual physical structure. The government project of sedentisation, of institutionalising in settlements people who previously roamed freely through their country, aimed to negate and overcome this inherent clash of values, using the house as a 'civilising tool'.

Following the Second World War, during the so-called era of Assimilation, 'transitional housing' was introduced in central Australian Aboriginal settlements. This entailed a vision of Western-style houses as a 'medium of uplift', and the idea was to move Aboriginal families through a series of domestic structures with increasing complexity. A 'first stage' house usually consisted of one room and a veranda, a 'stage two' house included additional rooms and a kitchen, and a 'stage three' house had added bathroom facilities, being equivalent to Housing Commission standard. A damning critique of transitional housing can be found in Heppell (1979b). Firstly, he says, living in 'staged' houses held little appeal, as they were not at all suited to the local climatic conditions. Made of concrete and corrugated iron, they were hotter in summer and colder in winter than humpies constructed of a combination of bush materials, corrugated iron and canvas, the other type of domestic structure available to Aboriginal people at the time. Another reason why transitional housing as a project failed was due to the fact that no instructions about how to use the houses were delivered, nor did families in actual fact ever move through the stages, as there were never adequate numbers of houses available. Ultimately, Heppel argues, in respect of Western styles of living and Aboriginal styles of living, the transitional housing scheme 'permits neither set of living practices, nor does it permit a compromise between the two' (Heppell 1979b: 15). Lastly, he points out the bizarreness of the idea that living Western-style can be taught by moving people through a series of increasingly complex architectural structures; this is certainly not how people in the West learn to live in their houses.

What interests me is the fact that houses are seen as instrumental in what was then called 'the civilising process', and in particular, the assumption that by living in a Western-style house, somehow one becomes Western or acquires Western social practices. This assumption was most starkly expressed during the era of Assimilation, but it has persisted.

Following the 1967 referendum, which gave the federal government a clear mandate to legislate on Aboriginal affairs, the policy of assimilation was succeeded by one of integration. While there was a greater emphasis on self-management and equal participation than before, the terms continued to be dictated by the Western majority, and in effect, policies were not inherently different from the former period. They shifted in focus towards those people considered 'able to integrate', and housing assistance for them was provided in White suburbs and on pastoral leases. Aboriginal people deemed 'not yet ready' were neglected in terms of housing provisions. This period was succeeded by the Labor government's early 1970s policy which sought to restore to Aboriginal people their lost power of 'self-determination'. In terms of housing policies this meant that

> Labor will give priority to a vigorous housing scheme in order to properly house all Aboriginal families within a period of 10 years. In compensation for the loss of traditional lands funds will be made available to assist Aborigines who wish to purchase their own homes. The personal wishes of Aborigines as to design and location will be taken into account (from the 1971 Launceston conference, cited in Heppell 1979b: 20).

During this period housing became to be perceived as causal within Aboriginal people's cycle of poverty, the common argument being that 'without housing, other conventional support systems such as education, health, and employment could have little impact' (Heppel 1979b: 20). Since the 1970s, in many instances adequate housing has not been provided, neither have the education, health, or employment statistics improved; nor, for that matter, have the arguments changed much. In contemporary times, the provision of housing to Aboriginal people, though not explicitly formulated as a 'civilising tool', is a point of contention of enormous proportions. A much-heard contemporary grumble by non-Indigenous Australians is that 'as long as they [Aboriginal people] don't know how to appreciate houses, no more money should be thrown at them'. On a more bureaucratic level, to this day education and health officials continue to maintain that improvements in their field can only flow from 'ordered living'; and health and education researchers continue to channel much of their research activity into housing surveys.

In short, Aboriginal housing policies have always implicitly and often explicitly endeavoured to 'civilise', and consecutive Australian governments have assumed that living in a Western-style house will magically turn residents into people with Western-style values and social practices.

Applying Heidegger's insights to this situation helps explain the failure of these policies in terms of their intended aims. There is no logical reason why provision of one element (building) of the series of building–dwelling–thinking should automatically produce the other two (dwelling and thinking, or social practices and ways of being in and looking at the world). As Heidegger specifies, each element of the series is produced in continual dialogue with the other two; the series as a whole is made up of processual, interconnected, interdependent processes. So rather than state-provided housing transforming Warlpiri people in a predictable and intended way, what happens is that the two series, the Western one and the Warlpiri one, intersect, with reverberations that shape the everyday at Yuendumu.

So how do Warlpiri people relate to houses at contemporary Yuendumu? Today most residences are located in and around Western-style houses, which come in a great variety of shapes and forms, reflecting stages in policy, from one-room tin houses to the latest suburban-style bungalows. The Warlpiri term for the physical structure of a house is *yuwarli*. However, independent of the kind of physical structure in and around which any Warlpiri residence at Yuendumu is located, it is called *camp* in Aboriginal English or ngurra in Warlpiri. That is today, a *camp* can be in a humpy or a suburban-style five-bedroom brick house.[7] Practices of dwelling in contemporary *camps* at Yuendumu follow as well as differ from those of the *olden days* in significant ways. Accordingly, the Warlpiri use of houses is inherently different from that of Kardiya.

Yapa ways of dwelling in houses

Nowadays, Yapa try to continue to follow the rules of how to set up *camp*, with many compromises. Yuendumu is a large settlement currently encompassing six Yapa-populated 'suburbs', and thus the aggregation of people and physical structures is too large to support the spatiality of the nightly residential separation of men, women, and married people, or of jangkayi, yupukarra, and jilimi (to the east, middle and west respectively). On a smaller scale, the Western-style houses in and around which most *camps* at Yuendumu are located make it equally hard to sustain this form of spatial ordering. In response, people uphold the rules of gender separation but are lenient with the rules of spatial orientation of gendered *camps*. Today, many contemporary houses are used either as a jilimi, a jangkayi, or a yupukarra, independent of their location within the settlement.[8] Other houses, however, have two or all three kinds of *camp* located in and around them. In these cases, different gendered yunta occupy different rooms when sleeping inside, or, and more frequently, when sleeping outside, they are located either on different sides of the house, or, at least at some considerable distance from each other.

Houses often interfere with the possibility of orienting the head to the east at night. Here, too, Yapa are pragmatic and if east orientation is possible, they adhere to it. If it is not, people are willing to sleep in other orientations.

In the 1990s, life in Yapa-occupied houses was oriented outwards rather than inward; most activity, including sleeping, cooking, eating, and socialising, took place in the yard and on the verandah.[9] This yard-orientedness of Warlpiri people leaves the house available to them as a space to put to other uses. In the pre-contact past people did not have more possessions than they could carry and store in their yalka. Nowadays, Warlpiri people own many more things, and the most prominent use of houses is for storage.

First among Yapa people's possessions are items of bedding. Each adult person has his or her own swag or mattress, a groundsheet and a number of blankets; and often people have two sets, one for home and one for travelling. Each adult person usually has at least one suitcase or large bag full of clothes, also stored inside houses.[10] Further items stored inside are personal belongings, such as towels, pannikins, crowbars, television sets, paints, tools, and ritual paraphernalia. Bedrooms as well as other rooms are used primarily for storage, and only secondarily for sleeping or socialising.[11]

No matter whether sleeping outside or inside, Yapa continue to sleep in yunta, rows. Sleeping normally takes place on the ground, although some camps have beds in them. However, beds usually change 'owners' quickly, and they also tend to move from camp to camp. Instead of moulds in the sand, sleeping positions today are made up of people's bedding, in the main swags or foam mattresses and blankets laid out on a groundsheet (usually plastic canvas). Rather than using a sheet, mattresses are covered with a blanket, providing extra warmth. Depending on the season and temperatures, people use between one and as many as six or seven blankets on top of them to keep warm. Usually, people do not change into sleepwear at night but keep their clothes on for extra warmth in winter, or take most of them off in the hot summer nights.

The windbreak above the sleepers' heads today can be anything from a 'proper' Warlpiri-style windbreak constructed out of leafy branches, to the wall of a room or verandah, a car or a suitcase, or it may just be there symbolically. Yunta are set up at nightfall, and in the morning the bedding is put out of sight.

41

These days, at Yuendumu, yarlu space and yard space surrounding a house are often conflated through the introduction of fences.[12] When I first came to Yuendumu in 1994, only some public areas and buildings, such as the school and the clinic and some non-Indigenous houses, had fences. Since then, fences have become immensely popular, and most Warlpiri *camps* nowadays have a fence surrounding them in a square yard-like enclosure. Yapa say they like fences 'because they keep out dogs and drunks' — while experience shows they are useless to keep out either.[13] The one thing that fences seem to achieve is awareness in non-Indigenous people about *camp* boundaries. Before the fences were erected, on many occasions I observed non-Indigenous people stumbling right into a *camp*, crossing the invisible boundaries dividing the public from the private, without ever noticing. Instead of those previous invisible and implicit yarlu boundaries, today, Warlpiri and non-Indigenous people alike often use the fence as the point of negotiation for entry into a *camp*.

Entry into the yarlu space is negotiated differently depending on degrees of closeness between people inside the *camp* and persons wanting to enter. If there is a fence, one stands next to it; if not, one stands at an appropriate distance from the closest yunta at the margin of the yarlu. If there is no response from anybody inside the *camp*, this is equivalent to a door not opened to an unwelcome visitor. Usually, though, people inside the *camp* acknowledge the presence of the person waiting outside the yarlu and negotiate the situation.

Depending on the relations between the person outside and those inside the *camp*, and the often known or suspected intentions of the visitor, there are several options. If the person is not wanted inside the *camp*, or their intentions do not warrant them entering, somebody from inside the *camp* may get up and walk over to the yarlu boundary where the person is waiting, to discuss the issues at hand (paralleling a conversation at the front door without inviting in). Should entry into the *camp* then seem desirable, they accompany the person inside and indicate to them where to sit. If the person is welcome into the *camp* without such negotiations, then people from within the *camp* simply shout over to them to come in. If the person wanting to enter is in a relatively close relationship to people inside the *camp* and sure of their welcome, they generally do not wait at the invisible threshold but walk into the *camp*. However, while they are doing this they address people inside to announce their approach. Often children are used to negotiate an entry of this kind. If the visitor has a child with them, they talk to the child in a clearly audible manner about who is inside the *camp*: 'Look, your granny there'. In this case, people inside the *camp* 'answer' by calling out, for example, 'Little Daryl is coming to visit his granny', thus implicitly sanctioning the entry. If a person comes visiting without being accompanied by a child but there are children present inside the *camp*, they greet the children by singing out, for example, 'Hello little nephew'. People inside the *camp* prompt the child to reply, for example, 'Paul, look, your auntie', again thus sanctioning the passage. If people close to the *camp* residents come to visit, they simply enter and sit next to the person(s) they came to see.

As in *olden days* etiquette, today the yunta present a further level of privacy within the yarlu (see also Spatial Diagram of activity areas within the yunta of Warlpiri jilimi in Keys 1999: 168). Yunta are only entered by people actually sleeping in them or people very close to them, as for example Tamsin was when she plopped herself down between Celeste and myself in our yunta, the night we watched *Who Wants To Be A Millionaire?* Without such established familiarity, entering uninvited into yunta space, even if one is inside the yarlu, is either rude or a downright threat. Normally only particularly close people or those invited in enter yunta space.

Equally, the yalka space between the sleeper's head and the windbreak (today just above, or sometimes underneath, the pillow) remains the most exclusive space within the *camp*. It is used for storage of essential items and prized possessions, such as water bottles, money, matches, handbags, talismans, tablets, photographs, tobacco and whatever else is important to the sleeper.[14] Nobody would ever go close to or take items from the yalka of another person unless explicitly asked to do so. Even though I have slept next to Celeste for years, she still asks me when she wants the water bottle in my yalka, rather than taking it when she is thirsty.

In terms of the yitipi and kulkurru positions of the sleepers within a yunta, nothing has changed, except that nowadays people may actually leave a yunta at night after it has been set up. For example, if a woman stayed with relatives while her husband was away and he returns late at night, she leaves the place she is sleeping at to move back with her husband. Or there might be an emergency somewhere and a person leaves to help out. In these cases, if the person leaving was positioned kulkurru, in the middle, their swag, if they are not taking it with them, is put back into storage, and the remaining swags are drawn together into an uninterrupted yunta. If on the other hand, one hopes to be picked up by a 'loverboy' at night, one would, if going to bed at all, sleep yitipi, on the outside, so one can disappear without causing a major disruption. In short, Yapa strive for 'gap-free' yunta.

Most significantly, today, as in the past, there is no concept of a single person yunta as a single *camp* on its own.[15] Close proximity when sleeping enables the sharing of dreams (see Dussart 2000: Chapter 4 and Poirier 2005), it deflects possible accusations of sorcery, and most importantly, it prevents 'loneliness'. To be without *marlpa* (company) is unthinkable and to be avoided at all costs.[16] Sleeping alone is an impossibility, not only because the 'lonely' person would be unhappy, but also because should something happen to that person, the ones who left them without marlpa, alone, would be the first to be blamed. This two-directional relationality — seeking the company of others for one's own comfort as well as to provide comfort to others — principally underpins the character of Aboriginal relations in central Australia, or, what I call Warlpiri forms of intimacy.[17]

Through their structure (the ease with which they were erected and unproblematic availability of required materials), or the way of building in Heidegger's sense, *olden days camps* accommodated for as well as generated mobility, intimacy and immediacy, the core values encapsulated in the concept of ngurra. Put differently, the particular structure of *camps* allowed for as well as generated particular forms of social practices (ways of dwelling, in Heidegger's sense). In tandem, these structures and these social practices embodied and produced Warlpiri ways of being in and thinking about the world. The ways in which the structures, the social practices and the ways of being in the world interconnect and create meaning can be iconographically summarised and metaphorically expressed through a set of concentric circles and the concept ngurra.

The values underlying the concept ngurra (mobility, intimacy and immediacy) clash with the values the house is imbued with (stability, privacy and future-orientation). Accordingly, when Warlpiri social practices interact with state-provided houses the result is something different to what Australian governments envisioned in the process of sedentisation. Instead, contemporary life in the settlement of Yuendumu continues along some of these parameters, and adapts continually to the presence of houses and what they imply. Following Moore, these changes in contemporary Warlpiri ways of dwelling in *camps* and in houses need to be understood as situated in a web of new readings of new and old practices — rather than a Warlpiri inability to comply with a particular way of living in Western-style housing. Following Robben, Warlpiri and Kardiya styles of dwelling in houses are not dependent on the structures, the houses, but on the appropriation of meaning through social practice.

CHAPTER 3

Transforming jilimi

Sedentisation, the creation of the settlement of Yuendumu and the provision of housing engendered the intersection of the Warlpiri and the Western series of building–dwelling–thinking. This intersection, in turn, set in motion any number of social processes which are manifest in, for example, the ways in which Warlpiri people engage with Western-style houses. These processes are multidirectional and may alter over time; and they feed back into ways of being in the world. An example of this is the jilimi, or women's *camp*. The social processes set in motion with the intersection of the two series of building–dwelling–thinking have substantially transformed jilimi from a gendered, spatially specified and single-purpose residential form into, as we will see, multipurpose, residentially complex and much larger domestic arrangements — often located in and around houses.

In the *olden days*, jilimi were temporary residential settings for the single purpose of mourning. Since sedentisation in 1946, Yapa social relations at Yuendumu have undergone significant transformations that are manifested in, among other things, the phenomenon of contemporary jilimi (see also Bell 1980a: 177, 1993: 139; Dussart 1992: 345; Hamilton 1981: 75–6; Peterson 1986: 139). Their original *olden days* purpose has been vastly extended and jilimi have increased in numbers and in size, and have also changed significantly in terms of residential composition and complexity. From a temporary residential arrangement for women during mourning they have been transformed into centres of sociality, not only for women but for children and men as well.[1]

Today, there is an ever-changing number of jilimi at Yuendumu, usually a handful or so of large ones and any number of smaller ones.

In the 1980s, for example, according to Dussart (1992: 345), there were six principal jilimi at Yuendumu. A decade later, Keys (1999: Appendix 5: Locations of jilimi in Yuendumu) details a total of thirty-two jilimi locations between February and October 1995, seventeen of which were spatially independent and fifteen of which were attached to or surrounded by yupukarra (married people's *camps*). During my research, the number of jilimi fluctuated significantly, with a minimum of six large and spatially independent ones and an ever-changing number of smaller ones at any one time. In contrast to Bell's characterisation of jilimi in the 1970s at Alekarenge (previously Warrabri) (1980a, 1993), those at Yuendumu are *not* land- and ritual-based, nor do they provide a power base for women (see also Dussart 2000: 44). Yet today's jilimi are focal points around which much of everyday life at Yuendumu revolves, and as such they are an excellent site to explore two aspects of the intersection of the Warlpiri and the Western series of building–dwelling–thinking at Yuendumu.

Firstly, I show how the transformation of jilimi from single-purpose mourning *camps* to large, numerous and socially complex contemporary *camps* needs to be understood in relation to changes that the institution of Warlpiri marriage has undergone in response to sedentisation and the resulting changes in circumstance. Jilimi in this regard are an example of how core concepts belonging to the Warlpiri series of building–dwelling–thinking are transforming.

Secondly, I introduce the actual jilimi that Nora, Joy, Polly, Celeste and I lived in, the one that was my home for over a year of fieldwork, and in which the ensuing case studies about mobility, immediacy and intimacy are set. This jilimi is located in and around a four-bedroom house, and I discuss how the four women relate to each other and the jilimi's four rooms. This interplay between a contemporary jilimi and the structure of a Western-style four-bedroom house illuminates how the first process (the transformation of jilimi*)* in turn feeds back into the intersection of the two series of building–dwelling–thinking and creates particular dynamics, played out in Warlpiri practices of dwelling in Western-style houses.

Changes in marriage and the jilimi

In the *olden days*, ideally, girls grew up in their parents' yupukarra, and at an early age (according to Meggitt 1962: 268–9, at eight or nine years) moved into a yupukarra with their (first and much older) husband. There they lived until widowed, when they spent the appropriate time for mourning in a jilimi, before remarrying and moving into yet another yupukarra with their next husband. With this ideal life cycle for women in pre-contact times, jilimi did not have a prominent position in everyday life, simply because women lived in yupukarra for most of their lives and stayed in jilimi rarely and only for the purpose of mourning.

The dramatic changes in prominence, number, size and purpose of contemporary jilimi result from changes in both residential practices (sedentisation) and the Warlpiri institution of marriage. What constitutes a marriage in Warlpiri eyes today? How has that changed from the past? And what do these changes mean in regard to the ways Warlpiri people live their lives today — and, specifically, how do these changes interact with Yapa ways of relating to domestic space?

In the *olden days*, marriages were living and economic arrangements between husband and wife, as much as they were (in a sense, contractual) arrangements between the husband and a woman's matriline, especially her mother's brothers. According to Meggitt, during the *olden* and the *early days*, there existed three ways for a man to legitimately acquire a wife, in the negotiations of all of which the matriline was instrumental. These three kinds of marriages came about 'through the levirate, through private negotiation with the women's kinsmen, and as a result of being circumcised by a man who becomes his father-in-law' (1962: 264). The third type, arrangements made during initiation, where the circumciser promises an as yet unborn daughter to the circumcised, according to Meggitt, was the 'ideal marriage arrangement, and indeed the most common' (Meggitt 1962: 266).[2]

Today, the few remaining examples of the first type of marriage, the levirate (where a man 'inherits' the wife/wives of his deceased brother), exist in the oldest generation of Warlpiri people alive. I am not aware of a continuation of this practice by the younger generations.

The second type, where negotiations between families, particularly matrilines, result in the marriage of a young girl, has also apparently been discontinued. In regards to the third type, initiation rituals continue to take place at Yuendumu almost every year, and marriage promises continue to be made during them. However, for a number of reasons, which seem to be working in tandem, today these promises rarely eventuate in actual marriages.

The first of these reasons is that matrilines, formerly instrumental in putting marriages into effect, seem to have lost their power, as the absence of the other two ways of 'legitimately acquiring a wife', among other things, indicates (see also Peterson 1969 on the roles of matrilines in marriage arrangements, and Dussart 1992 for recent changes).

Secondly, while the age difference between 'promised' potential spouses remains substantial, in actual marriages this has shrunk significantly. During Meggitt's research, the age difference between spouses at Yuendumu in their first marriage was on average twenty-one years (Meggitt 1965: 156); today it is less than five years amongst the youngest married generation. In the past, this age difference, in tandem with support of the girl's matriline, must have made enforcement of marriage (should a girl have been unwilling) easier for the much older husband.

Thirdly, the economic motivation to enter a marriage has waned. During the *olden days*, men and women combined their subsistence forays, and nuclear (and extended) families were tight economic units with clearly gender-defined rights and responsibilities. Sedentisation under colonial rule and ensuing post-colonial welfare arrangements led to crucial shifts in forms of subsistence and thereby a shift in roles and responsibilities of spouses. Economically, marriages are not of any crucial significance any more: quite the opposite. Through Australian welfare arrangements, women especially benefit financially from *not* being married (see Dussart 1992).

Fourthly, with a significant weakening of the contractual aspects of a marriage as between matrilines, room opened for more individualistic reasons underlying the choice of a spouse, chief amongst them love. This has been further underscored by enhanced mobility, and by the growth of larger, concentrated populations, which has led to an enormously increased choice of potential marriage partners.

The general picture Meggitt presents of Warlpiri marriages at the time of his research is one of stormy durability. On the one hand, he declares, that 'the Walbiri divorce-rate is much lower than that in a number of native societies' (Meggitt 1962: 103) and asserts that 'the norm of long-term unions is generally achieved' (ibid.). On the other, he elaborates that 'there is a high incidence of casual adultery' (Meggitt 1962: 104), and his ethnography is testament to that, providing numerous detailed case studies revolving around disputes to do with adultery. After presenting a number of vignettes concerned with adultery, Meggitt states:

It is impossible in the circumstances to estimate accurately the incidence of adultery among the Walbiri. To judge from their remarks to my wife and myself and from observed situations, most of them probably commit adultery several times during early married life, while for a few it is a pastime to be pursued on all occasions (Meggitt 1962: 107).

In relation to what Meggitt calls 'adultery', nothing much has changed. What has changed drastically is the impact of infatuation, love and lust upon marriages. In the past, marriages usually seem to have withstood the turbulences caused by adultery; today often they do not. This does not seem to be due to a change in adultery, but to changes in the nature of marriage.[3] That the stability of marriages has undergone substantial changes is illustrated in the following extract from my fieldnotes:

There are Thomas and Lillian, compared to many other Warlpiri marriages, theirs is a very close relationship, intimate, loving — sometimes. At other times it is real stormy, with lots of brooding, running away, and fighting. Netta's husband dotes on her although, or because (?), she is more child than woman, continually sulking, very much dependent, and very very demanding. 'You are a wife now', they sometimes tell her when she is grouchy, 'you have to behave yourself'. When Old Man's younger wife left him for a younger man, he told Maisy (her sister and co-wife): 'If I can't have her, I don't want you either'. Her sister was the one he loved. Now, Maisy says, she is *divorced*, but she lives with the old man, and looks after him. Viola's husband got himself a second wife and her and Viola had big jealousy fights. When Rosalind came to Nyirrpi to visit, Viola asked if she could come with her back to Yuendumu — yes. Later her husband said: 'I sent you to the shop, not to Yuendumu', and she should return to him, but she didn't want to. Did she have a boyfriend? Ih! [Emphatic no]. Years later and she quietly asks whether we are going to Laramba Sports (where her ex-husband will be, too) and she is always the first to jump into the car when we go to Nyirrpi (where he lives). Then there is Frederick and his two Glorias (one a wife, one a girlfriend) always fighting over him. Marsha who just 'talked' to Alex before they got married and their hours of quiet whispers every night; and how Walter burnt all his wife's belongings because he was jealous.

These observations are similar to Meggitt's vignettes about the tempestuous nature of Warlpiri marriages, but the crucial difference here is that two years after I wrote this, all of the marriages described had ended.

What has not dramatically changed, on the other hand, is the way in which a marriage is established. In the *olden days*, a marriage was simply announced by the woman joining her husband in his *camp*, forming a yupukarra:

> When a man thinks his betrothed is old enough to leave her mother — that is, when she is about eight or nine years old — he privately asks her father and mother's brother to send her to his shelter. The men instruct the girl's mother accordingly, and the girl joins her husband without any formality. Her father and mother's brother simply tell onlookers that the betrothal is consummated (Meggitt 1962: 268–9).

Significantly, especially in respect to contemporary practices at Yuendumu, Meggitt points out the following: [4]

> The statement that there is no wedding ceremony requires comment. The people regard the initial removal of the girl to her husband's dwelling at his request as the termination of the betrothal and the beginning of marriage. Her walking through the camp to join the man constitutes the public statement of fact (Meggitt 1962: 269).

In similar fashion, a marriage today is announced by the public moving of bedding into a yupukarra. Indeed, the only way of finding out whether or not two people were married at Yuendumu during my research, if they were not already known to be married, was to hear that 'X was now living in a yupukarra with Y'.[5]

Considering the ease with which a contemporary marriage is established, as well as the absence of power (or interest) of matrilines to enforce or prohibit a particular marriage, the absence of economic incentives to remain in a marriage, and the movement from contractual arrangement to individual choice, mean that today marriages can also be resolved more easily. In fact, aside from the emotional work required for most separations, the simple act of moving out of the *yupukarra* terminates a marriage.[6]

With the termination of a marriage, the former husband moves into a jangkayi and the former wife into a jilimi. Today, women live in the jilimi when they are in between marriages, or at any point in their life when they decide to remain single (this does not mean celibacy, as they may have one or more *boyfriends,* or *run around* from time to time). The increase in size, quantity and purpose of jilimi thus correlates directly to Warlpiri marriages being less stable today than they were in the past, meaning that women spend much less of their lives in yupukarra and much more in jilimi.[7] Moreover, children, who now constitute a further substantial part of the jilimi population, have also changed their residential patterns as a result of these developments in the institution of marriage. *If* the ideal of a stable marriage is achieved, then children grow up living in their parents' yupukarra.[8] However, as the *ideal* case is rarely the norm today, children also often live in jilimi, sometimes with their mothers, or more regularly with their grandmothers, who take up a carer's role.[9] Men, as well, who rarely live (that is, sleep) in jilimi, may nonetheless spend much more time there during the day than ever before. Considering the storminess of contemporary marriages, many young and middle-aged men come to the jilimi to receive food and financial support from their mothers. Accordingly, the presence of men in contemporary jilimi, especially around mealtimes and during early evening socialising, is by no means unusual.

Our jilimi

The flux in numbers and locations of contemporary jilimi at Yuendumu already indicates their lack of stability over time. This flux needs to be understood not only in terms of location, but also in terms of residential composition. As women decide to stay single, and the marriages of others dissolve or are being formed, they and their (unmarried) children move in and out of jilimi (creating some of the flow of residents through jilimi discussed in the next chapter). The six more permanent jilimi at Yuendumu are no exception.

I first knew ours as a long-established jilimi in this location when I began research at Yuendumu in 1994. However, the women and children who were some of its core residents in 1999 (the period of the case studies) did not live there five years earlier, nor did they live there just a year or so later. While the same locale remained a jilimi until 2005, it is now a yupukarra.

This jilimi is located in Yuendumu's Inner West Camp, within easy walking distance of the Park. Its most immediate neighbouring *camp* is yet another jilimi, while all other houses in its vicinity are occupied by yupukarra, sometimes with smaller jilimi attached to them (and the house across the road from the jilimi is the one in which the Catholic nuns live, known as 'Little Sisters'). The jilimi is situated in and around a house made of corrugated iron. This house has four identical-sized rooms (approximately 2.5 x 4 metres) adjacent to each other, which open onto a roofed verandah facing north (Figure 8). The verandah is separated from the yard by a wall about one metre high.

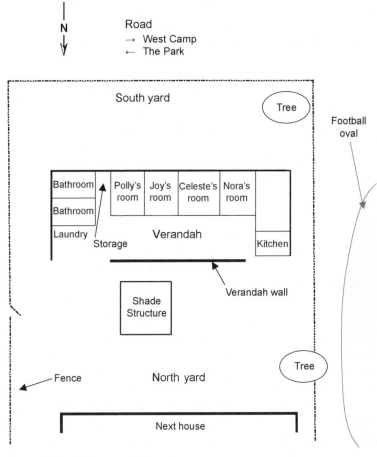

Figure 8: The jilimi — spatial layout

Each room has a louvred window to the south (always shut) and a door opening onto the veranda facing the north yard. At the western end of the structure is another (windowless) room, which opens onto the verandah without a door, and a (dysfunctional) kitchen. At the eastern end are a storage place, which can be locked, and two bathrooms with a shower, sink and toilet each, as well as a little laundry space with a tap and a washing machine. The house is located in the southern half of a yard. Nowadays, the yard is confined by a fence on three sides, about 25 metres long and 35 metres wide; and the back of an identical house on the northern side (the neighbouring jilimi). In the middle of the yard between the two houses is an iron structure which, when covered with canvas, provides shade and often has shelters and leafy branches for extra shade attached to it. To the north-west is a large tree providing further shade. The yard space south of the house is rarely used, mainly perhaps because it is not visible from the other spaces.[10] It does not usually comprise part of the jilimi's yarlu space. The yarlu space, in the main, is made up of the north yard and the verandah, where most of the social activity within the jilimi takes place. This is where in the evenings the yunta normally are arranged.

The vexed issue of room ownership

Not all jilimi are located in and around houses, but when they are, as ours was, then they face the same issues as all other *camps* which are located in houses. One of these issues revolves around the roles and functions of rooms. Conventional Western-style houses are normally divided into rooms with shared access (lounge, dining room, etc.) and private rooms (bedrooms). Bedrooms in Western-style houses are 'meant' to be used as private spaces; ideally, one room is allocated to one individual (or a couple). Practically, this is not feasible because of the ratio of people to bedrooms in Yapa-occupied houses (in 1999 the average was 4.5 persons per bedroom, see Musharbash 2001a: 6). Ideologically, this use is also not acceptable because of the preference for sleeping next to others (providing and receiving marlpa, company). *Olden days camps* had no rooms; each person had their spot in the yunta to sleep in and their yalka for storing personal belongings. There were no physical separators between these spaces; all could be seen and none differed from each other. How are bedrooms used, then?

Firstly, individuals hardly ever sleep in them alone (this is as rare as a one-person yunta). When rooms were used for sleeping, which happened in the jilimi only when it was very cold or rainy indeed, then a number of people slept in one room.[11] The jilimi house's four rooms were mainly used for storage, particularly (but not exclusively)for bedding during the day. This is a neat way of dealing with the contrast between permanence as a value underlying houses and mobility as a value underlying *camps*: While the house is there all the time, the yunta which create the *camp* are put up again each night (and during the day the bedding which creates the yunta is out of sight in the rooms).

However bedrooms are comparable in one way to those in Western-style houses, as not all jilimi residents have equal access to all four rooms. In fact each room is known to 'belong' to a particular woman at any one time. When I first moved into the jilimi in late November 1998, the jilimi's four rooms were said to belong respectively to Polly, Joy, Celeste and Nora.

This is not a kind of exclusive ownership in terms of rights over the room's space and use. It is more accurately described as an association between a room and a person. 'Celeste's room' for example was the one in which she stored most of her belongings and where she slept when it was cold. However, she never spent any time alone in it. She shared access to and use of the room with the people who stayed with her in the jilimi, as well as some of her relatives who lived in other *camps*. They stored their belongings in it, sometimes slept in it, and generally entered it without asking Celeste for permission. Other jilimi residents, however, would neither use nor enter it. Ultimately, when Celeste moved to another *camp*, 'her' room became somebody else's, and her association with it as well as her and her associates' access to the room ceased entirely.

While each room is associated with at least one main person at any one time (and these associations shifted), 'room ownership' in no way impacts upon access to and control over any of the other spaces in the jilimi (as it would in a non-Indigenous-occupied house, where only those people who have bedrooms generally have some 'say' about the rest of the space of the house). Nor did 'room ownership' add any weight to a woman's standing within the jilimi, i.e. no power was associated with this kind of 'ownership'. Apart from the rooms, access to the rest of the space of the jilimi is equally distributed to all residents present at any one time. This is not to say that disagreements between residents do not take place, but whether or not a woman 'has a room' in these cases has no impact on arguments.

What 'room ownership' did do for women while they 'held' a room was associate them directly with the jilimi — which was considered by them and others as their home. However, room ownership is in no way a requirement for considering the jilimi one's home. There are many people who lived in the jilimi and called it their home but who never 'owned' a room there. Neither was room ownership an exclusive symbol for social centrality in the jilimi; while Joy, Nora, Celeste and Polly were central to it, at least while they lived in the jilimi, so were a number of other people who did not own a room. To underscore the insignificance of room ownership in this regard, I know of at least one woman who, before Nora moved into her room, was said to 'own' this room while not actually living in the jilimi.

The issue of 'room ownership' alerts us to the fact that rooms can be ambiguous spaces. They are not easily and clearly related to persons; and their use throws up interesting issues in respect to the sociality of *camps* when set up in and around houses. Rather than following the Western series of building–dwelling–thinking and using bedrooms as spaces of privacy, Yapa seem pragmatic in their dealings with rooms, using them in such a way that it suits their purposes (which, of course, are built on the values underpinning the Warlpiri series of building–dwelling–thinking). Interesting in this context also is that the fifth room, the one on the western side without a door and with open access to and from the verandah, was at no stage said to 'belong' to any particular person, though in all other regards it was used in a similar fashion to the other rooms, i.e. for storage of bedding and sleeping in when rainy or cold, by a changing number of individuals. Since it had no door and no windows, however, it was never considered a 'proper' room. Nobody ever claimed it as theirs (even when using it over a period of months), nor was it ever verbally described as 'someone's' room.

Lastly, while these four rooms were said to belong to Polly, Nora, Joy and Celeste for a while, the respective rooms belonged to other persons before they moved into this particular jilimi (all at different times) and after they left. This hints at the process of forming and maintaining jilimi. They are not randomly formed by women and children who at any one time choose to live in one; rather, when a woman decides to move into a jilimi, she generally moves into one where relatives live already. This slow process of acquiring and losing core residents is what happened to our jilimi too, and because it was one of the larger ones, sheltering many more core residents than other jilimi, this is perhaps the reason for its comparative durability.

Polly, Nora, Celeste and Joy

To underscore the relationships between core residents, let me here outline as an example how Polly, Nora, Celeste and Joy related to each other (and note that they all arrived at the jilimi at different times, and also moved out at different times, except for Polly and Celeste, who moved out of this jilimi and into another one together). These four women were not the only core residents during the time they lived in it; all except Polly brought with them children they were caring for, some brought sisters and aunties, and lastly, there were other women as central as them who called the jilimi home and who were not close relatives.

Both Polly and Nora were widows in their seventies. Celeste and Joy were in their early and mid-forties respectively. Celeste had left her husband many years before and had been single since; Joy also often lived in a *camp* close by (on the other side of the Little Sisters) with her *divorced* husband (*divorced* here meaning that sexual relations had ended though the relationship continued). These four women are related to each other in a variety of ways (Figure 9).

Polly, Nora and Joy are what at Yuendumu is called 'close' sisters (the term 'close' qualifies an otherwise also possibly classificatory kin relationship as substantiated through biological, adoptive or similar connections). Joy's and Nora's fathers were brothers. Joy's and Polly's mothers were sisters. Polly's and Nora's mothers were co-wives of the same man (Nora's biological and Polly's social father; Polly's real father was a man her mother had an affair with). The bond between Polly and Joy was further reinforced through marriage and adoption links. They were married to two (close) brothers (Polly's husband was deceased by the time I met her). Following a common Warlpiri practice, Polly, who had eight children of her own, had given one of her sons to her sister Joy, who had none. Joy thus adopted and brought up one of Polly's sons, who passed away a number of years ago. Joy now looks after his children. These biological grandchildren of Polly's consider Joy their first grandmother and stay with her rather than Polly when they spend time

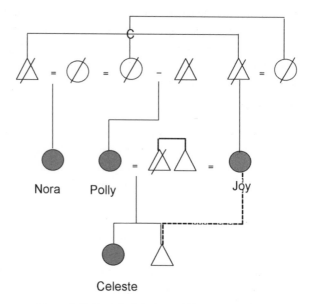

Figure 9: Polly, Joy, Celeste and Nora's genealogy

in the jilimi. Celeste is Polly's daughter; and Nora and Joy are thus 'close' mothers of hers.

These four women are connected by genealogical bonds, and share much of their life histories, as well as, during different periods of their lives, experiences of co-residency — thus drawing them together for the time that they all lived in the same jilimi. Let's look at the jilimi, then, and examine how the values of mobility, immediacy, and intimacy are integral in shaping its everyday.

CHAPTER 4

In the jilimi: mobility

The high residential mobility of Warlpiri people through the *camps* of Yuendumu, can be approached from two directions. One is to follow individuals on their trajectories through *camps*; the other is to take a *camp*-centric view and examine the flow of people through it. I here undertake the latter, and analyse mobility in the jilimi in which Celeste, Joy, Nora, Polly and I lived.

The flow of people is a reality in all kinds of *camps* at Yuendumu and is by no means exclusive to jilimi; however, its volume is particularly high in these. During the period I lived in the jilimi, for example, more than 160 other individuals stayed there, at different times and for different lengths of time. For a four-bedroom house, this is a staggering number of residents, even if not all were ever present at the one time.[1]

Moreover, none of this mobility was random. Each person arrived in and left the jilimi for their own reasons, which included choosing to stay at this particular jilimi because others they knew and related to were staying there.

In order to understand the patterns underlying mobility, we also need to examine the relationships between people. Our jilimi thus serves well to illuminate the entanglements of physical structures (a four-bedroom house), values underpinning particular ways of being in the world (here, mobility), and social practice (the relationships of Joy, Nora, Celeste and Polly to the house and the jilimi on the one hand, and their roles in facilitating the mobility of others through the jilimi on the other).

The magnitude and the nature of Warlpiri people's mobility through the *camps* of Yuendumu made it impossible for me to reconcile the reality I was observing (and participating in) with the analytical terms anthropologists commonly apply in similar contexts. For example, how can it be possible to find a social unit at Yuendumu that can be defined as 'a household' when people move so much? The constant flux in the social composition of people who sleep in any one *camp* does not at all lend itself to trying to draw boundaries around units. Yet many people who work in Aboriginal Australia use the term. It is habitually applied within the post-contact, on-going colonial and post-colonial contexts (rather than in reference to pre-contact *camps* where anthropologists commonly speak of bands and the domestic cycle, see amongst other Peterson 1978).

Much of the discussion about Aboriginal households is underwritten by an implicit and often explicit understanding of money and access to it as being the triggering force behind the dynamics of the formation of households as social units. Such studies stress the mutual interdependence of mobility and financial factors, and portray Aboriginal households as prone to cyclical changes induced by the vagaries of 'boom and bust' or 'prosperity and poverty' (see especially Finlayson 1991; Finlayson et al. 2000; Finlayson and Auld 1999). Generally, the practice of 'demand sharing' is seen to engender fluctuations in the social composition of Aboriginal residential arrangements.[2] Focussing on the mobility side of the equation, Sansom (1982) introduced the term 'concertina household' into the literature, used by Perth welfare workers to describe the high fluctuations common in dwellings occupied by Aboriginal people there. This fluctuating social composition, Sansom suggests, is a crucial feature of the contemporary Aboriginal commonality.[3] I agree, and maintain that in the face of this, the term 'household', with its suggestions of boundedness, is rendered meaningless.[4] Similarly, and almost three decades ago, Yanagisako, in her review of the extensive anthropological literature on households (1979: 200), concluded that terms such as household are 'merely "odd-job" words, which are useful in descriptive statements but unproductive tools for analysis and comparison'.[5] Outlining the analytical dilemmas associated with this term is important however, reaffirming as it does my reasons to maintain a methodological distinction between domestic space on the one hand and social practice relating to this space on the other. This distinction allows for an examination of mobility as process and value in its own right, rather than viewing mobility as effect on bounded categories (such as the household). Accordingly, the questions I address are: where do people come from, where do they go, why do they stay, why do they go, and what are the reasons and meanings underlying their mobility? To answer them I first outline the quantitative realities of mobility through the jilimi, and then analyse these statistical findings by contextualising them ethnographically.

Extent and volume of mobility in the jilimi

During my fieldwork, I took a census of who slept where and next to whom each morning when I woke up. I slept in this particular jilimi and recorded census data there for 221 nights, over a period of some 467 nights. This means that for 246 days of that period I have no data about who stayed at the jilimi because I stayed elsewhere. This is significant in itself, because while I considered the jilimi my home for this period of my fieldwork, the data shows that I spent fewer than half of those nights there. As my own mobility was largely determined by the mobility of the people I was living and working with, this may well be quite representative of the amount of time people generally spend 'at home' and 'elsewhere'.

As we have seen, more than 160 individuals slept in the jilimi during those 221 nights. Compared to an average four-bedroom house in non-Indigenous Australia, this is an astonishing number. Moreover, when I say 'at least 160' persons stayed in the jilimi over the census period, this is a conservative estimate. As I was by no means the first person up every morning, the chances are that I have failed to count people who left early in the morning. Further undercounting has, I suspect, occurred during the initial stages of fieldwork in relation to children, not all of whom I knew. More importantly, one difficulty arose out of the fact that initially I did not know the names of many of the people who lived in the jilimi.[6] The census data encompasses named individuals (105 in total) and three other categories: adults whose names I did not know (60), children whose names I did not know (146),[7] and *sorry mobs*. The latter term describes groups of people who travelled to Yuendumu from other settlements to participate in mortuary rituals, and stayed in or adjacent to the jilimi and accessed its facilities during the time mortuary rituals were performed. *Sorry mobs* comprised between ten and twenty people at any one time.

Including named and un-named individuals (but excluding *sorry mobs*), as indicated in Table 1, on average 17 people stayed in the jilimi every night, on average 12 adults and 5 children. Over the census period, the minimum number for adults was 6 and the highest 19. For children, the highest number was 11 and the minimum was one child present.

Table 1: Average numbers of adults and children sleeping in the jilimi over 221 nights

	Average	Highest	Lowest
Adults	12	19*	6
Children	5	11*	1
Total	17	30*	9**

*Note that this table does not include individuals from *sorry mobs*, in which case these numbers would be substantially higher.

**This is the lowest number of actual residents present at any one time, not the sum of lowest number of adults and children together.

Such averages have to be treated carefully, as they conceal another dimension. These average numbers encompass different people at different times, which distinguishes them from comparable non-Indigenous statistics. In a case study about another Yuendumu jilimi I presented elsewhere, there was an average of 22 people, but in actual fact:

> Over the fortnight there were a total of 27 different adults and 15 different children sleeping at the house; that is, a total of 42 different persons. Moreover, a 'core' of 11 persons (seven adults and four children) slept at the house for the whole two-week period. (Musharbash 2000: 59)

The point is that average numbers of residents conceal the actual flow of people through *camps*. The figures in Table 1 should thus be treated with caution and be read as indicating statistical realities rather than actual practice. The fact that more than 160 people stayed in the jilimi over the census period is at least as important as the fact that on average 17 of them were present on any one night. Further analysis of the figures draws attention to other features of the jilimi population. The graph in Figure 10 presents the number of nights the 105 named individuals spent in the jilimi on those 221 nights I slept there (the graph excludes both un-named individuals and *sorry mobs*).

Each column of the graph represents the number of nights a named individual slept at the jilimi. Because it is based on the nights I myself

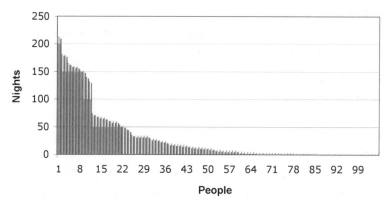

Figure 10: Nights/people in the jilimi

spent in the jilimi, the tallest column represents myself and the 221 nights I spent there. The next column in line represents the person who spent the next highest amount of nights in the jilimi, while I was there. It is important to keep in mind, however, that this person, like most others covered by the graph, would have been present on many of the nights I was not. The graph is skewed by my own mobility; it does not present data for a continuous period of time, and it may well under-represent some people and over-represent others (especially those like Celeste, for example, whose patterns of mobility I often followed). Nonetheless the data does reflect well the way people relate to the jilimi. In analysing the data in the graph it is helpful to divide the columns into four sections, splitting the 105 individuals into categories according to how many nights they spent in the jilimi.

The first section comprises eleven individuals who during the census period all slept in the jilimi more than 100 nights (133–221 nights), and distinctly more than everybody else. I call these the core residents and discuss them under this heading below. Then the curve takes a deep plunge, and the next section is comprised of those individuals who spent distinctly fewer nights in the jilimi than the core residents but distinctly more than the remaining individuals — these I call regular residents (44–76 nights/12 individuals). Then the curve peters out slowly and I divide it into two more sections, one comprising those individuals who slept in the jilimi on an on-and-off basis (8–36 nights/36 individuals) and the other those who slept there sporadically (1–6 nights/48 individuals).

Table 2: Types of residents

	Number of nights	Number of individuals
Core residents	100+	11
Regular residents	76–44	12
On-and-off residents	36–8	36
Sporadic residents	6–1	48

Core residents

These are the eleven individuals who stayed in the jilimi for distinctly more nights than all other residents over the same period, and who can be described as relating emotionally to the jilimi as 'home' for most or all of the census period. They would have thought of and talked about the jilimi as 'home' when they were sleeping there as well as on the many nights they slept elsewhere. In contrast to Bell's description of jilimi residents as senior, ritually active women (1980a, 1993), these eleven individuals belong to four generations and include children as well as elderly women beyond the state of social seniority (see Musharbash forthcoming on the loss of social seniority). Next to Polly, Joy, Celeste, Nora and I, the others are (see also Figure 11):

1) Neil (aged thirteen), who is the adopted son of Celeste, the biological son of Celeste's sister and Polly's grandson. Polly and Celeste, while co-residing, shared the responsibility of bringing up Neil.

2) Nangala (in her eighties), Joy's frail and blind mother, cared for by Joy, assisted by Polly and Celeste.

3) Kiara (aged ten), who lives with her adoptive grandmother Joy, and who is is the daughter of Polly's son whom Joy adopted, and thus is, in actual fact, Polly's grand-daughter and Celeste's niece.

4) Toby (aged twelve), one of Nora's grandsons, whom she looks after.

5) Pearl (in her seventies), a close sister of Nora's. These two, Pearl and Nora, co-resided and shared resources and time over long periods of their lives.

6) Annie (in her fifties), who is the daughter of a close brother of Polly's deceased and Joy's former husbands. Annie is not a co-dependant of any of the four women and in fact moved into Nora's room when she left, taking up a similar focal position in the jilimi as Nora held before.[8]

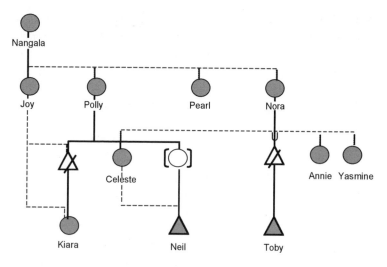

Figure 11: Genealogy of core residents

Who comes to stay at the jilimi, when, why and how long for, is largely, but not exclusively, determined through the relationships people have to any of these core residents. Based on age, social status and life history, Polly, Joy, Celeste, Nora and Annie in this regard certainly had a greater gravitational pull than the other core residents, and I describe them as focal in this regard (however, people also came to stay with Kiara, Toby, Neil, Nangala and myself, as well as with some of the less regular residents). In the following case studies, I provide some examples of why people came to stay in the jilimi, who they stayed with, how long for and so forth, by paying particular attention to the nature of the relationships between these residents and Polly, Joy, Celeste, and Nora respectively. In these case studies, I also discuss these residents' stays in regards to the classification by amount of nights slept in the jilimi during the census period.

Staying with Polly: Amy

Just counting close kin, Polly has many descendants: next to her own eight children, twenty-two grandchildren and nineteen great-grandchildren, she has also 'brought up' a number of other children. All of these and their respective children and grandchildren make up the substantial pool of her descendants. However, not all of them spend equal amounts of time with Polly, nor do they all have the same access to her resources. A few never stay with Polly, and the others are distributed across the four categories of residents. This fact hints at a crucial difference between types of residents: although people in one category may be equally closely related to a focal woman as those in another, they stay with her for different amounts of time and for different reasons. Residence may thus acquire different qualities depending upon the factors underlying it.

Polly is Amy's paternal grandmother; the reciprocal kin term for this emotionally often close, caring and comfortable relationship (between father's mother and son's children) is *yaparla*. Amy is in her late twenties, and she has been married twice. Her first marriage was to a man from Nyirrpi with whom she has a teenage daughter who spends most of her time with her paternal grandmother in Nyirrpi. Amy's second husband is from Kintore and she has a five-year-old son with him, who usually stays with Amy and sometimes with his paternal grandmother in Kintore. Amy herself mainly lives in one of the Alice Springs town camps.

Then Amy became gravely ill. She told us that after several checks at Alice Springs hospital, the doctors there decided they could not tell what was wrong with her. Since her illness could not be determined with certainty, everybody suspected sorcery, and Amy had to find a safe place to stay and be cared for (this case is study is further discussed in Musharbash 2008a). Neither the Alice Springs town camp, nor Kintore or Nyirrpi seemed good places, since in all of them lived affines (in-laws) of Amy — and affines, especially if marital relations are not too good and there are fights over children, are the first suspects in cases of sorcery. Since her parents are no longer alive, the place for her to go, then, was to her yaparla, Polly. During her sickness, Amy stayed physically close to Polly, sleeping next to her every night, and also shared her money and food with Polly. Polly in turn looked after Amy and organised a number of trips to go with her to other settlements to visit traditional healers to find out the causes of and cures for her grand-daughter's illness. Amy stayed in the jilimi for 36 nights (while I was there), while her son (Frederico) stayed with her for 28 nights.

In this instance, Amy and Frederico can be classified as on-and-off residents who have a particular reason for staying in the jilimi for a substantial period of time (Amy's illness). Once recovered, Amy went back to Alice Springs, and when she came to Yuendumu after that she generally stayed in other *camps*. During Amy's illness, her daughter

Cassandra came from Nyirrpi to visit her, but while in Yuendumu Cassandra often preferred to stay with some of her paternal relatives and only spent a total of six nights in the jilimi. Cassandra thus falls into the category of sporadic residents, and her example serves well to illustrate some core differences. Polly lived in the jilimi, Amy came to stay with Polly during the time of her illness and Polly, Amy and Frederico shared space and resources equally. Cassandra, who also is Polly's great-grand-daughter, sometimes came to stay with her mother, and although Amy looked after her while she was in the jilimi, Polly did not get involved much. Cassandra's access to the jilimi was conveyed through Amy and did not come from Polly. The fact that Cassandra spent fewer nights in the jilimi and more with her paternal relatives points to the reasons why she is here classified as a sporadic resident, while Frederico is classified as an on-and-off resident. Both Cassandra and Frederico are related to Polly in exactly the same way (both are children of Polly's grand-daughter Amy); however, Frederico is emotionally closer to Polly than Cassandra is (and there is more shared history between them) and Cassandra thus stays elsewhere more often.

Staying with Joy: Charity, Jenna and Megan

Joy's adopted son (Polly's actual son) had four children, all of whom were brought up by Joy, as was one of their sisters, Charity, daughter of the same mother but a different father (Charity is thus not a grandchild of Polly's). The youngest of these grandchildren, Kiara, stayed with Joy at all times (and was one of the jilimi's core residents). Her siblings are in their teens and early twenties, and most of them are involved in tempestuous marriages. Kiara's next eldest sister, Charity, was highly mobile and oscillated between her father's place, her young husband's parents' place, her close grandfather's place, her close sister's place and the jilimi. There, she spent 34 nights (during the census period) and is thus a typical example of an on-and-off resident. This kind of 'restless' or 'unsettled' residency behaviour is fairly common among young Warlpiri girls, who until they settle down with a husband and children are extremely mobile within a fairly stable and limited number of residences. Where Charity would sleep each night depended upon what happened during the day, with whom she spent time and where she ate dinner. If she had dinner in the jilimi, as she sometimes did, she might simply stay there. On other nights she would have spent time with Kiara at the disco and then came home with her, and so forth. The point is that in all her usual residences there would always be a place for her to stay, and if she felt like it she would come 'home' to the jilimi and simply crawl under the blankets with Joy and Kiara.

Kiara's and Charity's sister Jenna stayed in the jilimi for 18 nights, and like Charity, Jenna oscillated between a number of places: her young husband's parents' place, Mt Theo outstation and the jilimi.[9] Being in a somewhat more stable marriage than Charity, Jenna would only stay in the jilimi when fighting with her husband, or to be with her siblings if all of them were at the jilimi at the same time.

Megan, the eldest sister, stayed 20 nights in the jilimi. She falls into the category of on-and-off resident as well, but her story is somewhat different to the others. Megan had been married to a man from the south and lived there until their marriage deteriorated. When she returned to Yuendumu she moved in with Joy, and lived in the jilimi as a single woman until she got married again and moved with her new husband into her close grandfather's camp. Megan's and her sisters' patterns of and reasons for staying were quite different; however, they all can be classified as on-and-off residents and they all came to stay with Joy.

Staying with Celeste: Adrian and Stella, Jemima and Angelina

Many years ago, Celeste separated from her husband (who lives in Willowra) and has been living in a number of jilimi since. Celeste's son Adrian lived with her until his initiation, after which he began living in jangkayi (men's *camps*). When Adrian married Stella, a girl from Hermannsburg, they had to face the problem of where to live. Normally today, a young, newly married couple sets up their yupukarra in the *camp* of either partner's parents.[10] However, since they wanted to live in Yuendumu, where Adrian had employment, this was not possible: Stella's family lived in Hermannsburg, and all of Adrian's paternal relatives were in Willowra, while the older members of his maternal family at Yuendumu were women living in jilimi. At first, Adrian and Stella stayed in a derelict house close to the jilimi for a while, using the facilities of the jilimi and joined by a number of other young couples. Winter approached, and the derelict house provided almost no shelter and no warmth, so all but Adrian and Stella deserted it. Finally, without protection from the weather and without marlpa (company), they used Celeste's room in the jilimi as a yupukarra (married people's camp). Due to the substantial period they spent in the jilimi while looking for a new place (Adrian stayed for 48 nights and Stella for 54), they can be classified as regular residents. When Adrian was elsewhere, their yupukarra ceased to exist and Stella shared a yunta with other women in the jilimi. While the arrangement of having a yupukarra in the jilimi did not please anybody (neither the couple nor the other residents), everybody agreed that for the time being there was no other option. During the day, Adrian was at work at the Mining Company or away with his brothers and cousins, and he had previously, while unmarried, often been present in the jilimi at mealtimes anyway. The only difference during their stay in the jilimi was that the door to Celeste's room was closed at night and access to the room was restricted, symbolically marking the separation between jilimi and yupukarra.

Jemima and Angelina are the six-year-old twin daughters of Camilla, who is Celeste's deceased sister's daughter, making the twins Celeste's close grand-daughters and Polly's great-grand-daughters. Celeste and Camilla spend much time together and also work together at Yuendumu's Childcare Centre. When Camilla is away shopping in Alice Springs or taking courses at Batchelor College, she asks Celeste to look after her daughters. Angelina and Jemima spent 20 and 15 nights in the jilimi respectively. The difference between the two girls' stays is due to the fact that while Camilla looks after Angelina, her twin Jemima is being brought up by her paternal grandmother who spends substantial amounts of time in Murray Bridge. Thus Angelina sometimes comes to stay with Celeste on her own, while her twin Jemima is only ever in the jilimi when Angelina is there too. When they stay in the jilimi, they always stay with Celeste, not with Polly.

Staying with Nora: Sharon, Leah, Eva and Ray

Nora's daughter Sharon often came to visit the jilimi during the day, to gamble, gossip, and pass time. She also spent a substantial number of nights there because of her rather stormy marriage. Her husband often left Yuendumu for business trips that frequently turned into long absences. Whenever he left Yuendumu, or when they had a fight, Sharon would, according to Warlpiri practice, move into the jilimi. However, Sharon's relationship to her mother Nora was almost as stormy as that with her husband. She would thus move into the jilimi in which her mother was staying, but only stay in the same yunta as her mother when their relations were smooth. More often, she would set up her mattress next to some other people staying at the jilimi at the same time, for example with Polly's daughter Marion when she was staying in the jilimi, or with Joy's grandchildren. Sharon spent 29 nights in the jilimi, and is thus yet another on-and-off resident. But due to her age (she is in her early fifties) and her familiarity with the jilimi and its residents, she moved into the jilimi as a free agent as much as she did as Nora's daughter.

Nora's sister Leah (in her late fifties) and Joy's half-sister Eva (in her fifties), who have co-resided for many years, came to stay in the jilimi with Nora twice for different reasons. The first time they came to care for Nora, who had returned home from Alice Springs after having been hospitalised with pneumonia. The second time they came because of trouble at their former residence. Leah and Eva for a while had been living with Leah's daughter and her husband. However, that *camp* was known to be a locus of violence, and after things got out of control one too many times, they moved into the jilimi. With them came Ray, Nora's grandson and Toby's half-brother. Previously, Ray had moved between the two *camps*, and stayed alternately with Nora or with Leah, as a regular resident in either *camp*. Now, these women, together with their half-sister Pearl, who had been staying with Nora already, and Nora's grandsons, formed a tight-knit group, sharing resources between them and living in close proximity. In fact, when Nora received 'her own house', they all moved into that house together (except for Pearl who joined them there much later). In early 2005, they still lived in that *camp* joined by a continuous flow of people coming to stay with them in turn, and later that year moved en masse into another house because their previous one had come under a death-related taboo (*yarrkujuju*, see also Musharbash 2008b) when one of Nora's grandsons passed away.

Two things are interesting here. First, Eva, who is more closely related to Joy, stayed with Nora because Leah did so. This is a case were friendship ties, those between Leah and Eva, were more significant than kinship ties, those between Joy and Eva. Second, while Leah and Eva were on-and-off residents in the jilimi where they did not stay long and for necessity only, once they moved into the new house with Nora, all three of them, as well as their grandsons, became core residents there.

Residential categories and personal networks

As these case studies illustrate, many of the other jilimi residents are *some* of the relatives of the focal resident women, but by no means all. They constitute a relatively small number of the substantial pool of relatives and close associates that each of these women can draw upon. In relation to the focal women, the twelve regular residents (44–76 nights) in this jilimi and during the census period, were comprised of sisters (four), daughters (three), sons (two) and one son's son, father's sister, son's wife and daughter-in-law respectively. It needs to be kept in mind that each focal woman has a much larger number of people in each of these kinship relationships, and that it is only a few who regularly stay with them. This point is important as it underlines the fact that other factors are at work besides the kinship status of the people involved.[11]

There were more on-and-off and sporadic residents (36 and 48 respectively) than core and regular residents (11 and 12 respectively), underscoring the fact that people regularly stay in *camps* other than their home ones for short periods. While staying less often or for shorter periods in the jilimi than core and regular residents, on-and-off residents are nonetheless recruited from the same pool of kin surrounding the five focal women. In the main, on-and-off residents relate to these women as children, grandchildren, great-grandchildren, sisters and cousins. Further, there are some other individuals in this category whose relationships can be traced genealogically to the focal women but who are more accurately described by their relationship to the jilimi. Take Greta, for example. She used to be the 'owner' of one of the rooms; in her own words, 'the whole building' used to be hers.[12] While I was staying at the jilimi, she had two other main residences that she oscillated between, but she also frequently came to stay at the jilimi. Having once been a focal woman in this particular jilimi, she stayed in the jilimi because she felt it was her right to do so, and also to express her closeness to some of the more recent focal women through residing with them occasionally. Often when she came to stay, her grand-daughter and her sister joined her, and these two never came to stay in the jilimi without her.

Another woman in this category, Celia, moves backwards and forwards between Willowra and Yuendumu, and when in Yuendumu she stays for substantial periods of time in the jilimi. Although she often put up her yunta on the spatial margins of the jilimi, in many respects she paralleled the focal women in terms of access to rights and space within it, as well as through the gravitational position she was in. When living in the jilimi, she was often joined there by her daughter-in-law and a number of grandchildren.

A final woman in this category was a close sister of a former focal woman who had passed away some time ago. Since this woman was also a close classificatory relative of some of the current focal women, she continued to stay at the jilimi for a period before moving elsewhere for good.

The 48 sporadic residents (1–6 nights) are similar to the on-and-off residents in that they are made up of actual and close classificatory relatives of the focal women. Some differences between the two categories are that the former includes ex-focal women and that persons in the latter stayed in the jilimi less frequently and for shorter periods, often for one night only (during the census period, that is). It can safely be assumed that these patterns of occasional short stays were repeated at other times.

Those latter, most infrequent short-term stayers fall into two different kinds. Firstly, there were those who would have a number of other options to explore before staying at the jilimi, whereas for many individuals described as regular and on-and-off residents the jilimi would be the first choice — after their own 'home'. And secondly, such short-term stayers are also made up of those who came from other settlements and stayed in Yuendumu for brief periods only. While only a few individuals in the above categories have their usual place of residence elsewhere than Yuendumu, a striking difference about sporadic residents is that almost half of them are individuals usually based elsewhere. Many of these are grandchildren of the focal residential women visiting from other settlements, as well as sisters and cousins. And while no adult core resident is male (some of the children are, though), and the categories of regular and on-and-off residents contain one and two men respectively, four of the sporadic residents were men. Men do stay overnight in the jilimi, but not many and rarely for very long. These men were sons and grandsons of the focal women, and two were the husbands of the daughter and grand-daughter respectively of one of the focal women.

It is important to note that all these (named) residents can and do trace their relationships to people already staying in the jilimi, in many cases (but not exclusively) to the focal women. Apart from myself and possibly some people in the *sorry mobs*, there were no 'strangers' who came to stay in the jilimi. However, a genealogical link alone is not enough cause to come and stay in the jilimi; what matters is the actuality of such relationships. Such relationships need to be lived, sustained and continually affirmed — practices which create the formation of personal networks.

I discovered these personal networks through participation rather than by being told about them. Warlpiri people do not generally teach the anthropologist by answering questions; they insist on one *doing* things (see also Harris 1987; Morphy 1983; Myers 1986a: 294). 'You did this and now you know' were words I often heard. In respect to mobility and residence choices it is only in retrospect that I realise what I have learned, and created. When I now return to Yuendumu I have choices as to where and with whom to stay. There are those people I am closest to, but should they be elsewhere I would not be homeless. There are a number of others whose *camp* I could join with equal ease. I cannot approach somebody and tell them, 'I'll stay with you for a while' just because they are my classificatory mother, sister or daughter; however, I can do exactly that with somebody who is part of my personal network. Personal network relationships are based on shared experiences, shared residency in the past, and continued practice of reciprocal exchanges based on demand sharing. To be able to walk into a *camp* with one's swag and put it down next to a person there, to stay there for an unspecified period, is possible only once one knows from whom one can demand hospitality.

This perspective on the personal trajectories of people's residentiality alerts us to the fact that the classification into four types of residents according to the length of stay is arbitrary in some crucial regards. It only makes sense from a *camp*-centric perspective, during a specific period of time. Had I taken the same census a year later, people who were in one category might have been in another, or in none at all; others that did not stay there when I actually did take the census, stayed at the jilimi before or after, and so forth. Most importantly, if one examines the residential trajectories of individuals, one would find that each person falls into each category in different *camps* at different times. For example, while Polly, Joy, Celeste and Nora were core residents of the jilimi during the census period, they were not so a year before or after, and, what is more, during the census period they often stayed in other *camps* — where in turn they fell into one of the other residential categories.[13]

Both the *camp*-centric and the personal network perspectives provide crucial insights into contemporary mobility. The quantitative data presented here express the high rate of movement of people through the jilimi and are characteristic of social life throughout the settlement. The qualitative data suggest that people's mobility patterns reflect their need for sanctuary when ill or involved in marital disputes, their involvement in mortuary rituals, their visiting of relatives, their need for or provision of help, their arrangements for childcare, and simply socialising. Above and beyond the particular reasons for any move stands the common practice of creating and the need to maintain personal networks through face-to-face interaction, for Warlpiri social relations depend on such networks. Mobility is a taken-for-granted aspect of life; in order to create and maintain the conditions for one's own mobility one needs to accommodate the mobility of others.[14]

Thus, in order to truly understand mobility at Yuendumu, we must also take a step back and look at mobility not only as a practice but also as the value that it so obviously is. It shapes people's everyday experiences and their lives. Why should this be the case? A clue to this lies in the Aboriginal English term for 'staying at' or 'living with', which at Yuendumu is *stopping*. As Warlpiri residential patterns are processual, to *stop* is an apt term underscoring the halt that the flow of people through the *camps* comes to every night. In this vein, when I return to Yuendumu these days, my friends and I reminisce about 'that time we *stopped* in that jilimi', or, when giving somebody a lift home, a sensible question to ask first is 'where are you *stopping*?'. *Stopping* aptly characterises residential patterns in a life where they change on a regular basis.

In the *olden days* people moved from one place to the next, where they *stopped* and set up *camp* before moving on to the next place, where they *stopped* again, and so on. The contemporary settlement of Yuendumu is fixed in place, as are its houses. Yapa, however, continue moving — not across their country as in the *olden days* — but in such a way that each night, when putting up yunta, they *stop*, bring the events of the day to a halt and arrange themselves in ever-changing *camps* in and around the houses of the settlement.[15]

Conclusion

At Yuendumu, the flow of people is halted each night when people *stop*.
Warlpiri people move; nobody lives in the same place with the same
people permanently. Rather, people follow their own paths, which
continually crisscross and occasionally run parallel to those of others,
forming flows of people through *camps*. These flows of people through
the *camps* cannot be captured within the standard terminology. Applying
terms such as 'the household' in this context would entail the creation of
analytical boundedness in a situation where there is none.

Nonetheless, I would like to examine one last definition of the
household, or rather in this case, the 'residential group'[16] as it illustrates
its own non-applicability in the Warlpiri context in particularly pertinent
ways. This definition is the result of Verdon's (1979) effort to criticise
the original concept of the 'residential group'. He argues that it is futile
to define it by activities such as cooking, eating, pooling of resources
and labour, as they are commonly engaged in with others from other
dwellings. Instead, he proposes that the 'residential group' should be
defined by the only one activity shared exclusively by all people in
one dwelling, namely sleeping. Elaborating on the possible range of
relationships between sleepers, he says that

> in every society with residential groups, one thus observes a
> certain limit of internal complexity in their composition, some
> kind of 'breaking point' which is only exceeded in uncommon
> demographic, economic or physical circumstances (Verdon 1979:
> 420).

His proviso that this is true only for societies with residential groups
begs the question who these are. Maybe Warlpiri people do not fall into
this category. Or maybe the 'uncommon demographic, economic or
physical circumstances' of settlement life cause them to exceed 'certain
limits of internal complexity'. Or, to make a third suggestion, maybe our
obsession with searching for bounded categories blinds us to the possibility
that reality (in some circumstances) is better understood without them.
The extensive internal complexity of residence in Yuendumu *camps*, I
hope to have shown, is the result of focussed agency, rather than random
activity. There are as many reasons to *stop* in the jilimi as there are people

who do so on any one night. The flow of people through the *camps* of Yuendumu is an expression of social practice being lived out, it is the result of negotiated relationships, and we should interpret it as such. The volume and rapidity of residential mobility is a direct consequence of the way Warlpiri people organise their everyday life around relationships, while the particular shapes residential mobility takes today are formulated in dialogue with the permanent structures of houses and the settlement.

CHAPTER 5
In the jilimi: immediacy

As it gets dark, people in the *camps* of Yuendumu start making arrangements for the night. Fires are lit, bedding is taken outside (or down from the trees and shade roofs where it was stored during the day) and is laid out on the ground forming yunta (rows for sleeping). Who sleeps where and next to who changes, often on a nightly basis. The constant shifts and continual movement of yunta location, both within the yard of the jilimi and at other *camps* at Yuendumu, and the perpetual changes in the social composition of people sleeping within each yunta, are negotiated with little or no discussion while the yunta are set up (though the socio-spatial ordering may be discussed retrospectively).

Warlpiri sleeping arrangements are an excellent example of Moore's (1986) proposal to read (domestic) space as a text and to read physical activities and movement through it as revealing and reinforcing social meaning. To transplant that metaphor to the Warlpiri context, one could say that Warlpiri people inscribe domestic space as text with the positioning of their bodies each night, and every night a new text is produced. What is constant is that each night new 'texts' of sleeping arrangements appear across the Yapa *camps* of Yuendumu; what changes, nightly, is the composition of these 'texts'. Sleeping arrangements are neither static, durable, nor planned ahead; instead, they embody people's summaries of that day's occurrences. As responses to the events of the day, the ever-changing nightly sleeping arrangements in Yapa *camps* are an expression of immediacy, one of the three core values underpinning the Warlpiri series of building–dwelling–thinking.

I take sleeping arrangements as a way of working towards a conceptualisation of the particular Warlpiri form that immediacy takes at Yuendumu: to get a sense of its nature, how it is engendered by people's actions and how in return it shapes their lives. I do this by discussing how sleeping arrangements 'materialise', paying particular attention to those aspects verbally discussed (where to arrange yunta), and those tacitly understood (who sleeps in which yunta), detailing the latter through case studies of actual sleeping arrangements as they happened in our jilimi.

Verbal negotiations about sleeping arrangements

In the jilimi, as is true in other *camps*, there is a strong preference for sleeping outside if at all possible. Unless circumstances make it necessary, the four rooms of the jilimi's house are not used for sleeping. That leaves the long verandah and the yard space for putting up yunta. Where to put them is discussed every night (sometimes briefly, sometimes at great length). These explicit verbal discussions are about the influences of the weather, supernatural forces and other practical concerns to do with sleeping location, and illustrate how the nightly arrangements are made in response to immediate circumstances. The primary aim, today, is to decide whether to sleep inside or outside (of houses, or, in the case of the jilimi, in the rooms, on the verandah or in the yard), and if sleeping outside, where in the yard are the choicest places that night.

Weather is a major influence impacting on such discussions and decisions. Some other Yuendumu *camps* are located in or next to better built and equipped houses than our jilimi, and in those the weather may impact differently on the decision whether to sleep inside or outside. People living in *camps* that have houses with air-conditioning in working order sleep inside more frequently on hot summer nights, and people in *camps* with houses that have heating in working order in turn sleep inside in winter more often. However, the greater number of houses occupied by Warlpiri people at Yuendumu lack either or both, and decisions are made in the same way as described here. Most weather-related discussions are made either in terms of 'rain' or 'wind'.

Yuendumu experiences three different types of rain. Torrential rainstorms, although occurring rarely, can happen at any time. They can flood Yuendumu and its environs for up to a week, during which everybody who can shelters inside — without discussion.

The second type of rain, mostly occurring in summer, is more usual and consists of numbers of isolated individual rain clouds bringing highly localised rain. Sometimes it is possible to stand in Yuendumu and with a sweeping 360° view to spot up to eight different rain clouds in different directions raining in the distance. Some of them may pass over one or another of Yuendumu's Camps and may or may not bring rain, others will sweep by in the distance. If these kinds of rain clouds are in the sky, lengthy discussions always ensue at the time of putting up yunta. People present offer their reading of clouds, wind, and the probability of rain. The paths of all visible rain clouds will be projected, usually declaring that they will pass by Yuendumu but not directly over it: '*Ngapa kapu wantimi, mayi?* — '*Lawa, yatijarra yanirra.*'[1] 'It will rain, won't it?' — 'No, the clouds are moving north.'

These discussions are accompanied by gestures the jilimi's residents make to 'shoo' the rain clouds away. Only if it is raining heavily at the time, or clearly going to rain soon, are yunta put up on the verandah and/ or in the rooms. Most often, however, it is decided that it will not rain, and yunta are put up outside in the yard. Moving back onto the verandah due to rain in the middle of the night is by no means uncommon. When it does start raining at night, moving onto the verandah is postponed for as long as possible. If the rain starts as a drizzle, the move inside is only made when blankets become soaked. And even after a middle-of-the-night move back onto the verandah because of rain, when the rain stops, it is common for people to move back into the yard — and back again onto the verandah during the next shower.

The third kind of rain consists of large thunderstorms. These brew in a spectacular fashion, painting the sky in dark and violent colours. These storms roll in from all sides, depending on season and prevailing winds, with a large front of blackness to the east or west, and smaller individual black clouds to the north and south. These are called *kurdu-kurdu*, the children of the storm.[2] Thunder is called *kumparri* and lightning *wirnpa*. Taking shelter, by sleeping on the verandah or in the rooms, during thunderstorms is important, not only because of the rain. During a thunderstorm one cannot cook, especially meat, for fear of being struck by lightning. 'Wirnpa smells meat, it looks for fire and will kill you,' people often say. During thunderstorms, if at all possible, people sleep inside.

Similarly, discussions about whether to sleep inside or outside take place depending on the presence of certain types of wind. Yuendumu experiences severe winds, particularly during seasonal changes from hot to cold and from cold to hot weather. Often they turn into sandstorms, making sleeping outside rather unpleasant, and the rooms and the verandah are preferred options. However, often storms die down during the night, in which case the usual decision is to move outside — frequently to be awoken by small gusts full of sand in the morning. The hot storms announcing the end of the cold season and the beginning of summer, with the skies overcast and cloudy from the burning of surrounding country, are oppressive. During this time, people become cantankerous, suffer from headaches, and say that they generally *feel weak*. One informant described these winds as *karikurda* — 'upside-down-winds' — and because of them 'people get cranky and [have] lots of jealousy fights'. Sleeping on the verandah, if possible, is much preferred during this time and people announce this verbally. The same response is made when there are strong willywillies (whirlwinds), which sweep up and whirl around debris from a large area, turning items such as sheets of corrugated iron into dangerous projectiles.

Then, there are the cold winds, the ones announcing the cold season, but also 'freak' cold winds at other times. People detest cold winds, not only because of the physical unpleasantness of the actual winds, but because severe cold winds are associated with *bad news*: that is, death.[3] Age-graded ideas about causality in relations to cold winds are discussed by Keys, who says that 'younger women described changing weather conditions as *causing* deaths, older women saw the change in weather *resulting from* a series of deaths' (Keys 1999: 197, original emphasis). In my experience Warlpiri people generally are aware that the cold winds can cause illness, and especially so for the very young and the old and frail, but the main concern, regardless of age, is that strong cold winds are a harbinger of *bad news*. Cold winds make people want to sleep inside or in more protected areas where they feel sheltered from the piercing cold, but more importantly, people feel safer because they are sheltered from the winds and what they may bring.

A further issue triggering discussions and making people prefer to sleep inside or in a more sheltered position than usual is the presence of *jarnpa*; also commonly known throughout central Australia and the literature as *kurdaitcha*. The Warlpiri dictionary translates 'jarnpa' as 'a person who walks around at night in order to kill another person and make trouble, with special powers to make themselves invisible, who wears emu-feather foot covering to dissimulate tracks' (see Meggitt 1955 for a typology of jarnpa). Warlpiri people describe them as human-like beings covered in red ochre, and fear them greatly, as they bewitch innocent victims, making them sick, or even killing them. Jarnpa announce their presence by a whistling peculiar to them; alternatively, their presence is heralded by the singing of a particular bird. It sounds like *pakaka pakaka* and if the pitch and speed with which the bird sings increase, people know jarnpa are close. They yell at the bird '*Yantarra*!' — 'go away!' — in the hope that the jarnpa will follow the bird away from people. Warlpiri people claim that they cannot see jarnpa, they are invisible to them; however people from further afield and Kardiya are thought to be able to spot them. If jarnpa are sighted or heard, the rumour will spread through Yuendumu with speed. If they are detected near a *camp*, people may well abandon it, and people in *camps* close by will make sure they are more sheltered at night than usual. This procedure of sheltering is repeated inside the *camp*. People who sleep yitipi (on the outside of a yunta) are positioned to protect those on the inside, and when jarnpa are around, only senior and knowledgeable people choose to sleep yitipi; most people preferring to be located kulkurru (inside). Concern about jarnpa is regularly pronounced during windy time, as the winds make jarnpa tracks (as well as all other tracks) unreadable and jarnpa whistling inaudible (see also Keys 1999: 197). This is a time, then, when people feel much less safe than usual and look for safe shelter, often sleeping inside (of buildings) and seeking the inside of rows of swags (making for less but longer yunta).

Apart from issues to do with weather or jarnpa, the only other explicit verbal statements involved in putting up yunta have to do with practical concerns. For example, people may request help when carrying a particularly heavy mattress, or when laying out a large groundsheet when it is windy. They may have verbal exchanges when requesting the use of a bed, if one is present, and how to position it, as often happens when people are in pain or ill. There are comments about a yunta being too long and suggestions it be broken up into two, and criticism is voiced about yunta too haphazardly arranged and deviating from 'proper' orientation. Lastly, the placement of old and frail people, and of those who are considered *warungka* (not knowing), is matter-of-factly and verbally decided by others. 'Put that old Nangala there, next to Nakamarra and not too close to the fire', or, 'Leave that Nungarrayi on the verandah, she can sleep there with Napaljarri' are examples of such comments. Newcomers to the jilimi, too, may be given verbal advice. 'Don't sleep too close to the western fence, we saw a snake track there this morning', or, 'Stay away from the eastern side, that septic tank is smelly'. Apart from that, however, the orchestration of nightly sleeping arrangements happens by means of tacit understandings and without explicit verbal mediation.

Explicit verbal discussions about sleeping arrangements are about practical concerns, and in their own way illustrate the element of immediacy in the nightly arrangements of yunta. In Moore's terms (1986), they are not (so much) about the composition of the text (the social, emotional, and personal aspects of who sleeps in which yunta) but where the text within the space of the *camp* (and in relation to the house if present) is arranged. During more than three years of sleeping in the *camps* of Yuendumu, I have recorded fewer than twenty nights without any changes in the placing of yunta.

Tacit negotiations

Putting out bedding at night is not a communally orchestrated effort. Apart from the issues outlined above, it does not normally involve debate, nor indeed does it engender much comment. Mostly, these arrangements are made 'automatically', they simply 'happen'. Someone or other will get up first and get their bedding from a room or the verandah, drag it outside into the yard and put it up at a place of their choosing. Others follow in their own time and arrange their bedding in a location of their respective choice. The result, however, is not a random aggregation of swags strewn all over the yard, but a rather neat arrangement of a number of yunta distributed over the jilimi's space. All yunta are oriented so that the sleepers' heads point east (unless people are sleeping in rooms or on the verandah, where spatial orientation is dictated by walls and doors). Who sleeps next to whom in what yunta to a large extent reflects general social relations and more specifically what has happened during the day.

Logistics would be Celeste's calling. In the jilimi, she was the one who often ensured that there was enough firewood, that children were being fed, that old women slept in a good enough shelter, and, when going on trips, that all things necessary, from groundsheets to billycans and water, tea, and meat, would be taken. She organised trips out bush to get poles and branches to build proper windbreaks. Celeste was the only person who took an active role in organising sleeping arrangements and the only one I ever encountered to frequently give directions and make decisions about who should sleep where. Nobody else in the jilimi ever showed any great interest in these matters. While often it seemed they good-naturedly let Celeste take charge, when she was away or when she took up paid work and spent less time in the jilimi, complaints started arising. In particular a number of elderly women who were living in the jilimi at the time had come to depend on her. They protested about being neglected; general grumbling could be heard about the lack of firewood, and so on — none of these accusations would be aimed at anyone specific, but all lamented the absence of the kind of organisation that they had come to take for granted. When Celeste was present, things seemed to run more smoothly.

Most nights, after dinner, Celeste would get up and say to me, 'Come Napurrurla, let's get the swags'. The two of us would go to her room, get her large blue plastic groundsheet and take it onto the verandah or into the yard to the place Celeste chose for us that night. After putting out the groundsheet, making sure it was all smooth and in the right direction, we would get the swags, Celeste's first. She would put hers where she wanted to sleep. Then mine. 'Put it there', Celeste would direct, usually indicating either north or south of her own swag. Depending on who else was staying in the yunta with us that night, she would direct them too. 'Napaljarri can sleep here, and Nangala there.' Our activity would be a sign for the others present to get up from around the fire(s) and start their own preparations for the night. Their putting up swags into yunta however normally included little or no discussion. As Celeste had made a start, people not included in our yunta would set up theirs in a distance and orientation to ours, mirroring what suited them and, as I later learned, indicating their relations to us. Initially, however, these ever-changing arrangements puzzled me immensely.

In order to find and understand the patterns of the social dynamics underlying these continually changing sleeping arrangements, every morning I drew a map of the previous night's sleeping arrangements. These maps are made up of a mix of Warlpiri iconography and written directions. They include lines depicting individuals (shorter ones for children, and longer ones for adults) with the name of each individual written next to them. Horizontal lines above them describe the extent of each yunta. I marked cardinal directions, described the location of fires with asterisks, and if relevant, included indications where a fence, a verandah, or the walls of rooms were.

Looking at the notebooks of jilimi sleeping arrangement maps now, they remind me of the flip books I used to play with when a child. One can imagine, when flipping through the notebooks' pages, how these maps display a 'moving image' of the social composition of the jilimi, with its yunta continually expanding and contracting over time. In a manner comparable to time-lapse photography, they portray individuals arriving for their first night in the jilimi, staying, and then leaving. They show people moving through the space of the *camp*, sleeping in one yunta for a few nights, and then perhaps in another; next to this person first, and then next to somebody else. They show images of people within the *camp* moving closer together night after night, or moving away from each other. In other words, the maps show spatial representations of lived social experience. If one were to fill the maps with daily activity, with gossip, with the developments of relationships and with the fights that took place, they would start to approach quite closely some of the core aspects of contemporary everyday life at Yuendumu. By discussing a number of these maps here, I explore the relationship between the jilimi as a socio-spatial entity and the production and reproduction of Warlpiri sociality. I present the maps for my first nights in the jilimi, and then discuss further examples of such sleeping maps from the jilimi to illustrate how immediacy as a core value of the Warlpiri everyday is embodied in the ever-changing sleeping arrangements.

Maps of the first nights in the jilimi and how to read them

The night of 29 November 1998 was my first in the jilimi (Figure 12). It was clear but unusually cold for November, so rather than moving out into the yard, the old and frail women (Lydia, Bertha, Nellie and Lynne) stayed on the verandah and put up their swags next to the fire on which they had cooked dinner. Lynne had two little grand-daughters staying with her, and they slept next to her on the same mattress. Nora and her grandson Toby, who often had their own little yunta, had spent much of the day with the old ladies (who are Nora's sisters Lydia and Bertha and her father's sisters Nellie and Lynne). Since they were all getting along famously during the day, Nora and Toby put their yunta up right next to the old ladies, in front of Nora's room on the verandah. (Note that the alternative would have been for Nora and Toby to carry their bedding out of Nora's room past the old ladies and away from them, an action contrary to the events of the day.) Toby slept, as always, on the same

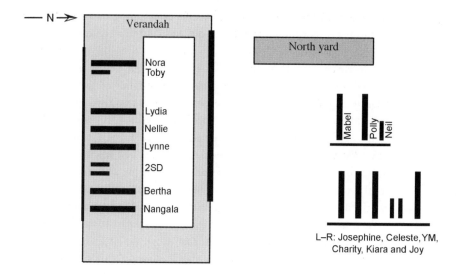

Figure 12: Sleeping arrangements for the night of 29 November 1998

mattress as Nora (his grandmother who was bringing him up). Since the verandah was warm and snug and there was marlpa (company) there, old Nangala was put next to one of the women there, rather than being taken out onto the yard to sleep next to her daughter Joy, close to whom she usually slept.

In the yard, Celeste shared a mattress with her sister's daughter Josephine, who often *stopped* with her. Normally, Celeste's 'son' Neil (Josephine's brother) slept under Celeste's blankets, but since Josephine took up his spot this night he stayed with his grandmother Polly. I slept with Celeste and Josephine on one side, and Joy and her grand-daughters on the other.

This was the first night I slept in the jilimi, and there were a number of reasons why Joy and I had moved there that day. Moving from our previous *camp*, where we had lived with Joy's (*divorced*) husband and a number of her grandchildren, to the jilimi somewhat decreased Joy's burden of looking after me. She was 'the owner' of one of the jilimi's rooms and closely acquainted with as well as related to the other core residents of the jilimi. She could expect them to help her look after me. This added help was doubly important as she had just switched from working part-time to full-time at the school's Literacy Centre, and thus had less time for me, especially considering that she was also looking after her old husband, her old and frail mother and a number of grandchildren.

Moreover, while Joy was my 'first mother', the person I knew best and who initially looked after me, tensions had begun to arise in our relationship. In retrospect, I suspect tensions had also mounted between Joy and the jilimi residents as they had observed her directly benefiting from and restricting from others' access to my resources. The move to the jilimi also meant that I became more of a 'shared commodity', pacifying others but in turn furthering tensions between Joy and myself. Use of my Toyota, access to which Joy had previously controlled tightly, caused much friction. When Joy and I moved to the jilimi she had asked Celeste to help look after me, that is, cook tea and damper in the mornings and generally share the responsibilities of ensuring I was all right and did not commit too many blunders.

Joy, wherever she went, usually had her grand-daughter Kiara with her and often some of Kiara's siblings. My sleeping position in between Celeste and her 'daughter' and Joy and her grand-daughters indicated my social position at the time. Sleeping in between them, connecting their two otherwise separate yunta indicated their shared responsibility: I was being looked after by both women and was not particularly close to either.

Further west in the yard that night was a third yunta, comprising Polly, Neil and Mabel. Mabel usually slept in her *camp* with her *divorced* husband and her daughter's family. At the time, however, Mabel was gravely ill and it was hoped that her stay in the jilimi would help her regain some of her strength, as there she could be looked after rather than having to look after others. Most nights, her sister Greta stayed with her, but as she was absent that night, Mabel shared a yunta with Polly.

The next night was even colder, and all jilimi residents (including Greta who had returned from another settlement) slept on the verandah (Figure 13). On the eastern end was old Nangala, who always slept yitipi (on the outside), 'so that she could make wee in the night on the side'. Joy and her grand-daughter slept next to Nangala, and I slept next to them, with Celeste, Josephine and Neil on my other side. West of them was Polly, and west of her the other old women who had slept the previous night on the verandah, together with the same grandchildren,

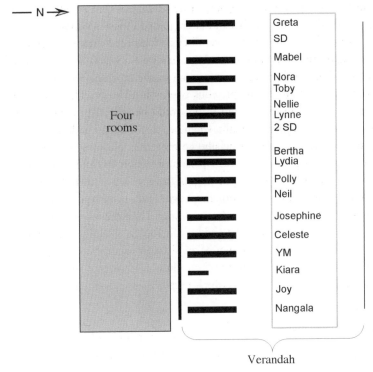

Figure 13: Sleeping arrangements for the night of 1 December 1998

and then Toby and Nora. At the furthest end were Mabel and her sister Greta and Greta's grand-daughter, who stayed with Greta in the same way as Toby did with Nora and Kiara with Joy.[4]

Variations of these two patterns — everybody on the verandah, or one yunta on the verandah and one or two yunta in the yard with similar social compositions — prevailed over the next week. Some small changes were made when new residents joined the jilimi. For example some of Joy's other grand-daughters and one of her close daughters joined her and Kiara, and another of Nora's grandsons, Ray, joined her and Toby.

The next major shift occurred when Nora had a minor fight with one of her sisters, and left the yunta of elderly women and instead made up a yunta with Mabel and Greta. A few days later, after yet another minor affray, Nora and her grandsons put up their yunta even further away from the old women, taking up their previous and often later repeated habit of having their own separate little yunta, this time equally far away from all other yunta. Mabel and Greta joined Celeste's yunta.

None of these moves were ever discussed, especially not when actually putting up the yunta in the evenings. In a way, it was as if the storing of the bedding inside or on the verandah in the morning wiped the slate clean of the affairs of the previous twenty-four hours. The day would begin, and whatever it would bring would be reflected in the sleeping arrangements of the next night, when people took their bedding out and placed it where they felt (socially) comfortable. Sleeping arrangements are a spatial expression of each person's reaction to, interpretation of, and statement about the happenings of the day, and as the following case studies suggest, are read by others as such. Since these readings are rarely discussed (but see below), and even though I had the maps, it took me a while to come to understand and be able to read sleeping arrangements myself. I can read the meanings of the sleeping arrangement maps of the first few months I spent in the jilimi only in retrospect, and only with the help of my notebooks in which I recorded the daily happenings.

Greta and Mabel

Greta is the woman mentioned previously as a former 'owner' of one of the jilimi's rooms, or, according to her, the whole house. At this stage, she had two other main residences, one where she shared a house with a Kardiya woman and looked after the house during the woman's long and frequent absences, and the other with her sister Mabel, in a *camp* not far away from the jilimi. When Mabel became ill and moved into the jilimi, Greta moved with her to look after her. During my first night in the jilimi described above, Mabel was in the jilimi without Greta and slept next to Polly. Then Greta returned, and as the next few nights were very cold and all residents made up one single yunta on the verandah, Greta and Mabel took up a position on the extreme western end. Once sleeping in the yard became possible again, the first night Greta and Mabel slept in the same yunta with the old ladies who before had slept on the verandah. The next night Mabel, Greta and her grand-daughter made up a yunta of their own, positioned north and west of the other yunta present in the jilimi. The next six nights they shared a yunta with Nora and her grandsons, and the following nights slept next to Celeste and me. A few nights later, in turn, they shared a yunta with Joy, and later slept in a yunta with Polly again.

These frequent moves from one yunta to the next were triggered by two separate objectives. The first was Greta's concern about Mabel's illness and her — successful — attempts to involve as many jilimi residents as possible in the care of Mabel. This raised awareness in different social sets about Mabel's needs and thus during the day, when Greta was absent, there were a number of different people who looked after and cared for Mabel. As a result, Greta and Mabel slept in different yunta on successive nights.

The second objective was to do with the fact that Greta had once been a core resident in the jilimi but was not any more. By sharing the yunta of all new focal women present on successive nights, she made an implicit statement about her relations to them: that she related to all of them in equally congenial ways, that she did not prefer any of the women to any others. In fact, her movements through the jilimi space are an explicit political statement about her wish to maintain good relations with all focal women of the individual yunta. Her spatial movements from yunta to yunta within the jilimi also attest to her personality, as a woman who seriously cared about the maintenance of amicable and harmonious relations of all around her.

Joy and Yasmine

The second example of a retrospective reading of the sleeping arrangements of the early months in the jilimi involves my first mother Joy and myself, and is rather less amiable. By the time we moved into the jilimi, our relationship had become increasingly fraught. We were both frustrated, and there were occasional minor outbursts on both our parts. Joy's decision to move into the jilimi and ask Celeste to help look after me initially meant that some of the strain was taken off Joy, while at the same time she did not have to worry about 'losing' me and access to my resources. After all, for years Celeste had generously helped Joy look after her old and frail mother, Nangala, and that arrangement worked just fine for all three of them. The first weeks in the jilimi, I, the only one who needed directions when putting up yunta, was directed to put up my swag either next to Joy or next to Celeste. More often than not, the other would put up her swag on the other side. Joy and whoever was staying with her, and Celeste and whoever was staying with her would form one large yunta, connected by me in the middle. These sleeping arrangements reflected exactly the arrangements agreed upon by Joy and Celeste: that both would look after me and 'shared' access to my resources. Accordingly (as indicated in Table 3), during the first 60 nights I *stopped* in the jilimi, I spent 23 nights sleeping in the middle between Joy's yunta and Celeste's yunta, combining the two into one long yunta. For 14 nights I was sleeping next to Joy; for 20 nights next to Celeste; and three nights I slept next to other people in their yunta.

Table 3: My positioning in the jilimi for the first 60 nights

Positioning	Number of nights
Joy one side — Celeste other side	23 nights
next to Celeste	20 nights
next to Joy	14 nights
next to neither	3 nights

However, in spite of Joy's hope that our relationship would improve through our move to the jilimi, relations between Joy and me steadily deteriorated. I continued to call her *ngati* (Mum); she continued to call me her daughter; and others continued to refer to me as 'belonging to Joy'. I also continued to share my resources with Joy as much as possible. However, as I became more independent and my own personal networks expanded, there was a greater circle of people with whom I shared money, food, and the Toyota, and as a result, Joy's share increasingly shrank. Joy was tremendously hurt whenever I rejected one of her requests, and this happened more and more frequently. In turn, I became more and more irritated with her frequent demands, which I read as attempts to control me. As time progressed, I slept more often next to Celeste and less often next to Joy. At the time, I was not at all conscious of the analogy between sleeping arrangements and the state of social relations. However, looking through those notebooks of sleeping arrangements now, one can see Joy and me slowly, from one night to the next, creating increasing distance between us in our sleeping arrangements, and so foreshadowing the turn our relationship was taking. Indeed, with one exception, after the first 60 nights I never slept in a yunta with Joy again. Our ceasing to sleep next to each other was a spatial indicator of the decline of amicable relations.

In May 1999 Celeste was away for a course at Batchelor College and Joy made one last attempt to repair our relationship. During Celeste's absence, two Kardiya women disseminated rumours that I had written scandalous reports about Yapa *camps* in Alice Springs newspapers. My relations to the people I was working with deteriorated because of these rumours, and I spent much time and effort assuring people that they were untrue. To my immense gratitude, Joy took an instrumental role in helping me and rallying for support. However, because Joy had taken on the responsibility of 'looking after' me in this instance, this gave her license to ask for something in return. And when Stella, Josephine and Tamsin asked me whether I would sleep with them in Celeste's room that night, Joy said, 'That's too loud', and suggested I sleep in her room on her bed. After what she had done for me that day, I could not refuse, even though I was aware of what her invitation implied. It was her attempt to convince me that I was better off with her (who could offer me the comfort of a quiet room, her own bed to sleep on, and her superior and just proven skills of looking after me) rather than with Celeste. I ended up sleeping in Joy's room for five nights until Celeste returned. Each night, Joy tried to talk me into moving out of the jilimi. As Nora was on the top of the Council list as the first person to receive one of the newly built houses, Joy suggested, I should move with Nora and her until Joy's house was ready. I had no intention of moving with either Joy or Nora and I kept repeating this — and our five nights together were vexing and frustrating for both of us. This shows clearly in the maps of our sleeping arrangements for these nights (see Figure 14). While life in the jilimi and for its other residents followed its usual paths, during those five nights it was as though Joy and I were trapped in her room, arguing and not being able to come to an agreement acceptable to both of us. And although we slept in the same room, in the sleeping arrangements for these nights it seems almost as if we were dancing around each other. While in that small room we never slept next to each other, but as far away from each other as possible. Shortly after these events, Joy and I had our 'big fight', and Joy 'dis-adopted' me, as described previously.

The reason for describing this case study in such detail is that it illustrates so well the opposite of Mabel and Greta's sleeping arrangements, described in the previous case study. Their movement from one yunta to the next reflected the creation of social and personal intimacy, expressing Mabel and Greta's desire for and achievement of harmonious relations with all jilimi residents. Joy's and my movements away from each other, on the other hand, were spatial expressions of our increasingly discordant relationship, demonstrating on a nightly basis the waning of our intimacy.

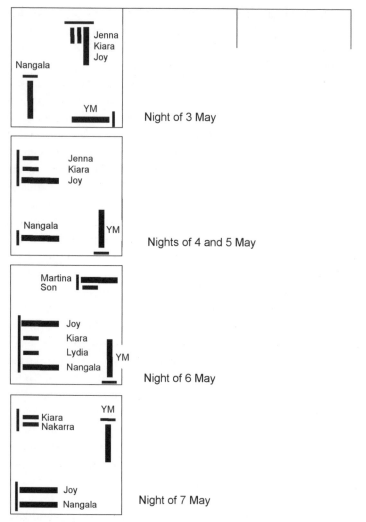

Figure 14: Sleeping arrangements in Joy's room for the nights of 3–7 May 1999.

Reading sleeping arrangements

When Yapa recount events, no matter whether they involved camping out bush on a hunting trip or sleeping next to the road on the way to another settlement, in an Alice Springs motel room, or in the jilimi, they supplement them with sand drawings. In these drawings, the sleeping position of every person present is indicated by a vertical line in the sand, while recounting their names, and the yunta is drawn by a horizontal line above them.

Had a sand story been recounted about the night of 29–30 November 1998, the lines would have been drawn into the sand exactly as they are represented in Figure 12, and the respective names would have been spoken while each line was drawn into the sand: 'Joy Napaljarri, and the two Nakamarra here, then Napurrurla, Celeste, Josephine. And there Mabel, Polly and that Japangardi. And on the verandah ...'. Even a question such as, 'Who went to Papunya Sports Weekend?' would generate a large sand drawing. This sand drawing would outline where exactly different people from Yuendumu put up their yunta, how these were positioned to each other, and where people from other settlements camped. The speaker would always include a detailed description of the actual sleeping order of people in the yunta he or she slept in, as well as those other yunta the speaker had knowledge of.

While the explicit description of who slept next to whom and in which yunta is an essential part of Yapa story-telling, it is of utmost importance to note that neither in these stories nor during the actual putting up of yunta are the meanings of the composition of yunta ever enlarged upon. Actual sleeping arrangements and sand stories themselves reveal these meanings, as everybody who sees them or listens to them recounted knows everybody involved. A person who was not present learns a lot from such a sand story. Warlpiri listeners can easily make many deductions by being told that X slept next to Y, and that Z did not. There is no need to *verbally* and publicly analyse the implicit meanings, as they are all equally clear to all — and this rather oblique way of relating stories of social relations has great appeal to Warlpiri people in general.

The nightly sleeping arrangements are thus understood (but not discussed) as summary statements about the impact of that day's occurrences upon webs of social relations and about the way each person related to the others present — on that night. As much as people understand the meanings implicit in nightly arrangements, they are aware that both the meanings and the order may change as a response to the social interactions the next day will bring. Verbal interpretation would thus not only contradict Warlpiri decorum in terms of being explicit rather than oblique, but also and rather unsubtly make a statement about something that is constantly in flux.

Sleeping arrangements change on a nightly basis as an immediate response to the physicality of that actual night. They also inevitably change because of social mobility. Most importantly, they change because as texts in Moore's sense they reflect Warlpiri practices of engaging with domestic space, and the underlying principle of this is that a *camp* is formed as a result of the happenings of the day. Reading consecutive maps of sleeping arrangements over time shows how the space comprising a *camp* is constantly being reformulated, and how the negotiations, divisions, invasions, withdrawals, uses and appropriations of this physical space can be read as analogous to those of social relations. These processes are subtle, implicit, and tacit. Greta, for example, did not move her and Mabel's bedding from yunta to yunta in a calculated and deliberate manner, it was simply the right thing to do. Similarly, at no time did I think that I had to (or wanted to) increase spatial distance between Joy and myself; the fact that I slept more and more often next to Celeste was more an automatic result of us spending the day together. The order that unfolds nightly in Warlpiri *camps* is tacitly achieved, it is never verbally negotiated, or, for all that I could find out, consciously decided upon. Yet, although creation of this order is always undertaken tacitly, its meanings do get actively read, and all participants understand how sleeping arrangements illustrate how relations are negotiated, manifested, created, transformed, broken, and reinvented.

As the day comes to a close, people *stop* in *camps* and within them in yunta in a manner that reflects where they should be. Sleeping arrangements at Yuendumu are not about group identity, rather they are an expression of the current state of interpersonal relations, of how people present related to each other on *that* day. Yunta thus understood are an expression of immediacy — they are physical manifestations of how people experience and react to the here and now rather than a continuation of the immediate past or a perceived future. People do not sleep next to people because they did so the night before, nor do they plan to sleep next to a particular person, on, say next Tuesday. The storing of bedding inside in the morning wipes the slate clean of the affairs of the previous twenty-four hours. The new day will begin and whatever it will bring is going to be reflected in the sleeping arrangements of the coming night — when people place themselves where they feel comfortable. As each day differs from the next, so each night there are new arrangements in the social composition of the yunta in the *camps* of Yuendumu.

CHAPTER 6

In the jilimi: intimacy

One of Bourdieu's paramount insights is that the body is a vehicle through which we experience and create the world (see especially 1990 and 2000: 89–96). As he says:

> But it is in the dialectical relationship between the body and a space structured according to the mythico-ritual oppositions that one finds the form par excellence of the structural apprenticeship which leads to the em-bodying of the structures of the world, that is, the appropriating by the world of a body thus enabled to appropriate the world. (Bourdieu 2000: 89)

This is not so different from Heidegger's series of building–dwelling–thinking. The processes of creating and structuring the world and being created and structured by the thus created world are the same; what differs is the role of the body. It is absent in all but an abstract sense in Heidegger, present as a active/passive force in Bourdieu, where the body acts, experiences, and is acted upon. What is missing in both theories is the person. We find generic man in Heidegger, man and woman as opposites in Bourdieu, but we do not encounter individuals. Yet, it is in exactly this nexus of embodied structures and rules (married people sleep in yupukarra, socially senior people sleep on the outside of a yunta, and so forth) and the actual bodies of actual people doing things in the real world, that Warlpiri intimacy arises.

A most helpful approach to this bridging of the body, the person and the world is found in the French sociologist Marcel Mauss's idea of body techniques (1979, first published in 1934). He describes body techniques as 'physio-psycho-sociological assemblages of action' (Mauss

1979: 120), alerting us to the fact that the body is employed (and read) on three interconnected levels: the physiological, the sociological and the psychological. He provides a list of body techniques in which, listed under 'sleep', there is an inventory of sleeping positions and contexts: sleeping lying down or standing up, on a horse, in a bed, on a mat, on the ground, under a blanket, alone, with others, in a circle, and so on. He adds that 'hundreds of things still remain to be discovered' (Mauss 1979: 112). In exploring Warlpiri intimacy through ways of sleeping, I am following Mauss's call to sociologically investigate sleep.

Sleep is a physiological need. Our bodies must sleep in order to live, we get cranky when we are tired, we feel great after a long deep sleep, and so forth. Sleep is sociologically (or socio-culturally) organised, or, as Mauss said, 'the notion that going to bed is something natural is totally inaccurate' (Mauss 1979: 112). Sleep in this regard approximates most closely some of Bourdieu's ideas about embodiment, as sleep is socio-culturally organised in terms of space, gender, protection, ritualisation and forth.

In socio-cultural contexts in which ideas of separating private and public, for example, are given moral priority, the sleeping person is protected through various thresholds and institutions, and the acts of preparing for sleep and re-entering waking life are ritualised (see among others, Aubert and White 1959a, 1959b and Schwartz 1970). At Yuendumu, sociality is formed through webs of personal networks, each of which is established through numerous person-to-person relationships. The distinction of public and private cannot play the same role in a context in which relationships are extensive and always personal, and formed around the tensions of autonomy and relatedness, or being *boss for oneself* and looking after others.[1] As a result, sleep is shared, within certain limits. Marital status and gender dictate some of the spatial aspects of sleep everywhere, through the ways in which marriage and gender are conceptualised and spatially organised in everyday life. At Yuendumu, as we saw, this happens through the separation of jilimi, yupukarra and jangkayi. Marital sexual relations and marital sleep take place at night in yupukarra, extra-marital sexual relations take place during the day and away from yupukarra. As Warlpiri sexuality is defined purely through heterosexual relations, all other non-sexual sleep, by implication, happens in jilimi and jangkayi, reinforced through the simple fact that in these places, blankets and mattresses are shared without connotations of sexual activity. Put differently, conceptually aligning yupukarra with sexual relations means that there is no need to flag the absence of sexual relations in other types of *camps*, there is no need for walls or physical distance regimenting sleep — as long as unmarried men and unmarried women sleep in separate *camps*. This allows for expressions of intimacy that are socio-culturally particular as well as indicative of what Mauss calls the psychological.

Significantly, Mauss placed the psychological in between the other two in his concept of 'physio-psycho-sociological assemblages of action'. The lens of the psychological as linked to both the physiological and the social throws light on Warlpiri notions of intimacy through examining Warlpiri practices of sleeping (which, of course, is one of many body techniques, all of which could be analysed in similar ways). It allows for exploration of both the meaning of choice within conforming to socio-cultural norms and individuality in physio-psychological terms.

Two issues in regards to sleep thus defined bring into relief the Warlpiri notion of intimacy. Firstly, the over-arching socio-cultural structures allow for (and are perpetuated by) mobility and immediacy, which in practice mean that Yapa co-sleep with a much greater number of others than, say, Kardiya do. This affords Yapa an intimate knowledge of a greater number of other people's bodies. Secondly, the individual choices specific persons make within the over-arching socio-cultural structures exemplify to themselves and to others their idiosyncratic individuality. Put differently, intimate knowledge is acquired by living in close proximity with others, by paying attention to their bodies, and to how individuals use and position their bodies. Sleeping arrangements are one of many Warlpiri practices of living in close proximity, and I examine them to approach an understanding of Warlpiri forms of intimacy in Bachelard's sense; I interpret sleeping arrangements as communicating aspects of the innermost protected idea of selfhood, of ways of being and seeing oneself. I begin with a description of the sensuality of knowing other people's bodies and the sensuality of sleep in the jilimi, and then analyse the particular choices Polly, Joy, Nora and Celeste made in their sleeping arrangements during my first sixty nights in the jilimi.

The sensuality of knowing the bodies of others

When I first arrived at Yuendumu I memorised people by their faces and sometimes by their clothes (bad mistake, as clothes are swapped frequently). As a result, I had great difficulties recognising people at night. When we sat around the fire telling stories and someone or another came toward us in the dark, I used to be perplexed by everybody but me recognising who was approaching long before I could see their faces in the firelight. However, it was not Warlpiri people's night vision that was superior to mine, but their knowledge of others, and of others' bodies.

Celeste does not need to see Tamsin's face to recognise Tamsin; she can identify her by her shape, the way she walks, by her foot tracks, her voice, her breathing, the way she smells, by the way she flicks her hand, by any number of clues deduced from Tamsin's body. Accordingly, she can identify how Tamsin feels, what mood she is in, if she is ill or healthy, happy, sad, or angry, by the smallest signs. The same is probably true for most intimate relationships (such as mother– child, husband– wife) around the world. At Yuendumu, however, people possess such intimate knowledge about others from a much greater circle of people. Such intimate knowledge is imparted and acquired through many practices. Here I single out sleeping in the jilimi. I am not concerned with the intimacy of sexual relations (in yupukarra), but that of women and children sharing mattresses and blankets in the yunta of the jilimi.

Familiarity finds expression in closeness. The degree of physical proximity of bodies inside a yunta is up to the individuals, and differs from night to night, depending who one is sleeping next to. Parallel to the way in which individual yunta are distributed across the yarlu of the jilimi and spatially express social closeness and distance to each other, so within each yunta sleepers arrange themselves in different degrees of physical closeness to each other. Snuggling up to others provides comfort, expresses sentiments of marlpa, and in the jilimi (as well as in jangkayi) has no sexual connotations. There are no age or generational limitations on who might share blankets with whom: adult sisters, adult mothers and adult daughters, anybody can and does — if they feel comfortable. Children generally climb under their mother's blankets, or, if they are being looked after by a grandmother, especially a yaparla (paternal grandmother), they grow up sharing the blankets with her. In fact, co-sleeping arrangements between yaparla are one reason why many senior women 'adopt' one of their son's children. In Nora's case for example, one of the benefits to her close yaparla relationship with Toby was the marlpa (company) he provided, including at night as a co-sleeper. Independent of the nature of Nora's current relations to any of the other jilimi residents, looking after Toby meant that there was always at least one other body in her swag at night.

Because of the extensive flow of people through *camps*, and because of the ever-changing nightly arrangements of yunta, who sleeps next to whom and how also is in constant flux. This in turn means that everybody has experiences of co-sleeping with a large (but varying) number of people, resulting in intimate knowledge of those people's bodies.

Having shared blankets with them, I know how Tamsin will wind her legs around mine, I know what Greta's arm over my hip feels like, and Monroe snuggling under my arm, I know that Zack will kick off the blankets in the middle of the night, that Marion grinds her teeth when dreaming. Having slept many times next to them, I can imitate Joy's snore, can pinpoint when Camilla will turn her body around after a particularly loud snore, I know Kiara's little grunts, and I would be able to identify Celeste's breathing anywhere. I know the smell of Neil's hair and how he tosses and turns until he falls into deep sleep, I know the feel of Polly's skin, I know whose skin is dry, whose feet get sweaty, I know how many blankets Annie likes on a cold winter's day and on a mild night. I know all these things about all these people because I have co-slept with them.[2] This knowledge is part of the reason why today I, too, can tell who is approaching our fire at night, or, even with my eyes shut, who has just entered the yunta, or, just by their breathing, who is asleep and who is awake.

Warlpiri people's knowledge, of course, is much more extensive than mine in terms of the things they know about others (and their bodies) and the numbers of others they possess such knowledge about, as they co-sleep and socialise every day and night of their lives. Because of the ways in which mobility and immediacy underpin their everyday lives, intimacy in the shape of such intimate knowledge about others becomes an inherent part of relating to others and, as a result, of experiencing life. These sensuous ways of knowing others (see also Stoller 1989) and of expressing the self are but a part of how personhood is expressed. Knowledge of others builds on the physiological, such as others' bodies' shapes, the particular way they move their bodies, their individual smells, the characteristic sounds they produce and so forth, but also far exceeds these innate features. What one knows about others and who one reveals oneself to, and in what shape, depends as much on personal choices, which are communicated in socio-culturally understandable ways.

Sleeping position choices and intimacy

One form of intimacy, of knowing others and expressing the self, can be found in the choices individuals make in the positioning of their bodies at night. The idiosyncratic nature of such choices and what they say about the person can be illustrated by examining how Joy, Polly, Nora and Celeste positioned their bodies. The four women are well suited for comparison, as they share many socio-culturally determining factors. Since none of them are children, they have more choices of where to sleep and who to sleep next to; since they are not married they do not live in yupukarra, but all four live in the jilimi; and within the jilimi all four hold gravitational positions in respect to the flow of people through the jilimi. Lastly, Polly and Nora are of similar age (in their seventies) as are Joy and Celeste (in their forties). To illustrate forms of intimacy, I compare the choices Joy, Polly, Nora and Celeste made firstly in terms of who (and how many people) they slept next to, and secondly where within the yunta they positioned themselves.

The data on which I base these comparisons derive from the sleeping arrangement maps of my first sixty nights in the jilimi — the same nights of the case studies from the previous chapter. Of those sixty nights, Nora spent 41 nights in the jilimi, Polly 44, Celeste 48 and Joy 55.[3] Put differently, during the sixty nights, these women were absent from the jilimi for anything between five nights and almost three weeks, underscoring my earlier point about the frequent absences from what one calls 'home'.

Their gravitational positions in the jilimi meant that Polly, Nora, Celeste and Joy often had their own separate yunta, sharing it with whoever was staying with them. There were only three exceptions to this. First, on the above-described nights, Joy's and Celeste's usually separate yunta combined with me in the middle at the first stage of my stay in the jilimi. Second, when it was cold or rainy, sometimes all jilimi residents formed a single yunta on the verandah. And third, while each of these four women's yunta seemed to move around the jilimi space according to their own inclinations and usually at some distance to the other women's yunta, Polly's and Celeste's yunta were combined or spatially much closer to each other more often than the others.

Choices of who to sleep next to and what these imply

Collated data for the four women and those people who slept immediately next to them during the sixty nights is shown in Table 4 (p. 102).[4] In the second column, next to the names of the women, it gives the total number of other people a woman slept immediately next to over the recorded nights. The third column indicates the name(s) of the main person(s) a woman slept next to, and provides the number of nights and genealogical relationship, and the fourth supplies information about the genealogical relationships between each of the four women and their respective immediate sleeping companions.

Looking at the numbers of immediate sleeping companions, Polly and Joy stand out as opposite poles in this table. Polly has 22 sleeping companions, more than twice as many as Joy, exactly twice as many as Nora and distinctly more than Celeste. Joy, who has the lowest number of sleeping companions, spent the most nights (55) of the four women in the jilimi, which puts these numbers further into perspective. These quantitative data can, at least tentatively, be imbued with social meaning. That Polly sleeps next to more people than the other three women, and that she sleeps next to distinctly more people than Nora and Joy, says something about Polly and the range of her personal network, as much as it does about Joy and Nora. The number of sleeping companions can be interpreted as indicative of the range of a person's personal network, and that there are degrees of scale to these networks.

Polly also stands out as having spent significantly fewer nights sleeping next to one particular person compared to the others. The person she slept next to more often than anybody else, her grandson Neil, spent 15 nights next to her, less than half as many nights as the other three women slept next to their main person. This contrasts sharply with Joy and Nora, each of whom slept 40 nights (out of 55 and 41 nights respectively) next to the same persons: Joy next to Kiara and Nora next to Toby and/or Ray.[5] In their cases, their choices attest to the strong yaparla bond between Nora and her grandsons, and Joy and her granddaughter. Celeste, on the other hand slept three-quarters of her nights next to Neil, her sister's son whom she was bringing up. Neil, however, was of course also the person Polly slept next to most often (15 nights), suggesting firstly that neither Celeste nor Polly had as strong a bond with Neil as, for example, Nora had with Toby and Ray (40 out of 41 nights); and secondly that Polly and Celeste shared the upbringing of Neil.

Table 4: Sleeping companions*

	Number of people slept next to	Person(s) slept next to most often, relationship and number of nights	Relationships to immediate sleeping companions
Polly	22 persons	Neil (DS) – 15	6 D
			3 M
			3 SD
			3 DSD
			2 Z
			2 DD
			1 SS
			1 DS
			1 SW
Celeste	15 persons	Neil (S) – 31	3 Z
		Me (Z)– 20	2 M
		Josephine (D) – 8	2 BS
			2 BD
			2 ZSD
			1 DS
			1 MFZ
			1 ZDD
			1 ?
Joy	8 persons	Kiara (SD) – 40	2 D
		Nangala (M) – 12	2 Z
		Me (D) – 8	1 M
			2 SD
			1 SSW
Nora	11 persons	Toby/Ray (SS) – 40	3 D
			2 SD
			2 SS
			1 Z
			1 M
			1FSD
			1SW

* For abbreviations, see Note on spelling and orthography, p. x.

Joy and Celeste contrast with Nora and Polly by having more than one main immediate sleeping partner. Partly, this is due to the fact (discussed in more depth below) that these two slept kulkurru (in the middle of their yunta) more often than did the other two, and hence had more people sleeping next to them anyway. Moreover, in both cases I was one of their immediate sleeping companions (attesting to my initial lack of independence more than to their closeness to me at the time, I suspect).

In terms of the relationships between each woman and her immediate sleeping companions, there are a number of noteworthy similarities. Firstly, and underscoring the fact that the data derive from a jilimi, there are few affinal sleeping companions: one daughter-in-law each, in Nora's and Polly's cases, and one son's son's wife in Joy's case. The most prominent companions amongst all four women are mothers, sisters and daughter, and grandchildren. Beyond this, Polly's and Celeste's companions come from a wider range than do Nora's and Joy's, encompassing more generations and more complex genealogical relationships.

Contextualising these statistical data with ethnographic background, what do they disclose about these four women? Celeste's entries in the table are a testament to her intensely social nature and her desire to be surrounded by people, especially younger relatives of hers. This is attested by the number of people she slept next to, distinctly more than Joy and Nora and from a wider range of relationships. Further, a lot of these sleeping companions were from descending generations and a lot younger than herself, underscoring the fact that she especially likes looking after children. When putting up yunta Celeste often makes conscious efforts of grouping as many people around her as possible — very successfully.

What stands out about Joy and her data is the small number of people she slept next to and the narrow range of their relationships to her. It is this small sample of sleeping companions that says much about her as a person. To explicate upon the list of relationships: the two 'daughters' who slept next to her were Lydia, her sister's daughter whom she had brought up, and myself. The two sisters were Nora and Polly, next to whom she slept one time each when there was a long yunta on the verandah. The mother was Old Nangala. Her two son's daughters were Kiara, who stayed with her the largest number of times, and Kiara's sister Charity, who stayed with Joy often. And lastly, Joy once slept next to

Martina, her grandson's wife, when she was staying in the jilimi. These people come from a small and very close range of relations, attesting to the fact that the 'gravitational pull' described for the four women was much less intense in Joy's case than for the others.

Polly's entries in the table are illustrative of her independence and her capacity to both be *boss for herself* and look after people.[6] Polly is a widow in her seventies, fully in control of her life and resources. Other Warlpiri women of her situation and constitution often choose to form close relationships with another person. They share their lives with either another woman, particularly a close sister, in a similar age and position to themselves, or with a grandchild, most often a son's child, yaparla (as for example do Joy and Kiara, Nora and Toby, and Greta and her grand-daughter). These women tend to sleep next to and move about with either their sisters and/or their grandchildren. Polly chose not to, and by this exhibits a tendency toward more autonomous and independent behaviour than most. As she often said, she had had two husbands and brought up many children and grandchildren. Now she tremendously enjoyed being her own boss without responsibilities for another person. While she was keenly interested in what was going on in the jilimi and what was happening in the lives of her large number of descendants and age-mates, whenever possible she preferred to be in the position of observer rather than participant. She also lacked the patience to deal in great depth with or spend much time on things she considered trifles in the larger scheme of things. Because she had experienced and witnessed almost everything in her own life, a daughter with a philandering husband, for example, could not expect sympathy from her but only a 'leave it, and find somebody else'. Her sense of judgment however is keen and greatly admired and this is part of her independence: she is a person other people seek but who does not seek nor *needs* to seek others herself.

Generally speaking, Nora exhibited more solitary behaviour than the other women (unlike Joy, who had fewer people around her but spent more time with them). Unless it rained, or there were particularly amicable relations, Nora did not join up with other yunta and neither was her yunta regularly joined by others. Largely this was due to the fact that she saw her stay in the jilimi as of short duration and not due to her choice. She was waiting for 'her' new house to be built, into which she would move with two of her younger sisters once it was completed. In the meantime, these younger sisters lived in the *camp* of one of their daughters, which Nora would not join because of differences between her and the daughter's husband. As she was a widow and some of her older sisters were living in this particular jilimi, this was the obvious residence of choice.

However, Nora, who formerly was a powerful *business woman* (ritual leader) at Yuendumu, as well as having been keenly involved in community politics, was getting older. She often complained about being constrained by physical ailments from continuing her previously active lifestyle. To be living with her old sisters, who had given up on all that and 'passed their days gossiping in the jilimi' to use Meggitt's phrase,[7] to not be going anywhere, was hard for her to bear. She consciously chose a peripheral position in the jilimi to mark that she did not really belong, that she was just there for a little while, waiting for her house in the hope of regaining her previous lifestyle. Her sleeping arrangements attest to her rallying against approaching old age; they are a statement of her not giving in (yet), and of not wanting to be associated with those who are warungka — old and without control.[8]

What sleeping yitipi or kulkurru says about the person

I delve deeper into these issues of personhood and intimacy by analysing and comparing the positioning Nora, Joy, Celeste and Polly took in the yunta they slept in during those same sixty nights. Yitipi is the name for the sleeping position on the far side of a yunta, and kulkurru means to sleep inside, or in the middle of a yunta. The yitipi sleepers protect the kulkurru sleepers from dangers from outside. Such dangers include trivial things like a pack of dogs chasing across the yunta to more serious threats like snakes, malevolent spirits and jarnpa. More often than not, a yunta includes more than four people, so there are more kulkurru positions available each night than there are yitipi ones. Note also that today, the decision whether to sleep yitipi or kulkurru is more influenced by and dependent upon the weather than it was before. In the jilimi, for example, when it rained, when it was too windy or particularly cold, people often slept in one long yunta on the verandah, and consequently on those nights there were only two yitipi positions available.

Individual women's preferences in and choices of the yitipi and kulkurru positions indicate likenesses in their social and gender status on the one hand, and differences which reflect upon them as persons on the other. Table 5 provides information about the relative sleeping positions the women took within a yunta: that is, how often each woman slept yitipi and kulkurru. The first row lists the number of nights each woman was present in the jilimi during the sixty nights. The second and third rows give the number and percentage of nights each woman slept yitipi and kulkurru respectively. The last row provides additional relevant information about positioning, noting, for example, when women slept in a single-person yunta or in a room, in which case yitipi/kulkurru positioning could not be determined.

Table 5: Sleeping positions

	Polly	Celeste	Joy	Nora
Nights present of 60 nights total	44	48	55	41
Yitipi (nights/per cent)	22 nights 50%	5 nights 11%	24 nights 44%	27 nights 65%
Kulkurru (nights/per cent)	18 nights 41%	35 nights 73%	31 nights 56%	13 nights 31%
Other (nights/per cent)	4 nights alone 9%	8 nights in room with children: 16%	0 nights	1 night alone 3%

Table 5 shows more kulkurru positions than might be expected because this sample was taken in summer, and there often were rainy (and some unexpectedly cold nights) when all jilimi residents slept in one long yunta on the verandah. In these cases, Joy's mother Nangala always was positioned on the eastern end (so she could 'make wee on the side'),[9] and Nora most often on the western end.

Apart from Celeste, who slept overwhelmingly kulkurru, the other women chose yitipi (outside) positions frequently (and much more often than all the other jilimi residents present during this period). Their high rates of yitipi sleeping underscore their gravitational roles within the jilimi. At night, when it was time to put up yunta, these women would take their swags out and put them up in the place of their choice — and the people staying with them would arrange their bedding next to them. While all the activity of putting up yunta would go on, as described previously, without discussion, the fact that these women sleep yitipi so often points towards their authoritative role within the nightly arrangements of the jilimi. The yitipi position is generally taken up by those people requiring the least protection and able to provide others with the maximum amount of security — both in the social and physical senses. As these women are 'at home' in the jilimi, they are more acquainted with it and therefore more often sleep yitipi, sheltering those who have come to stay with them. Further, their yitipi positioning is also a manifestation of their social seniority; they are mothers and grandmothers, and with the exception of Joy, active in the ritual sphere, hence knowledgeable in dealing with spiritual threats. They frequently sheltered people in the kulkurru positions who were either younger or much older than themselves, and in both cases the responsibility of looking after lay with them, due to their relative age and their social standing.

From this angle, and considering Celeste's considerable pull of residents into the jilimi, her low rates of yitipi sleeping are peculiar (she slept yitipi only five nights). She slept kulkurru much more often, having been on the inside position 73 per cent of the nights, which is a much higher rate than any of the other women display (more than twice as often as Nora and distinctly more often than Joy and Polly). These choices, however, underscore Celeste's nature quite well. Her sleeping kulkurru, in the middle, so often is an expression of her achieving what to her is her ideal of domestic bliss: a neat yunta, snug and warm, filled with people she is close to and ideally with herself in the middle (= surrounded by others). It also points towards another trait: namely, that in daily social interaction Celeste sees herself and is seen by others as less senior and authoritative than, for example, the other three women. Her sleeping kulkurru so much more often than the others testifies to her relative lack of authority.

A further reason why Celeste mainly slept kulkurru is that her yunta was regularly connected to Polly's. In these cases, Polly would be yitipi on one end, Celeste somewhere in the middle and somebody staying with her on the other yitipi end. While independent of each other in most respects (except for their shared responsibilities in bringing up Neil), Celeste and Polly relied on each other for resources in times of need; and often also pooled resources when people came to stay with both of them. Since they are mother and daughter, many of the people who came to stay with them were equally related to both of them. In the case of adults — for example Marion, who is Celeste's sister and Polly's daughter — this did not cause them to move close together and share. Rather, Marion would take up yunta with one or the other. However, there were many instances of children from other settlements coming to *stop* with them. Generally, these were Celeste's nieces and nephews and Polly's grandchildren, and in these cases Polly and Celeste often formed a yunta together. Significantly, this never caused either of them to move into the same yunta with Joy, whose visiting grandchildren were Celeste's actual nieces and nephews and Polly's actual grandchildren, but who were socially considered Joy's by all, since she had adopted and brought up their father, Polly's son.

Polly's positioning in yunta attests to her popularity and her capacity to look after people when needed, as well as her independence. This achievement is clearly visible in her sleeping patterns: she often sleeps yitipi, in the position those people sleep who are able to offer the greatest amount of protection. Moreover, she sometimes sleeps in single-person yunta, always of course within the jilimi, as sleeping in a camp on one's own would be anti-social indeed. Her little yunta, when sleeping alone was always positioned close to another yunta, thus not expressing social disconnection but just independence. Her sleeping patterns illustrate her highly successful (and idiosyncratic) management of the complementary pulls between *looking after* and *being boss for herself*. Not only is there a great number and range of people she sleeps next to, by far surpassing the other three women, but she sleeps yitipi often, and sometimes even in her own yunta.

Neither Joy nor Celeste ever slept in their own single yunta (nor can I imagine them contemplating this), Nora did once. While in Polly's case this kind of sleeping pattern was a choice and a positive expression of independence, in Nora's case it was an instance of expressing displeasure about and disconnection from the other jilimi residents (on a night that her grandsons were absent). Nora slept yitipi much more often than the other women (65 per cent, as opposed to 50 per cent in Polly's, 44 per cent in Joy's and 11 per cent in Celeste's case) because she slept in small yunta much more often than the other women. On many nights she shared her yunta just with one or both of her grandsons, often at some considerable distance from the other yunta in the jilimi.

Lastly, how can Joy's statistics be interpreted? Again, we find an idiosyncratic explanation for the fact that she slept kulkurru slightly more often than yitipi. This explanation relates to both circumstance and personality. It is partly determined by the fact that she often had no choice but to sleep with her old mother Nangala on the yitipi side (so she could assist Nangala if she needed help at night), thereby necessitating her grand-daughter's positioning on her other side. Furthermore, the fact that her personal network was much less extensive than those of the other women perpetuated this sleeping pattern. Her main social contacts were with certain members of her close family and some of her colleagues from work. Her personal network was a lot less extensive than that of most others of her age, partly due to her inclinations, but also allowing for as well as caused by her thriftiness. Through her ceaseless attempts to keep a tight lid on her resources, as well as through her lack of interest in participating in ritual, she manoeuvred herself to some extent into a bit of an outsider's position. She did not often find people who would help her with Nangala (Celeste would when Joy was away, but not when she was *stopping* in the jilimi), and as there were less people *stopping* with her than with the others, she had fewer choices of positioning. Her sleeping patterns attest to her peculiarities in this regard.

Conclusion

In the introduction to this book, I said that clues to understanding the view(s) people take of the world can be revealed by analysing the most routine issues of everyday life; and in this and the two preceding chapters I have used the mundane occurrences of the flow of people through the jilimi, the social composition of yunta and the positioning of individuals within yunta to explicate on mobility, immediacy and intimacy respectively. Naturally, the flow, the composition and the positioning can only be separated in analysis; in real life they happen in tandem. Equally, the three values — mobility, immediacy and intimacy — feed into each other; none can exist in their contemporary shape and form without the others.

Warlpiri people use their bodies to continually communicate these values, to themselves, to others and to the world. The content of this communication is about the state of social affairs. What is expressed from a person-centric view, however, is the internal state of things. Where one sleeps, how close to another one sleeps, where one eats, how one walks, next to whom one sits, and a myriad of other actions express, but never spell out, how one feels — about oneself, about others, and about the world. It seems vital to me that Warlpiri forms of intimacy are understood through the subtlety of the 'texts' in which they are expressed, and the oblique manner in which they are performed.

The 'texts' themselves are scripted through the series of building–dwelling–thinking; they are contained within and written through the structure of *camps*. As Bourdieu says:

> The house, an *opus operatum*, lends itself as such to a deciphering but only to a deciphering which does not forget that the 'book' from which the children learn their vision of the world is read with the body, in and through the movements and displacements which make the space within which they are enacted as much as they are made by it. (Bourdieu 2000: 90)

The *camp* does this as well, and in similar ways; it is the contents of the 'book' which differ. Warlpiri people through and with their bodies learn 'their vision of the world'. In regards to intimacy this means that living in *camps*, no matter whether in *olden days* or contemporary ones, fosters, imparts and teaches intimacy. Sleeping is one of many possible practices, or, in Mauss's terms, body techniques, and is both socio-culturally regulated and a sphere for self-expression. That is, the body is not only an instrument of learning but also an instrument that is 'played'. Nobody is slave to the embodied rules, but everybody finds room within them to express themselves — and the rules allow for others to read such expressions. How much one engages in the pursuit of such knowledge and how many people one opens the self to changes from one person to the next.

As the comparisons suggest, Polly's positioning in the world is vastly different from that of, say, Joy — a difference that is both expressed in her sleeping arrangements and perpetuated through them. The small numbers of Joy's co-sleepers are a manifestation of the size of her personal network, which is dwarfed by the size of Polly's. Personal choice, personal inclination, personal ability as well as age are all contributing factors.

Intimacy, at Yuendumu, means knowing others through understanding (being able to read) how they position their body in the world, and, expressing one's own selfhood in the same subtle way. This is not to say that verbal communication does not serve similar purposes, but that there are specific ways in which Warlpiri people engage through their bodies with domestic space and the world, as the example of sleeping suggests.

Knowing Celeste, I can make sense of her positioning herself kulkurru more often than yitipi, despite her gravitational pull of others into the jilimi. However, knowing Celeste's sleeping patterns in turn assists me in making sense of Celeste as a person. And while I communicate such knowing verbally in a book as this, when I am in Yuendumu, it means that I put my swag in the yitipi position if I am sleeping in a yunta with Celeste because I know that she prefers sleeping kulkurru. Equally, if Polly, as happened one day, puts her swag in between Celeste's and mine, this act alerted us more urgently than words probably could have, that Polly was not feeling well.

This kind of knowing others, or form of intimacy, incorporates understandings of how a person *is* (whether they are young or old, male or female, what they look like, what they smell like, and so forth), how a person *acts* (whether they are caring, selfish, sociable, easily angered, and so forth), and how at any point in time they *feel* (whether they are cheerful or miserable, tired, healthy, and so forth). Such knowing is acquired through extensive shared experience and physical closeness. The amount, size and extent of such knowing is particular to each person; it differs depending on the nature and depths of the relationships a person has with others, as well as on how many others they have relationships with.

CHAPTER 7

Intimacy, mobility and immediacy during the day

At night, the jilimi (or any other *camp*) shelters its residents, those people who sleep there. Who sleeps in which *camp* and next to who, I previously declared, is related to social engagement during the day. Here, I present and analyse examples of such daytime social engagements of jilimi residents (and others), showing how these interactions cultivate — and are cultivated by — mobility, immediacy and intimacy.

The relationship of daytime activity and the restfulness of night has also been elaborated upon by Sansom in regard to the relationship between spatiality and sociality in Darwin fringe camps, about which he says:

> Although there is a day and night contrast between the camp doing and reforming and the camp resting and formed, people in both the active and the resting state should locate themselves in places where they have reason and business to be. Unrolling a swag 'one side' and spending long day-time hours 'other side' are contrary allocations of time. They raise the issue: 'Which way you bloody think you goin?' (Sansom 1980: 111)

Correspondingly, my aim here is twofold. On the one hand, I follow jilimi residents (and others) through the day (and often, away from their *camps)*. On the other hand, I am interested in the mutations the jilimi undergoes during the day through the contractions and expansions in terms of presence of people in it.

I analyse the daytime spatial and social restructuring of the jilimi by drawing on Munro and Madigan's (1999) concept of time zoning, developed to analyse spatial uses of domestic space during different times of the day. Based on research in Scottish suburban homes, they transcend the truism that the inside of a house is private and the outside public, proposing that private/public distinctions operate inside the house as well and are not only spatially defined but also, and importantly, temporally. They argue that the spatial division in Western houses into shared rooms (such as living rooms and bathrooms) with greater public access and private rooms (such as bedrooms and study) can be further extended temporally. Different people use these spaces, especially the shared ones, differently at different times. The living room, for example, after being the realm of the 'housewife' for the early part of the day, may be taken over by children and teenagers in the late afternoon, then the entire family, and later in the evening by husband and wife and perhaps guests. Time-zoning in the sense of Munro and Madigan (1999) is the negotiation of relationships inside the private domain of the home by allocating space temporally to different persons and for different purposes. I find, with certain caveats (e.g. different definitions of privacy are at work in the Scottish and the Warlpiri contexts), the concept of time zoning works well transposed to Warlpiri *camps*.[1] A *camp* is a different place at different times of the day (or night) because different people congregate and perform different activities within it.

I pursue these issues by first outlining the daily cycle of an ordinary day from a *camp*-centric perspective, and then present ethnographic examples of breakfasts, of mobility during the course of the day, concluding, as the day does, in the late afternoon back in the jilimi, with a discussion of negotiations about firewood.

The daily cycle

The daily cycle as described here is an ideal representation. Normally, of course, the everyday is interrupted by any number of occurrences and events, from fights to mortuary rituals, Sports Weekends, initiation ceremonies and so forth.[2] On a normal day without exceptional events or interruptions, then, as the sun comes up (*mungalyurru-rla*), the *camp* slowly comes to life. The rustling of senior women starting the cooking fires announces the beginning of the day. As the women prepare tea and damper, the remaining sleepers get up in their own time and congregate around the cooking fires.[3]

Sitting in groups around the fire in the morning is a social activity much cherished, both for the warmth provided by the fire and for its sociality. This is the time when the first visitors from other *camps* might come over to share breakfast (or people leave the *camp* to do so themselves elsewhere). Breakfast is a sociable time, with people eating, chatting, and discussing their nightly dreams or their plans for the day. Once breakfast is finished the cooking fires are allowed to burn down, unless it is cold, in which case they are turned into warmth fires for those residents remaining in the *camp*. Bedding is put away, and residents with a job, a hunting trip planned or any other task at hand leave the *camp*. Usually only the old and infirm and young children remain in the *camp*, with a few people to look after them and keep them marlpa (company). They pass the time chatting, playing cards, working on acrylic paintings, making carvings and so on. Older children go to school, play in the *camp* or may go to find friends to play with — and often take off not to be seen again until dinnertime.

Around lunchtime (*kala-rla*) the *camp* fills up again. Many eat lunch away from the *camp* at work, or at the shop's Take Away. For those who come home to the *camp*, lunch is a more individual and briefer affair than either breakfast or dinner, and not highly structured. Sometimes a large pot of soup is made, from which everybody who comes to the *camp* for lunch serves him or herself. After lunch, some people return to their jobs, or go hunting or for a drive or walk around the settlement to see what is going on, and the remaining people stay in the *camp*. Especially in summer when it is overpoweringly hot, a *camp* after lunchtime is made up of groups of people congregating on blankets in any available shaded place, dozing, reading magazines, de-lousing each other, discussing what happened earlier in the day and gossiping.

As the afternoon (*wuraji*) wears on, many people who had been elsewhere return to the *camp*, and others from other *camp*s may come visiting. By now there will be large groups of people sitting on blankets, socialising; this is also the time to start getting firewood. As it gets dark, most visitors leave the *camp* they are visiting for their own *camps*, and the cooking fires are started again. Dinner is a more intimate affair of people gathering around 'their' cooking fires in small groups, sharing food and company. A large billy of tea is cooked on each and shared by the group of people using that particular fire. Individual women around one fire put meat they each bought (or received as gifts) on the fire and then share it with those they are *looking after*.[4]

After sunset (*wuraji-wuraji*) and following dinner, there is again an intense period of visiting: people coming and going to visit from *camp* to *camp* for *story time*. *Story time* means sitting around a fire with close friends and relatives and exchanging news and gossip, remembering events from the past, planning trips, and joking. If there are groups of senior women present, *story time* often turns into singing of *jukurrpa* (Dreaming) songs and telling *olden days* or *early days* stories.

At night-time (*munga-ngka*), swags and bedding are brought out and put into yunta, and people start retiring onto their mattresses, while continuing conversations started during *story time*, or watching television (television sets are often brought out at night and put up in front of a yunta; alternatively, people watch inside the house and then come outside to sleep). One by one people fall sleep when they get tired, disturbed by nothing but the occasional need to push a log further into a warmth fire, and maybe a pack of dogs howling now and again (unless there are disturbances such as fights or drunks coming home late and making a racket).

In a 24-hour period a *camp* experiences quiet times, such as at night when people are asleep and in the mornings after most residents have left after breakfast. Other times are intensely social, such as breakfast, late afternoons and *story time*. Others again are distinguished by their intimacy, like dinnertime.[5] These 'moods' are dependent on who is present, how these people are distributed across the yarlu of the *camp*, and, of course, the types of activities they are engaged in.

Breakfast and the importance of damper

Depending upon weather, the availability of firewood, and the availability of food, breakfast is cooked and eaten outside. Typically, the morning in the jilimi begins by some of the older, but not the very old women, starting cooking fires to boil the billy for tea and for the hot water required for making dough for damper.[6] This signals the first step from resting to being active. It is during breakfast that an initial *camp*-internal reshuffling of sociality occurs, when the spatiality of sleeping arrangements in yunta reforms into the spatiality of seating arrangements around the breakfast fires. Significantly, visitors start to arrive in the *camps* around breakfast-time. They may only spend a few minutes in the jilimi, e.g. a man picking up damper from a mother or grandmother, or the whole day, e.g. an old lady coming to visit a resident old lady to pass the day with her.

There may be one breakfast fire to each yunta; however this is unusual. More frequently only one or two fires are lit. Fires are located a little distance from the yunta, so as not to wake up the sleepers with the clatter and the smoke. By and by, as the other sleepers wake up, they gather around the breakfast fires according to their closeness and the state of relations to the damper-making women. Seating arrangements around breakfast fires could be mapped in a parallel way to sleeping arrangements in yunta. In retrospect, I wish I had taken regular maps of the number and locations of breakfast fires, and especially of seating arrangements around these fires. But breakfast-time was when I wrote up my fieldnotes. It was the only time I was able to write without being interrupted, and accordingly I scribbled madly while drinking my tea and eating damper, without time to note too closely what was going on around me. As soon as I put the pen down 'the day started proper' and I was too busy for further note-taking, and breakfast was over in any case. I therefore cannot produce any such maps, only some general statements about breakfast fires and seating arrangements that such maps would have provided and underscored.

Unless relations between yunta are really bad, there are fewer breakfast fires than there are yunta. The reordering of people from a number of yunta where they slept to a smaller number of breakfast fires where they eat points towards a beginning of an increase in the volume of sociality. The state of restfulness of the night is lifted by opening up the more intimate formations of yunta. Breakfast fires invite people to begin the day through increasing contact with more people.

Which fire to choose and where to sit depends on similar issues to — and is conducted in an equally non-verbal manner as — the nightly establishment of yunta. Invitations are not issued. People get up from their yunta and walk over to a fire of their choice. This choice depends upon who else is sitting there, who one would like to sit next to or not sit next to, how much room there is around individual fires, which way the wind and smoke are blowing, and similar issues.

Sometimes (especially after the redistribution of flour after ritual, discussed below), there may be a number of breakfast fires in the jilimi, on all of which tea is cooked, and around each of which people sit and eat their breakfast, but only one fire for the production of damper. In this case, people eating breakfast at one of the other fires get up, get their damper from the damper-making woman, and return to share and eat it at their fire. Other food items such as butter or jam are generally shared by the people around one fire, and if relations between different fires are good, may also be passed from one fire to the next. People from neighbouring *camps* may also come over to ask for some butter, jam, sugar or salt.[7] Closely related people residing in another part of Yuendumu may drive over to request one of these items if they need them and know that they are available in the jilimi.[8]

The fire one chooses to sit at is the fire where one eats. Parallel to the way one sleeps in only one yunta, one eats at only one fire. A major difference to yunta is that breakfast fires may be joined by people from other *camps*, especially by younger people coming to receive their share of their older (always female) relatives' food. Others who come to pick up damper from a breakfast fire to take over to their own *camp* may briefly join in; however they usually eat elsewhere.

The mood around a breakfast fire depends upon a number of issues. If relations are good, or there is enough firewood available for a number of breakfast fires, breakfast can (and usually is) a sociable yet homely affair. If relations between yunta are uneasy and a shortage of firewood forces people to share a breakfast fire despite their personal inclinations, then people tend to cut breakfast-time short. Lastly, as happens frequently, particularly towards the end of the fortnightly pay period, there may not be any food in the jilimi, and in this case only tea is boiled and quickly drunk, and then the fires are left.

Flour, damper, and gender

Damper is not the only food eaten at breakfast, and neither is it eaten every day. Other breakfast foods include porridge or weetbix, often toast, tinned meat or jam, and fresh meat. Damper however was the most common breakfast staple during my fieldwork, and as such it provides valuable insights into the dynamics of breakfasts and how they relate to sociality at Yuendumu. Whether or not damper is made in the mornings in the main depends on the availability of firewood and flour. Here I look at flour, at who is involved in the production of damper, and how it gets distributed. While my description mainly arises from observations made in the jilimi it needs to be mentioned that many yupukarra also are places of damper production. These are yupukarra with senior women resident in them. Younger women tend either to buy bread or to get damper for themselves and their charges from their mothers or grandmothers. Damper production is not only age-graded but also gendered in that it is exclusively women who make damper; I have never seen a man make damper.[9]

While all women know how to make damper, only a few do so regularly. In the main, they are senior women who *look after* others. The people they *look after* with damper comprise children and grandchildren, particularly male ones, husbands if they have any, and often also older female relatives. The latter usually 'pay' for their services with flour. For example Pearl and Bertha, Nora's older sisters, always bought 20-kilogram buckets of flour as soon as their pension cheques arrived, but never made damper themselves. They usually passed the flour, and with it the damper-making responsibilities, to either Nora or Polly. The woman who received their flour in return made damper for them, for herself, and for her charges out of it. Not only do the old woman 'pay' for the labour involved with more flour than they receive back in damper form, but the damper-producing women factor the receipt of such flour into their budgeting.

Polly was regularly the first person in the jilimi to start a breakfast fire, for several reasons. She always woke up early, and making damper gave her something to do, but more importantly she saw it as her responsibility to produce damper for the many people she knew depended upon her. In fact, we all came to rely on Polly so much so that one entry in my notebooks reads: 'Great confusion this morning, Polly didn't make a fire, and no-one in the jilimi has damper or tea'. Her damper-making responsibilities encompassed not only older sisters staying in the jilimi, but usually also Celeste and myself, and any number of her grandchildren staying with her or with Celeste. Many of her descendants would come to the jilimi in the mornings to pick up 'their' damper. In Polly's case, grandsons living in jangkayi, men's *camps*, regularly came for damper in the mornings; in Nora's case her sons would often do the same.

The seniority of the damper-making woman and her role in nurturing those dependent on her (both younger, e.g. children and grandchildren, and older, e.g. older sisters, and sometimes husbands) can be illustrated by Polly's and Celeste's co-operation in these matters. Normally, Celeste and her direct charges were encompassed in the much larger number of people Polly catered for, with Polly and Celeste pooling their flour and Polly normally being in charge of production. Thus, when Joy initially asked Celeste to help her look after me, including my breakfast provisions, Celeste often did not *make* the damper herself, but got it for me from Polly.[10] However, when Polly was absent, Celeste took over her role and produced damper for her own as well as for Polly's charges. Although I cannot be absolutely certain, to the best of my knowledge I cannot remember Polly and Celeste ever making damper at the same time. Other senior women in the jilimi at times also pooled flour and responsibilities with Polly, and at other times they did not, depending upon relations between them. For example, Polly sometimes made damper with Joy's flour for Joy and her charges. More often, however, both women made damper at the same time, on different fires.

The gendered nature of damper production is expressed not only through the non-existence of male-produced damper, but through distribution and production itself. Individual men receive their daily morning damper ration from their wives, mothers or grandmothers. In the case of some large ceremonies, the gendered nature of damper production and distribution becomes even clearer. During these ceremonies, men and women camp on separate sides of the ceremonial ground (men to the east, women to the west). Just after dawn, the beginning of the day is signalled by a number of women walking to the middle of the ceremonial ground to hand over a large amount of damper to a few men who carry the damper to their side for break-fast. Significantly, *all* women present are required to rise when the fires are lit before dawn, either to participate in or at least be wit-ness to this damper production, underscoring the link between women and damper.

At Yuendumu, there are two 'kinds' of flour: privately bought and owned flour and flour received after ritual. Women who make damper try to ensure in their budgeting that they have enough flour for the fortnight between one pay or pension cheque and the next. The damper produced from this flour is theirs to eat and distribute. The 'other' flour arrives in the jilimi (and other *camps* where senior women reside) as a result of distributions undertaken during ritual, most often mortuary rituals. Mortuary rituals end with a distribution of large quantities of blankets, flour, tea and sugar to the mother's brothers of the deceased. This second 'kind' of flour undergoes a number of significant transformations and exchanges before it gets consumed in damper form (see Figure 15).

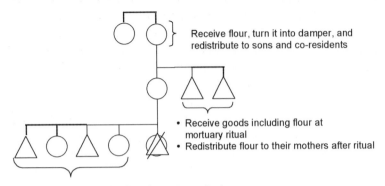

Figure 15: Flour distribution during mortuary rituals

In mortuary rituals, ideally, the siblings of the deceased pool their resources to sponsor the goods, including flour, to be distributed to the deceased's mother's brothers at the end of the ritual. The siblings are in turn supported by their close relatives, and today by grants for these purposes. Yuendumu Big Shop (which is set up as a Social Club, aiming to redistribute profits) often also 'donates' large quantities of flour (and tea, sugar and blankets) for mortuary rituals.[11] During the course of the ritual, which may take anything from a few days to two weeks, increasing amounts of goods are stored in the *sorry camp* where the key mourners sleep and live. These goods are said to have originated exclusively from the siblings, but with their storage in the *sorry camps* they become a 'public good' in the context of the ritual. At the end of the ritual this 'public good' is redistributed to the deceased's mother's brothers and thus transformed into 'private goods'. While the deceased's mother's brothers may keep items such as blankets and previous belongings of the deceased (which are part of the distributed goods) for themselves, they pass the flour on to their mothers.

'Private' flour turns into 'public' flour once the deceased's siblings bring it to the *sorry camps*; it turns 'private' again when the deceased's mother's brothers receive it. Once the mother's brothers pass it on to their own mothers, this flour not only becomes transformed into damper, but also into a good with a different redistribution status. The damper the mothers (of the deceased's mother's brothers) produce from this flour, in turn, is more public than damper made from privately owned flour, and less public than the damper distributed in central gendered ritual distributions described above. Firstly, it is passed on to all the residents in the jilimi, and to the sons who had passed on the flour in the first place. They come to the jilimi every morning to receive damper for themselves and residents of their respective *camps* while the flour lasts. Neighbouring *camp* residents may also come over and ask for a damper or two, if their senior female residents did not receive flour from the ritual. This goes on every morning for as long as the flour lasts (as this kind of flour often comes in numbers of 20-kilogram buckets, it may last for a week or two).

It is after mortuary rituals and other ceremonies involving the distribution of items such as flour that the above described central damper production takes place in the jilimi (and other *camps*), where all damper is produced on one fire and eaten around many. One woman is responsible for turning this flour into damper, and the damper rather than the flour will thus be further redistributed. Damper made from this flour is not public in the sense that it passes to all and sundry, but its distribution is more extensive, and crosses more *camp* boundaries, than that of damper made from privately owned flour. Once this flour is gone women fall back on their own flour, and distribution of damper made from this is much more limited.

Breakfast at Napperby

To further illustrate the significance of damper production, I describe a breakfast we made and ate at Napperby (also called Laramba), a mainly Anmatyerre settlement about 100 kilometres east of Yuendumu. Polly, who has part Anmatyerre heritage herself, and many of her close descendants, try and go to the Laramba Sports Weekend every year, as they have many relatives there. I went with Polly, Celeste and some of their close relatives to Laramba Sports Weekend in late August 2000, and we camped in the creek, just near the entrance of the settlement.

Napperby Creek is a magnificent camping spot, wide enough to allow for the comfortable putting up of many yunta, with large ghost gums providing shade. All people who came 'for Sports' from Yuendumu camped in the creek, and we took up a position at the northern end, furthest away from the road that crosses the creek into the settlement. Our *camp* was made up of a number of yunta, all sheltering close descendants of Polly. Polly herself, in a yunta with Neil and Amy, was in the middle of our *camp*. North of hers was a yunta with Gladys, her close sister, and Gladys's daughter Sandra, and Sandra's son Pete. North-east of them were Polly's daughter Marion and her husband. South of Polly was a yunta with Celeste, her 'son' Brian, and myself. South-east of us slept Gladys's other daughter Kate in a yunta with Polly's granddaughter Camilla, her husband, and their daughters Angelina and Jemima, and south of them was Celeste's adopted daughter Tamsin and her husband.

In the morning, we congregated around one breakfast fire and were joined by more of Polly's relatives: two of her grown-up grandsons and their children, and a son of Gladys's, his wife and child. Polly sat in the middle, surrounded by her relatives, next to the fire and positively turned into a damper-producing machine. The breakfast party quickly transformed into a carnivalesque scene with everyone shouting for more damper, the jam, some tin-of-meat; demanding spaghetti, the knife, tea, sugar; passing salt one way and meat the other; becoming louder and louder, everybody talking over everybody else and, most memorably, lots and lots of laughter. At some point, Camilla said to me, 'Oh, I am happy. All the family together. This is good!'

I found that this breakfast was a celebration of relatedness. The sharing of food and the space around the breakfast fire, being grouped around Polly who churned out the damper, created a euphoric feeling of togetherness. Polly was central to this in a number of ways. Literally, she sat in the middle, next to the fire. She was also the common link through which all persons present could trace their relationships. And while everybody contributed to the breakfast with additional items such as tinned meat and jam, the staple, damper, came from her. The celebratory mood this breakfast projected was due to it being an anomaly. Not only was there an abundance of food (very unusual), enough for everybody to truly fill themselves, but there was an abundance of closely related people who did not usually share their breakfast with each other. In fact, with slightly varying compositions, the only other times I experienced breakfasts similar to this one were at other Sport Weekends, which is when relatives living afar meet in great numbers.

Polly's centrality as a damper-producing woman, and, in this case, her role of 'matriarch', is what bound people together. Goodale (1996) has described the role of senior wives and female heads of households, so-called *taramaguti*, in the Tiwi Islands.[12] There men tried to acquire large numbers of wives, resulting in establishments comprised of up to one hundred individuals, and taramaguti acquired the role of matriarch by becoming the matrifocal heads to these large establishments. The term matriarch sits somewhat uneasily with Warlpiri ethnography, as polygamy rarely exceeds two wives, neither of which would be distinguished from the other as first wife with more power in any case. However, the fact that the age discrepancy between husband and wife (or wives) used to be rather substantial meant that women usually survived their (first) husbands, and as they aged they turned into central figures for their descendants. In the main, this does not provide them with any 'power' but rather with a great number of responsibilities, such as *looking after* people, of which damper production is a central expression.

It is senior women in these positions who usually are the 'damper-producing' ones. And the damper they produce moves along their lines of descent. Elsewhere (Musharbash 2004) I have compared women in different age groups in respect to the food they distribute and are identified with, suggesting that the oldest ones alive are associated with bush foods, the older generation with damper, and younger women more often with 'new food', such as store-bought bread, salads, and stove-cooked meals. Damper, it needs to be remembered, is an introduced food item, closely associated with colonisation (see also Rowse 1998), and next to meat currently (still) the main staple in people's diet at Yuendumu. The contemporary damper production going on in jilimi almost daily (provided flour is available) is a reminder of the centrality of these senior women, and what they stand for.[13] Women in the jilimi make damper to feed themselves and their co-residents, and to provide sustenance to those they are close to, starting the day by inviting the network of people across *camp* boundaries based on descent. The day begins with children and grandchildren dropping in to pick up 'their' damper. Breakfast can be seen as a launching pad into the gradually intensifying sociality of the day, and damper as having a central role in this, as it travels along the lines of connections between people before it is consumed.

Daytime mobility throughout the settlement

If breakfast is the opening up or loosening of the restfulness of the night and the positions established there, then the end of breakfast signals the beginning of the 'day proper'. From now until the yunta are put up again in the evening there is a steady increase in interaction with others. Naturally, this takes many forms and shapes. After breakfast, those who have a job leave for their offices, classrooms, or workshops. Children too young or not going to school (that day) form gangs and play in the vicinity of their *camp*, or, if older, also at quite considerable distances. The old and more immobile women in the jilimi start doing some craftwork or similar activity if they are up to it, or play cards, and receive the first of the day's long flow of visitors. Those that do not have a specific task at hand usually do one of two things: go hunting (if transport is available) or go *cruising* (i.e. driving or walking around the settlement, checking out what is going on elsewhere, and visiting).

As I have already said, of the more than 1000 kilometres I drove each week, a lot was done close to Yuendumu (getting firewood, going hunting or swimming) and most of it in Yuendumu itself. Indeed, I spent many more hours driving around Yuendumu, than from Yuendumu to some other place. A lot of that driving was taken up by what is called *cruising*, and much of the rest by driving around before leaving Yuendumu for some other destination, or, what I call 'hithering and thithering'. I examine these practices with a view to how they foster the ways in which people socialise with others and how they shape, create and reaffirm webs of relations.

Cruising I

When a person has no particular task at hand, the thing to do is to go *cruising*. At Yuendumu the usage of the term *cruising* is largely limited to describing the activity while driving around in a car. There is no specific word to designate the same activity performed on foot, and I use *cruising* to describe both.[14] *Cruising* is more exhilarating and more fun in a car, but since cars are not always readily available, it is more regularly performed on foot. *Cruising* entails leaving the home *camp* and heading towards one's usual stops: *camps* of close relatives, the shop, or the locations of specific organisations and institutions where one knows or expects to find people to talk to and hang out with. From the first stop one is propelled on to the next depending on who is there, what kind of news and gossip are exchanged and what is going on at the time. This is repeated at the next stop. To give an example:

> In the morning after breakfast, Lydia, who did not have anything planned for that day, decided to start the day by walking over

to Warlpiri Media. There she was hoping to find Delilah, who works as a radio announcer. Delilah indeed was there, and Lydia watched and helped her work, listening to music and answering some phone requests. Other people dropped by, and someone mentioned that Lydia's cousin Megan had arrived back in Yuendumu from Alice Springs late last night. Lydia decided to walk over to their place and see what they had brought with them. At Megan's place she marvelled at the new pram they had bought and sat down for a chat and for news about relatives in Alice Springs.

After a while, she and Megan decided to walk over to Megan's sister Charity, who they knew would be 'happy for company' and who had not yet seen the new pram either. Lydia, Megan and her daughter walked over to Charity's, where they sat down and exchanged and discussed their news. Then they, with Charity and her daughter, walked to the shop to buy drinks. At the shop they were exchanging Alice Springs news with some people there, when all heard yelling and shouting coming from in front of the council office, where a fight had broken out. Everybody ran over to watch. As the fight died down, Megan and Charity with their daughters decided to go and visit their sister Kiara, and Lydia went back to the shop in the hope of finding her mother there.

The best metaphor to describe cruising from a personal perspective is a pinball game (albeit with a ball that has its own mind): when cruising, one is being propelled from one place to the next by a conglomerate of reasons, moving from one point of the settlement to the next, carried forward on the impulse of news and gossip, and intercepted in one's path by others. For example Lydia, Charity, Megan and their daughters each followed their own paths of cruising: overlapping and running parallel for a while, then diverting and splitting, while simultaneously each of their paths were crisscrossed again and again by other people in the same pursuit. Unless big events, such as fights, draw the paths of many people cruising at the same time to the one place/event, each cruising individual follows their own trail. This is determined by his or her inclinations that day, through their personal networks, and their objectives. Often paths overlap, or run parallel for a while (as did Lydia's and Megan's and then Lydia's, Megan's and Charity's) but over the span of a day each of the three women's cruising paths would have been individual and idiosyncratic.

Cruising at the level of the person is a spatial expression of personal networks and one's reaction to 'what is going on'; on a general level it is an activity connecting people over the course of the day. Looking at it from a perspective of the dissemination of news and gossip, it must be said that *cruising* is part of why the mythologised 'bush telegraph' works so well. Any piece of news is distributed all over Yuendumu with enormous speed as it radiates out from its point of origin along the intersecting cruising paths of individuals. It is through cruising and related practices that it can be guaranteed that any important information is known all over the settlement within minutes, which, in terms of intimacy, also means that it is hard to keep a secret in Yuendumu and everybody knows everybody else's business.

Cruising II

From a personal perspective, the trajectories of cruising take an individual from place to place in their personal fashion. From a spatial perspective, the practice of cruising means that people's trajectories cross and overlap in some places more than in others, making them points of convergence for a great number of individual cruising paths. At Yuendumu, the Big Shop is such a place of intensified sociality due to overlapping cruising trajectories. Since most people shop for each meal, there already is much coming and going at Big Shop. People also go there to cash in cheques they have received, to spend money they have been given, to ask people there for money, and quite simply to see who else is there already. Another such main centre is the front of the Council building on mail days, especially on paydays. People go there to pick up their cheques, and other people go to receive (demand share) money from those who received cheques. Others go because many people are there already, and it is a good place to 'hang out' for a while and catch up on news. Other places where trajectories meet in a concentrated manner at various times are the buildings where Warlukurlangu Artists Aboriginal Association is housed, Warlpiri Media, the Women's Centre, and around 'smoko' the front of the school. And, some *camps* equally become the focus of many individuals' trajectories, the jilimi chief amongst them.

The jilimi I lived in was empty only under rare circumstances (when a death occurred in the jilimi or when, very unusually, all residents went away from Yuendumu at the same time). Many of the older women resident in the jilimi stayed there during most of the day, attracting older women from other *camps* to come and stay with them, *marlpa-ku* (for company), so that both the resident old women and the visiting old women had company. These aggregations of old women in turn attract younger women, who come past to chitchat with their mothers, aunties or grandmothers for a while, which in turn attracts more young women and children.

Paydays always meant that card games were played throughout Yuendumu.[15] These games in turn attract more people to come, either as spectators or as participants, and turn into 'gambling schools' easily encompassing more than thirty people or so. The jilimi regularly hosted 'gambling schools', causing frequent tension. On the one hand, residents were happy about the diversion, participating themselves in the gambling, and enjoying watching the games when the stakes were getting high. On the other hand, after each such event complaints mounted as the *camp* became 'dirty' with so many people being hosted, who 'just leave their rubbish' and 'use toilet all the time'. Moreover, these gambling schools often continued all through the day and late into the night, hindering the jilimi residents from getting any sleep. One woman or another would turn the main electricity switch off and declare that the power meter, which in Yuendumu needs to be fed by 'power cards' was empty — but the gamblers always saw through the trick. Getting up in the morning after a night of no sleep, with no money left and in a *camp* littered with soft drink cans and chips packets, caused jilimi residents on a fortnightly basis to declare 'no more cards in this jilimi'. But, with most of them being gamblers themselves all this was forgotten the next time cruising patterns caused the jilimi to be the locus of big gambling schools.

Hithering and thithering

Before going on a trip, no matter whether a hunting trip for a few hours or a trip to a place 500 kilometres away for a week, the car(s) to take the travellers drive(s) around Yuendumu, from one *camp* to the shop, to another *camp*, back to the first one, and so on usually for at least half an hour, often much longer. Although every anthropologist I know who has worked in central Australia is aware of this practice, and often impatient with it, I could find neither a name for it nor any anthropological discussions of it. In my notebooks I called this practice 'hithering & thithering', which I abbreviated in entries to 'h&t', so that there are daily entries such as '2 hours of h&t before we got out'.

'H&t' used to drive me crazy. I failed to understand its internal reasoning and its purpose, interpreting it instead as 'disorganised' behaviour. All that is needed for a hunting trip, I thought, is a car, people, crowbars, water, and some food (just in case). Considering that logistically this should be quite easy to organise, initially I used to despair about the amount of time it took from having the first person hop into the car to finally being out on the road. It took me a while to get used to 'h&t', and even longer to fully comprehend its meanings. Largely, this impatience was due to me, as the driver, having a different idea about the purpose of driving to that of the passengers. Focussing on the destination of the trip, 'h&t' became a chore, something that invariably and inevitably happened *before* we 'hit the road'. While driving around Yuendumu impatient for getting to where we were heading, I did not at first realise that 'h&t' was as much part of the trip as was driving from Yuendumu to X. The first time I realised this, significantly, was when I was a passenger myself in a car driven by another Kardiya person in preparation for a trip to a site west of Yuendumu. All of a sudden, I was the one giving instructions as to which *camp* we needed to drive to next, that another stop at the shop had become necessary, and so forth. After this, I began paying more attention to 'h&t', and started seeing it as an end in itself, not only as part of the exasperating preliminaries to a trip.

Any kind of trip away from Yuendumu requires 'h&t'. I focus here on hunting trips, but the general points are true independently of destination and purpose. A hunting trip often is 'planned' in advance by people suggesting 'we might go hunting, might be tomorrow?' hoping that something will develop out of it. Planning to go hunting first of all poses the problem of *where* to go hunting. Even if the initial suggestion is 'we might go hunting at Wayililinypa, full up with yam',[16] this needs to be confirmed, okayed, and verified. Povinelli (1993) has described the 'language of indeterminacy' that permeates the decision-making of Belyuen women as they 'decide' where to go hunting and what for. She notes that an 'important dimension to the sociality of hunting is the relationship among knowledge claims, responsibility – culpability, and authority – status' (1993: 685), drawing out the fields underlying women's hesitancy in determining the cause of action. The situation at Yuendumu is identical. The decision of *where* to hunt is not one easily made and partly underlies the 'hithering and thithering' illustrated in the following case study.

Yams were in season at Wayililinypa and Leah from South Camp had suggested to me a few days earlier that we could go hunting 'might be anytime', i.e. when it suited. A few days later in the jilimi during breakfast, I recalled her invitation and announced my plan to take her up on it that day. Polly and Celeste asked if they could come along marlpa-ku (for company). 'Sure', I said, and they and Neil hopped into the Toyota. The four of us drove over to South Camp to pick up Leah. She suggested that we also take her daughter Rita, her sister Eva, and her young grandson Marcel. From Leah's *camp*, now eight of us in the car, we drove over to East Camp, to the *camp* where a number of Nampijinpa women at that time lived. Wayililinypa is their country and we wanted to let them know that we were going there. Most of them had already left to go hunting themselves earlier that day, but Lina and Delilah Nampijinpa had not got a lift and were keen on going too. Polly said in that case she would stay behind so there would be enough room for them. We drove back from East Camp to the jilimi in Inner West Camp to drop off Polly and then returned to East Camp to pick up Lina; Delilah had already gone to her *camp* to pack. Lina's crowbar was at her husband's *camp* in South Camp, so we drove there from East Camp to pick it up, and then on to North Camp to fetch Delilah and two of her little granddaughters. While at Delilah's *camp* in North Camp, Neil chatted to one of the boys there and heard that Camilla had bought a new video, so he asked to be dropped off at her place in East Camp where they were watching it (also, the car by now was not only full to the brim, but full with women. Neil chose a polite way of opting out of the trip). After dropping him off in East Camp, we went to the shop so everybody could buy drinks and oranges, and ran into Moira who asked whether she could come along.

There were now ten people in the car (some of them large women), and some discussion ensued about what to do. Moira's hunting skills are legendary and she would be fun to take along, so it was decided that Eva, who 'is cripple anyway', might as well stay behind. We drove back to South Camp to drop off Eva, back to the shop to pick up Moira and then to West Camp where she was living to pick up her crowbar. On the way back we stopped at our jilimi in Inner West Camp to get our own crowbars and the big jerry can for water, only to discover that somebody had borrowed it. Lina said she had one in South Camp so we went there and got her jerry can, returned to the shop to fill up with diesel and then were on our way to Wayililinypa.

Figure 16 shows the paths we took during this 'h&t' for a short hunting trip mapped onto a mud map of Yuendumu. Drawing a map of the paths a car follows during the 'h&t' before any one (hunting) trip, one inevitably comes up with something similar to this, namely, a representation of a finely spun web connecting a number of *camps* and other places distributed over several of Yuendumu's Camps, and often spanning over the whole geography of the settlement. The *Oxford English Dictionary* translates the expression 'to hither and thither' as 'to go to and fro; to move about in various directions'. And rather than disorganisation being the root of this practice, it is the purposeful moving about in various directions, the tying of connections, that underlies it.

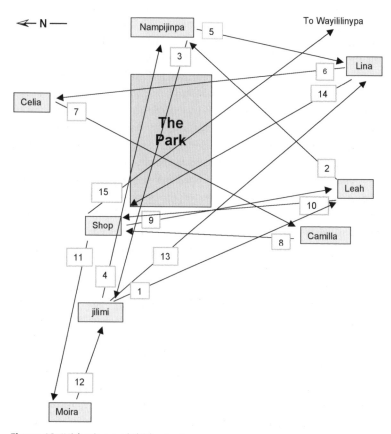

Figure 16: 'Hithering and thithering'

The actual paths taken and the connections created through them are important, as is the activity that takes place at each stop. Usually a stop, for example, at a *camp* so crowbars can be picked up, involves intense discursive activity between the people in the car and the people in the *camp*. During these brief (and sometimes not so brief) periods, all sorts of 'essential' information is exchanged, and if need be new decisions pertaining to the planned trip are made. The people in the car broadcast their intentions, the anticipated itinerary the trip will take, the intended composition of people going, ideas about the time of return and so on. From the people in the *camp* they receive similar information about other trips in preparation, as well as any other news and gossip the people in the *camp* have received from others passing by on their respective itineraries of cruising and 'h&t'. Information about other hunting parties as well as other gossip is 'exchanged' and updated in turn at the next stop so that within the one hour or so of 'h&t' both the people in the car as well as most people in *camps* at Yuendumu will have been filled in on anything that there is to know. This is one reason why 'h&t' often includes quick stops at any of Yuendumu's organisations and institutions, to quickly inform those who are at work of something just found out that may concern them.

To believe 'hithering and thithering' is caused by lack of organisation is to utterly fail to understand this practice, which fulfils a range of vital purposes. It is a central social practice shaping both social relations and the everyday. It underscores the fact that approval needs to be sought for most actions, however implicitly, e.g. in the case study approval needed to be sought for the purpose and destination from those people responsible for the country the trip was going to be made to. The 'h&t' in the first instance informs all people with a right to know of the intended trip and gauges its acceptability in terms of destination, itinerary and composition of people going. Highlighting the importance of this approval seeking is the fact that regularly after a bit of 'h&t' the planned destination and/or itinerary and/or the composition of people in the car change. It is not uncommon at all to start off with four people in a car planning to go hunting out east and end up with seven other people going west instead. 'Hithering and thithering' is about connecting people and places. The map in Figure 16 outlines the paths taken, and presents a visual image of the web thus spun during one particular episode of 'h&t'. Realistically, what needs to also be taken into account is the fact that simultaneously to us driving around, other cars with other people in them were occupied in the same activity, as well as the numerous paths taken by people involved in cruising. If one were to draw a map of the entire extent of 'h&t' and cruising taking place at Yuendumu during one hour, the illustration would be black with lines, underscoring the intensity of lived sociality and the multitude of social interconnections interweaving with each other at Yuendumu during the day.

Ending the day: firewood

As the day comes to its close, the intensity of sociality lessens and subsides gradually. The focus shifts from settlement-wide interactions to spatially and socially more concentrated ones. I discuss this refocus to domesticity at the end of the day by examining issues surrounding the gathering of *warlu* (firewood).[17] The example of firewood underscores this refocus as well as the previously made point about the often-occurring fractionisation of *camp* residents and reinforces issues about relatedness negotiated over commodities. Negotiations revolving around firewood are a central everyday occurrence at Yuendumu.

Only a small number of *camps*/houses, populated by people in their mid-twenties and younger, use firewood rarely, while almost all other *camps* use firewood regularly, and many of them depend exclusively on firewood for both cooking and warmth. Firewood is not available within walking distance of the settlement, and transport is necessary to acquire it — making it a valuable and often scarce commodity in high demand. The Council, CDEP, and the Old People's Program all have commitments towards providing Yuendumu residents with firewood; however, this is a task often neglected. *Camps* whose residents are overwhelmingly old and/ or female, which are in the main also the *camps* most heavily dependent on firewood, have particular difficulties in obtaining amounts adequate to their needs, due to a lack of access to transport. Residents in these *camps* have to rely on being able to persuade relatives owning cars to help them, which may put strains on these relationships, especially in winter, when daily firewood trips become necessary to meet all the needs for warmth and cooking. The negotiations revolving around firewood throw light on sharing, asking, distribution, and conflict. Starting with the rare examples of two situations of an abundance of firewood and what happened, I work towards the more 'normal' scenario of firewood supply being scarce but present, concluding with examples of social tensions being expressed through negotiations about firewood 'ownership'.

The social limitations on the capability to accumulate

While *stopping* in the jilimi, I was involved in daily trips for firewood, both for the jilimi and for a number of other *camps* in which resided people I was working with. In the winter of 1999, as it became colder and colder, requests for firewood trips increased to such an extent that they hindered me from doing other work. The jilimi residents, more aware of this than others, suggested I borrow a large trailer so that I could get a week's supply for them which would help free me up to do other work. We went out three times with the trailer, piling it up high each time, resulting in an enormous amount of firewood in the jilimi. Very pleased with the thought of at least no more jilimi firewood trips for a while I was able to spend the day elsewhere in Yuendumu following up other issues. By the time I returned to the jilimi in the late afternoon all the firewood had disappeared. Getting such an enormous amount in fact meant that it lasted less time than a small pile normally did. This was because all the neighbours of the jilimi, like us dependent on firewood and undersupplied, saw the enormous pile and many came over to ask for 'just a little'. The news that there was a huge pile of firewood in the jilimi spread like wildfire and people from a bit further away came too. Nobody could be refused any firewood, on two accounts. First, the jilimi had heaps, and therefore giving a little to others was the only decent thing to do. Second, since many others had received 'their share', nobody else who asked could be refused. By late afternoon we had nothing left ourselves, and I had to go out again to get some more.

It is simply not possible to store a large supply of something that is in demand by others for one's own use. My frustration about firewood that day was paralleled earlier by Joy's frustration about butter. She declared: 'I will not buy butter again. I eat a little and then, put it in the fridge, somebody will eat it. Leave it outside the dogs will eat it or it will melt in the sun. Buying butter is a complete waste. Someone will take it anyway.' The point in both cases is that if one has more than one needs for immediate use, others will use it. The traditionalist hunter-gatherer literature has for long argued whether one or the other of two preferred moralities underlie this phenomenon (see among many others Bird-David 1992; Hawkes 1993; Hiatt 1982; Ingold et al. 1988; Lee and DeVore 1968; Sahlins 1972; Testart 1987; Williams and Hunn 1981; Woodburn 1982). Is this simply a manifestation of an altruistic ethic of generosity or is it a more calculated sharing of things in abundance with a view to receiving returns later when in need? This argument was developed further by Peterson (1993; 1997) who argued for a reconsideration of the meaning of 'generosity' and postulated the practice of 'demand sharing' to be essential to any understanding of such activities.[18] This often overlooked practice not only sheds light on vernacular ideas about generosity but is an intrinsic element of Aboriginal social life as interpersonal relations are structured around it. Peterson says:

> Demand sharing is a complex behavior that is not predicated simply on need. Depending on the particular context, it may incorporate one, some or all of the following elements. It may in part be a testing behavior to establish the state of a relationship in social systems where relationships have to be constantly produced and maintained by social action and cannot be taken for granted. It may in part be assertive behavior, coercing a person into making a response. It may in part be a substantiating behavior to make people recognize the demander's rights. And, paradoxically, a demand in the context of an egalitarian society can also be a gift: it freely creates a status asymmetry, albeit of varying duration and significance. (Peterson 1993: 870–1)

The case of what happened to the jilimi's huge pile of firewood in the middle of winter when everybody around was complaining about their lack of firewood incorporates all the above-mentioned elements. The residents of the jilimi felt there was no option but to respond to all demands made on them for firewood until they were out of firewood themselves — in the light of the huge pile previously visible to all who came past, the only polite way to refuse further requests was to be able to say honestly that there was 'nothing left' and therefore nothing to give. This giving of firewood did indeed create asymmetry, and return demands by jilimi residents over the next weeks were generally answered (often not in kind, as there are many things to demand). It was a peculiar situation, however, since such a 'flaunting' of a scarce good is rather unusual, and stimulated increased requests from others for a share to such an extent that nothing was left for jilimi residents themselves. This example contrasts starkly with the following case.

A few weeks later that winter, CDEP organised some firewood runs, involving the labour of a number of men and a large CDEP truck. They dropped off truckloads of firewood at specific *camps*, chosen because of their residential composition, which put them in a higher 'need' category than other *camps*. Because of its large proportion of older women, our jilimi was one of the recipient *camps*, as was the jilimi right next door to it. This created a situation where two neighbouring *camps* in Inner West Camp each received a truckload of firewood while none of the surrounding *camps* received any (this situation was mirrored in other parts of Yuendumu). The CDEP objective was made public and everybody knew that this particular firewood was for 'the old and needy' only. Demand sharing happened to a much smaller degree and these truckloads of firewood lasted for a little over a week.

During this time Celia came from Willowra for one of her frequent stays in the jilimi. She had gathered some firewood on the way to Yuendumu and brought this with her. The day after her arrival she took me aside and asked whether we could go on a firewood trip. I replied that there was a large pile there and why did she not use some of that? 'No,' she answered, 'that one CDEP warlu [firewood], it belongs to the jilimi, I can't use him'. Celia and I went out to get her some firewood, which she kept in a small pile next to her yunta.

During this time Celia often used and sat around other residents' breakfast and dinner fires (fuelled by CDEP firewood). However, she used her own wood for the warmth fire at night, thus making implicit statements both about different uses of different types of firewood and about her relationship to the jilimi and its other residents. Her refusal to use for her own purposes the firewood delivered by CDEP for the jilimi, of which she was a resident, makes an interesting contrast to the almost public demand sharing which consumed the above described pile of jilimi firewood within hours. Hers was a declaration both about her independence (not using the wood of 'the old and needy') as much as about her usual residential status. Being from Willowra meant that although she regularly stayed in Yuendumu, she did not use the wood provided for Yuendumu old people by Yuendumu CDEP, fully aware of the implications this would have had for her if fights had arisen. Further, this is a case of firewood being distinguished into different kinds, the CDEP pile being reserved for specific people and purposes, and her own one allowing her to use it as she pleased.

My firewood, your firewood, our firewood

Often, the jilimi had one pile of firewood only, which all residents used. As long as relations in the jilimi were amicable this worked well. However, when tensions arose this became 'visible' by people's behaviour towards firewood before they were verbally aired. An increasing number of piles of firewood in the one *camp* indicates that things are running less smoothly than is ideal. I discuss three separate firewood trips to illustrate the relationship between firewood and sociality.

While Celia was still staying in the jilimi, I went on a firewood trip with her, Joy, and two other women from two *camps* in East Camp. We drove to an area north of Yuendumu through which a bushfire had recently gone (in the desert, firewood collection is easier after a bushfire, not only because the spinifex grass is burnt down but also because large and heavy trees, wood from which burns longer than the dry wood normally gathered, are more easily breakable). I parked the car and the four women and I went off in different directions in search of good firewood. About half an hour later, I loaded up my wood and then drove past their respective piles and we loaded them unto the back of the Toyota, all the while making sure that wood from different piles did not mix. I first dropped off the other two women and their piles at their respective *camps*, then we drove to Joy's *divorced* husband's *camp* where she dropped off half of her pile. As Joy moved between his *camp* and the jilimi (mostly sleeping in the latter and eating in the former), she was responsible for firewood in both. Then we drove to the jilimi and unloaded our piles in three separate locations: Celia's next to her yunta along the eastern fence of the jilimi yard, Joy's wood on the eastern side of the verandah, where her yunta was located at the time, and mine in front of the kitchen for the use of the remaining jilimi residents.

A second firewood trip later that week did not end quite so peacefully. This time, I dropped off Polly, Nora and Celia half way on the road to Mt Allan, where I was heading with Pearl to collect her pension cheque.[19] On the way back we picked up the others and loaded the wood they had gathered onto the back of the Toyota. Nora had standard firewood only, while Polly had also gathered some wood for producing artefacts to sell on a planned trip to Melbourne, and both Polly and Celia had found some extra heavy long-burning firewood. While I was loading the wood onto the Toyota all three women gave minute instructions as to where to put it, which was basically that each woman's logs were to be put as far away as possible from the others'. When we arrived in the jilimi, a fight broke out between Polly and Celia, with accusations flying about wood theft. While they were fighting, Nora proceeded to unload, and (accidentally?) took some of the coveted heavy wood, in turn drawing her into the argument as well. The yelling and screaming over that particular load of wood, containing lots of 'this one's my wood', 'that one's your wood', stands in stark contrast to the idea of demand sharing in connection to firewood described above. This particular case of fighting over firewood was fuelled by the emotions about a trip to Melbourne. Originally all three women were to go on the trip but earlier that morning the Kardiya woman who was organising the trip had told them that there was only enough money for Polly to travel. Celia's and Nora's anger, due to their disappointment about not being able to go, and some envy because Polly was, did not get played out verbally. Instead the emotions about it were transferred to the issue of 'wood ownership'.

Lastly, as often as there were separate piles of firewood in the jilimi, we had only one communal pile. This happened when relations between residents were relaxed and amicable. On these days, people from different yunta came on the one firewood trip and the firewood was randomly piled onto the Toyota and then unloaded as one pile somewhere central in the jilimi — for everybody's use. The use of and negotiations about firewood thus parallel other markers of the nature of social relations: ideally, firewood is shared by all within the jilimi. Just as often, though, rifts in social relations are expressed through the separation of firewood into different piles for the uses of different social fractions.

Night-time, daytime and webs of sociality

The state of restfulness of the night stands in stark contrast to the intensity of daytime social engagement. During the day, the boundary of the jilimi (and for that matter, that of any other *camp*) is highly permeable, accommodating flows of visitors in and out of the jilimi as well as residents' own movements. Daytime social practice, rather than being *camp*-focussed, is about social engagement settlement-wide. This engagement takes an elliptical course, beginning slowly in the morning with a *camp* internal reordering for breakfast and first inter-*camp* visitation, then increases steadily to heightened hive-like activity with which the settlement 'hums' during the day, to the diminishing volume of interactions toward the evening with a refocus on domestic matters. Individual *camps* and the settlement space complement each other in terms of being locales of social interaction. During the day and throughout the settlement, webs of sociality are created, lived, and reinvented, which are at night 'recorded' in the sleeping arrangements in individual yunta in the *camps*. The settlement thus needs to be factored into any discussion of 'domestic space' as it operates as a daytime extension of Yuendumu's *camps*.

During the day and across the settlement, webs of sociality are created through social practices that are part of the Warlpiri series of building–dwelling–thinking. These webs of sociality are incessantly spun, maintained, broken, repaired, expanded, and renewed through the crisscrossing paths of mobility. People are constantly on the move, *cruising* and 'hithering and thithering', interconnecting with others, exchanging, discussing, finding out, thus creating the 'feel' of immediacy. Intimacy is drawn upon and generated by connecting people along the lines of damper distribution, visiting, through exchanges of gossip and news, co-*cruising*, and being in the same places. Lived out together in daily interaction and social practice, the values of mobility, immediacy and intimacy engender the very stuff that makes the Yuendumu everyday so distinct. As a result, Yuendumu as the physical manifestation of a remote settlement is a space which is neither fully part of the Western series of building–dwelling–thinking nor fully part of the Warlpiri series of building–dwelling–thinking, but one that encapsulates the intersection of both.

CHAPTER 8

Tamsin's fantasy

Let's return to the beginning. There we were — Celeste, Tamsin, Greta, myself and the others — lounging on those swags in front of the television. Tamsin had just made her extraordinary pronouncement that if she had she a million dollars, she wanted a house filled with copious quantities of desirable items, which was to be inaccessible to others, in which she wanted to live alone in peace and quiet, and she wanted that house right there, in the middle of Yuendumu. I tackle the questions arising out of this puzzling desire by examining elements of Tamsin's life history and by drawing upon the core points I have raised throughout this book.

Personal networks

When Tamsin's mother Chloe was a little girl, she was 'given' to Polly by her mother, Polly's close sister. Celeste, Polly's own daughter, and Chloe, Polly's adopted daughter, grew up together (with their other siblings) and later married their promised husbands: two brothers, Basil and Rory. Chloe, who in turn had seven children, gave her eldest daughter, Tamsin, to Celeste, who only had one son herself (see Figure 17).

Tamsin's emotional relationships with these four close parental figures, who brought her up and looked after her at various times and to varying degrees, are complex. She grew up with Celeste and Basil while they were married, and after their marriage deteriorated, mainly in a number of jilimi with Celeste. However, she regularly went (and continues to go) to Willowra, where Basil and his next wife live, to *stop* with them, or with her yaparla, Basil's and Rory's mother. She also regularly *stops* with her biological parents, Chloe and Rory — or, when they are involved in one of their frequent marital disputes, with one of the two.

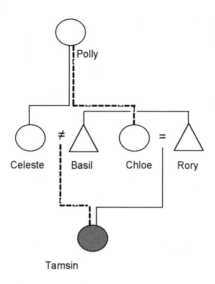

Figure 17: Tamsin's genealogy

Every so often, Tamsin goes to Papunya where one of her older brothers is married and *stops* with him and his in-laws. She has a large number of close and classificatory siblings and cousins with whom she socialises, changing in closeness from one to another over time. Lastly, Tamsin is in a stormy marriage with a man a few years older than herself. Her husband is from Hermannsburg, and when they are together, he and Tamsin sometimes live there, sometimes with other members of his family in Alice Springs, and sometimes in Yuendumu.[1]

Together, these people make up her most intimate circle of relations, or — to put it differently — they are the core of her personal network. These are the people she interacts with on an almost daily basis, the ones she can make demands on (for unrestricted admission to domestic space, food, money, commodities, lifts, care, intimacy, and time in their company) and who demand from her.

As Myers and Sansom argue elsewhere and I have put forward throughout this book, personal networks are the bedrock of Warlpiri sociality. In his discussion of Pintupi sociality Myers emphasises that 'the mobility of individuals is a primary feature of the social structure' (1986a: 71). He goes on to say that the formation of a group should be seen as a social accomplishment, not simply taken for granted. Furthermore, the significance of individual mobility in Pintupi social life does not mean that all enduring structures are lacking. The ego-centred qualities of Pintupi society are themselves social facts, the products of a larger system. To grasp these dialectical relations, one must start with individual action, as the Pintupi do (Myers 1986a: 72).

Similarly, Sansom examines 'mob' formation in Darwin fringe camps as a realisation in time. He says that mobs 'are collections of people brought together in places where social purpose is not established in the long term but shifts instead in time' (Sansom 1980: 14), and, that 'mobs brought into being in this way are not entities as are corporations. Rather a mob brought into being in this way is, at any moment of its existence, a realisation' (1980: 16).

Both Myers and Sansom were concerned with the way in which social aggregations of people are *achieved*. This book has looked at the realisations of social aggregations by examining them through the lens of one of the jilimi at Yuendumu. By investigating mobility from the perspective of the flow of people through the jilimi, and by focussing on the negotiations around nightly sleeping arrangements and daytime time-zoning, I have attempted to show how Warlpiri social relations are manifested, created, transformed, broken, achieved, reinvented, and negotiated as a continuous social process. Such process necessarily requires focussing on individuals and social networks rather than on fixed social units.[2] Children are socialised into these networks from an early age onwards, first into those of their main carer(s), then gradually expanding their own network, in ways depending at least partly upon their own choices and inclinations.[3]

The case studies suggested that some individuals' personal networks are more extensive than others. Some individuals crystallise as focal points in a large number of other people's networks. Polly, Celeste, Joy and Nora were introduced as focal to varying degrees and in different ways. Ultimately, they are focal within these networks, rather than being 'the core' of the jilimi in a durable sense, as they all ceased living in the jilimi at some point in time. There are differences between the expansiveness of their networks, and I have suggested that Polly in this respect was 'more focal' than the other women. A girl of Tamsin's age, on the other hand, does not command anything like this focality. While firmly anchored within her personal network, she is still at the beginning of expanding it and has relatively little influence within it. Moreover, emotionally, economically and socially she is highly dependent upon other people in her network — being looked after rather than looking after. The frustration that goes with this is voiced in her fantasy, where she owns everything she wants and does not need to ask anybody for anything.

Performative kinship

Relationships within these egocentric networks are, as are relations at Yuendumu generally, always formulated as kin relations. However, the classificatory nature of the Warlpiri kinship system, as well as the extensive use of subsection terminology in everyday discourse, effectively veil the finer nuances of how these networks are created. Sansom has analysed similar realties in terms of performative kinship, which he says is the north Australian mode:

> Its spectacular features receive less than due emphasis in the literature because most contributors evince interest in what they call kinship structures, kinship systems and social organisation where these umbrella terms shelter everything that pertains to kinship save the conduct of relationships of kinship between persons (Sansom 1988: 172).

Sansom presents parent–child and husband–wife relations to illustrate his understanding of performative kinship, recounting how parenthood is ascribed to a whole range of people who at various times of their life 'grew up' a person, and how it can be denied to biological parents if they did not 'look after' their children, as well as how marriages 'are sustained only by and through adequate performance' (Sansom 1988: 171).[4] Both examples are true in Tamsin's case, who ascribes fatherhood much more regularly to Basil than to Rory (her biological father), and who from time to time has violent fights with Chloe (her birth mother) centring exactly around negating the latter's motherhood: 'She is not my mother, she did not look after me'.[5] Her marriage as well fluctuates wildly between being 'on', when she and her husband live in a yupukarra, and 'off' when they do not. The performative aspects of kinship are significant indeed at Yuendumu and are so in respect to everybody. Relations are activated, validated and maintained through sharing of resources, sharing of time, and as this book outlined extensively, sharing of domestic space. They are fractured, split and broken for a great number of reasons, and these ruptures are expressed through fights, moving away, ceasing to share and so forth.

However, performative kinship does not capture the nature of relations at Yuendumu in full. It is not only the question of whether or not for example a sister relationship is 'activated' through interaction or is lying dormant; a multitude of gradations exists within these relationships, involving a range of interactions. At Yuendumu kinship is a paradigm concealing the realities of personal relations. Genealogical and classificatory kin ties are meaningful but by no means crucial in determining who lives with whom, who shares with whom, and who spends time with whom. After all, most Warlpiri people can trace genealogical links to each other in one way or another, and all of them can trace a classificatory link, but not all of them live together — or even like each other, for that matter. Through the subsection system, a Nangala gets to call every other person called Nangala in her generation 'sister'. But obviously, not all persons called Nangala get along with each other in the same way, even if they all call each other 'sister'. They may live together and share lots of time and resources with each other; or they may not even be on speaking terms with each other. Thus when I describe two sisters living together, it means that these two women are simultaneously *not* living with other women who are in the same kinship relationship to them. There is a subtle but significant difference between the paradigmatic meaning of the term 'sister' and the different realisations of that relationship in everyday life, or, as Bird-David (1994: 594) so succinctly puts it: 'relating makes relatives — not a pre-given link in a logical template of fixed relationships'.

The reason I chose to present people in this book by describing their kin relations to each other is that this represents everyday Warlpiri practice; it is the way yapa themselves describe everyday realities. But I hope to have illuminated the nature of some of the actual personal relationships and to have made it abundantly clear that closeness of relations depends at least as much on 'friendships' and animosities, on life histories, on personalities and inclinations as on kinship.[6] I have drawn attention to the fact that Warlpiri relationships, and often especially close relationships, are fraught with tensions. Two sisters may share a camp, a yunta, and their blankets harmoniously for a while, but if relations deteriorate, they will gradually increase the distance between them by moving into separate yunta within the same camp, by pooling resources to a lesser degree, by beginning to use separate piles of firewood and so on. These are ways in which a slow drifting apart from each other is expressed spatially and socially. On the other hand, relations can also be ruptured swiftly and suddenly, tensions may erupt in fights, and new social distance is marked by packing one's swag and leaving. Many of Tamsin's relationships are emotionally volatile, underscored by and perpetuating her high residential mobility. The fantasy of a house of her own, a space of 'peace and quiet' just for herself, must be contextualised by the nature of her relationships to others.

Testing relationships

Demand sharing is a one of the social practices that on the one hand underscores the nature of certain relationships and on the other serves to test the nature of relations. The demands made in demand sharing take on different qualities depending on the relations between people and the item requested. Between close people a simple '*yungka-ju* X!' ('give me X!') suffices, as both the person demanding and the person giving are aware that the transaction is part of their everyday way of relating to each other. If the item demanded is something more than food, small amounts of money, a dress or some such thing, then the demand is more carefully formulated, as it is in the case of the person demanding and the person asked not being quite so close to each other. However, while the placing of demands is normally conducted in a socially accepted manner it is also fraught with possible friction. To demand something too big, to demand something inappropriate from another person, or to place demands too incessantly may cause refusal. This creates anger both in the person refusing and in the person refused. Indeed, Myers links anger to compassion and says it is aroused 'by a perceived rejection of relatedness [and an assertion] of autonomy in the face of loss' (Myers 1988b: 596).

This took a comical turn in the above-recounted conversation with Tamsin. When she said that she will keep the door locked and not let anybody in, I said, 'What? Not even me?' 'Oh, okay', Tamsin answered, 'you can come and visit, but not Celeste!' She said this within earshot of Celeste, who was lying right next to Tamsin and following our conversation. Tamsin was fully aware that Celeste was listening and said it in order to tease her. Celeste replied, 'You can keep your house, you are not my daughter anyway' — playing along with the joke built around a refusal to share and the subsequent negation of the relationship.

There is another element to Tamsin's fantasy about her house full of coveted items, where 'every room has furniture in it. Sofas, and beds, new blankets, and tables and chairs. And every room has a stereo in it, and a television, and a video player and a playstation.' These are not the little things given in everyday demand sharing, like a handful of chips, five dollars, a T-shirt, or half of one's soft drink, these are the things she sometimes tries to demand from Celeste and especially from Basil. 'Can I get a playstation, get me a playstation.' They are also the things she would declare Chloe or Rory would never get her. They are items much more expensive than anything Tamsin can afford on her own — they are not something she is in a position to give, they are something that she wants. Wanting them in her fantasy house, owning them on her own terms, thus also expresses a frustration with reality, where she is utterly dependent on others for those big things (that, moreover, these senior others often cannot afford themselves).

Demand sharing is one of many social practices of testing, establishing, maintaining and breaking relationships; however the subtleties of the actual relationships are worked and reworked also in more intricate and more obliquely expressed ways.

Intimacy and obliqueness

Explicit exegesis of sleeping arrangements is not only unnecessary; it would in fact be considered highly inelegant. What Warlpiri ways of sleeping seem to have in common with other body techniques, as well as with Desert Art ('dot paintings') and most Warlpiri verbal communication, is that they are highly abstracted, while simultaneously — if you are knowledgeable, that is — their meaning is abundantly clear. Others have also noted the value of obliqueness in Aboriginal interaction (see amongst others Liberman 1985, Sansom 1980). Aboriginal interaction in this vein has been described by Kendon as having a 'highly complex and delicate character' (1988: 455) and he argues for the prominence of sign language 'because signing is silent, less intimate, and perhaps less complex in information than speech, [and therefore] particularly well suited for the indirect, semi-explicit, communication that is so often required in Aboriginal interaction' (1988: 443). This indirectness is necessitated by the

> aggregate character of Aboriginal sociality, the negotiable nature of interpersonal relations, the continual need to maintain personal autonomy and equality in the face of generational hierarchy, the need to sustain relatedness and identity and the highly public character of daily life. (Kendon 1988: 451)

Above and beyond verbal language, and the more subtle manual sign language, Warlpiri people use their bodies to continually communicate with others and the world. The content of this communication is about the state of (social) affairs. What is expressed, from a person-centric view however, is the internal state of things. Where one sleeps, how close to another one sleeps, where one eats, how one walks, next to whom one sits, and a myriad of other actions express, but never spell out, how one feels — about oneself, about others, and about the world. These are subtly accomplished statements about the state of relations whose diplomacy derives from their non-verbal execution. Through movement, within camps and yunta as well as between and out of camps both autonomy and relatedness are tactfully expressed. This was further explored in the circumspect way in which during 'hithering and thithering' consensus is sought for any planned activity (see also Povinelli 1993). It seems vital to me that Warlpiri forms of intimacy are understood through the subtlety of the 'texts' in which they are expressed, and the oblique manner in which they are performed.

How then to interpret Tamsin's bold statement of wishing for 'peace and quiet' inside a house, a placing of her body (and self) away from those that surround her daily, by locking them out and herself in?

The immediacy of sociality

Warlpiri everyday life at Yuendumu is highly public. At night, people prefer sleeping outside so they have visual control over what is going on around them — in turn being observed by others. During the day Yuendumu is a hive of social activity, humming with news, and everybody knows everybody else's business, from fights they are involved in to who they were 'running around with' last night. These circumstances have been summarised by Kendon, who says that 'People must live out their lives in continual co-presence. Individuals are almost never alone and there is almost no privacy' (1988: 446).

More, they all know each other. The meaning of sand stories in which people recount sleeping arrangements when they were away on a trip are read implicitly; there is never any need to spell out why X did or did not sleep next to Y — the fact that they did tells the listeners all they need to know. Immediacy in this sense has been described by Bird-David for indigenous Nayaka in India (and comparatively for Pintupi and Inuit) as the basic principle around which social relations are organised. She says, 'mutual help and sharing are underwritten not by kinship ties but by immediacy' (Bird-David 1994: 593) — and this is certainly true for Yuendumu as well.

The fact that Tamsin's fantasy house is stocked with all she needs (from blankets to videos) frees her from having to ask others for things, and the closed door frees her from having to share with others in return — it frees her from *engaging*. That the house is locked and access is denied to those close to her (and others) underscores the stress of the intense levels of socialising that almost all Warlpiri people are involved in. The immediacy of sociality defines Tamsin's life. Tamsin lives in constant engagement with others every minute of every day of her life, and often these relationships are not what she would like them to be, nor does she have the degree of autonomy she would like. What she rebels against when dreaming about the impossible is the constancy and immediacy of sociality, which, especially if one is not altogether happy and secure in one's relationships, is not entirely a blessing — it can also be a burden.[7] Yuendumu's then (Kardiya) school principal summarised this, to the amusement of Warlpiri people, in 1999 during a staff meeting, where he said to the Kardiya teachers: 'You have to understand that the Yapa teachers have two jobs. They work as teachers at the school and when they go home they have to be Yapa. Being Yapa is hard work.'[8] Specifically he was referring to the fact that during that week (as on many others) many people in the settlement were exhausted because they had just returned from a large *sorry business* at Lajamanu, a trip that involved many hundreds of people making a return journey of more than 1000 kilometres, that lasted five days. He understood 'being Yapa' as essentially defined through the stresses of having to constantly engage with others, with no possibility of excluding the self from social activity. And much of this activity embraces mobility.

Sociality and mobility

Mobility is a constituent part of Warlpiri sociality. In order to relate to others one has to be with them. And Warlpiri networks reach far — throughout the settlement, to other settlements and places all around Australia. This book has focused on intra-settlement mobility by analysing residential movement, and identifying four kinds of residents: core, regular, sporadic and on-and-off residents. Every person falls into each category at different times and places. Another kind of mobility is inter-community mobility, and, of course, mobility is caused by Sport Weekends, big sorry businesses and other events. Through movement people live their relations to others. Movement is halted at night when people *stop* in camps, and movement defines relations in that moving into a yupukarra constitutes a marriage and moving out of it the end of the marriage.[9]

Tamsin, like all Warlpiri people, is highly mobile, between certain points defined by her network. One can expect her at any one time to be in Yuendumu, Willowra, Papunya, Alice Springs or Hermannsburg. In each of those places, again, she can be found in a specific set of domestic arrangements of any of her close relatives or in-laws. Significantly, what she lacks is 'a place of her own', a *camp* where she is a 'core resident'. Instead she is always *stopping* in other people's *camps* for brief periods of time.

As a teenager Tamsin was sent to Kormilda College in Darwin, as happens to many bright pupils from Yuendumu School. She stayed at Kormilda as long as one of her close cousins did, but often complained about 'loneliness' and 'homesickness'. When her cousin left Kormilda, she left as well and returned to Yuendumu. Around the time we had the above-recounted conversation she had started to work at Yuendumu's Childcare Centre, where Celeste also worked. Together they went frequently to Batchelor to participate in early childhood training courses. Tamsin always looked forward to trips further away, as they promised excitement as well as an escape from the familiar. Significantly, however, in the same breath as voicing her excitement, she always mentioned people from Yuendumu, regularly including Celeste, who were going with her, no matter whether to Batchelor, Darwin or Adelaide. The same applies to trips she has undertaken in the past or is planning for the future. For example when talking about how the senior girls of Yuendumu School had travelled together to Adelaide, she always mentions who she stayed closest to, or when making plans to visit me upon my return to Canberra: 'I'll come and visit you, and Celeste, and Chloe, and Neil, and Polly, we'll all come together'. Thus, while there is a willingness, and sometimes even an eagerness in Tamsin to travel beyond the points she knows and is familiar with, she does not seem to want to go on her own.

Why then locate the fantasy house in Yuendumu?

Tamsin is keenly aware that Yuendumu is the centre of her universe, not only spatially, but socially. Yuendumu is the place most of her close relatives live, where her networks are the strongest and most supportive, where she will always have people to fall back on, people whom she cares about and is intimately linked to. Yuendumu is where she is from; spatially and socially it is her home. Importantly, I think, her answer to my questions encapsulates the desire not to escape the realities of Yuendumu, but to have a life she is in control of and happy with exactly at Yuendumu. It stems out of an implicit awareness that going to some other place will not change anything, that the most difficult thing, the 'biggest challenge' (to use *Who wants to be a Millionaire* terminology) for her is to achieve independence rather than interdependence, to make come true her wish for a calm centre of protected selfhood situated in the middle of life as she knows it. The ultimate fantasy is not to have full control over her resources, personhood, domestic space, but to have all this *at* Yuendumu.

Conclusion

Following Bachelard's dictum that the metaphoric power of the house lies in its potential as a psychological diagram 'that guide[s] writers and poets in their analysis of intimacy' (Bachelard 1994: 38), in the preceding chapter I interpreted the imagery of Tamsin's fantasy, the space of her dream house, as exemplifying Bachelard's idea of innermost protected selfhood. By drawing on the ethnography of this book, I related Tamsin's fantasy house to her experiences of immediacy, intimacy and mobility, the core values shaping the contemporary everyday at Yuendumu. I suggested that her fantasy house intimates the way in which she desires to be in the world — if the impossible was possible. That interpretation of Tamsin's fantasy was grounded in the analyses of Warlpiri engagements in and with the settlement of Yuendumu I presented in the body of this book; it approached her fantasy on the level of social practice and personal life history.

In this conclusion I offer a reinterpretation of Tamsin's fantasy. Here I am concerned with Tamsin's choice of imagery — the house — and the meanings of this imagery in the context of contemporary Yuendumu. Houses have consistently been central and financially dominant in Australian Indigenous policy over many decades; and while over time significant differences in the actual practices of distribution of houses have taken place, the underlying assumptions and expectations that come with the provision of Western-style houses seem to have remained the same. Viewed from the perspective of the Western series of building–dwelling–thinking, Yuendumu houses stand for the expectations the state has of Indigenous people — that they become like 'us'. Moreover, the always 'overcrowded', often dysfunctional and partly derelict houses at Yuendumu become an expression of the Warlpiri 'failure' to comply, and, a failure to be in the world in 'acceptable' ways.

Yet Warlpiri people want Western-style houses. Council meetings to discuss housing allocation are by far the most heated as well as the best attended meetings; living in a suburban-style house with curtains, a lawn, flowers and an orange tree in the garden was one of Joy's biggest aspirations; and Tamsin, asked what she would do with a million dollars, answers she wants a house. The question is, why do Warlpiri people want those suburban houses so badly, seeing that their practices of dwelling and their ways of thinking about and being in the world conflict so starkly with the values that houses are imbued with in the West? To answer this question, I employ Tamsin's fantasy to explore in more depth the underpinnings of the intersection of the Warlpiri and the Western series of building–dwelling–thinking at Yuendumu. I do so by analysing Warlpiri and Western entanglements in each of the elements of the series, beginning with building, followed by dwelling, and then thinking.

Building

'We attain to dwelling', Heidegger says, 'so it seems, only by means of building' (Heidegger 1993: 347). In order to dwell, in order to live the way we live, we need physical structures to live in, structures which allow us to live the way we do. As Heidegger elaborates: 'Building as dwelling, that is, as being on earth, however, remains for man's everyday experience that which is from the outset "habitual" — we inhabit it, as our language says so beautifully: it is the *Gewohnte*' (Heidegger 1993: 349).[1]

This deeply embodied sense of continuation between the structures we live in, the way we live in them, the way we think about them, and the way in which, as a result, we build them, is manifest in both the Warlpiri and the Western series of building–dwelling–thinking. Houses through their very structure allow for and perpetuate stability, privacy and future-orientation; while *camps* through their very structure allow for and perpetuate mobility, intimacy and immediacy.

At Yuendumu today, Yapa live in and around Western-style houses, the built structures of the Western series of building–dwelling–thinking. This situation is somewhat reminiscent of Robben's (1989) study of canoe fishermen and boat fishermen, who lived in houses that were physically exactly the same, but lived in them in crucially different ways. The Yuendumu situation diverges from Robben's example in that the Brazilian fishermen, of both canoes and boats, even though living somewhat differently in their respective houses, both live within the same series of building–dwelling–thinking. Their respective differences can be and are accommodated within (and inside) their houses, because their differences are variations of the values underpinning their shared series of building–dwelling–thinking. At Yuendumu, on the other hand, the practices and values jar with the structures.

The reasons for this become clearer if we look at what exactly Heidegger meant by 'building'. Building does not mean that one has to build one's abode with one's own hands, but that building is done in a way that reflects practices of dwelling and thinking. At Yuendumu (and in other Aboriginal settlements across Australia) however, houses reflecting the Western series of building–dwelling–thinking have been provided. At no point in time has there been any consideration for accommodating Yapa practices of dwelling in the provision of houses; building thus cannot be said to have happened by Yapa in Heidegger's sense. Houses are 'built for' not 'built by' Warlpiri people.

Depending upon funding, every year or two a few new houses are built at Yuendumu — and they are much coveted. Everybody wants one, and accordingly meetings about their allocation are probably the best attended and certainly the liveliest meetings held by the Yuendumu Council. There exists a long, much discussed and ever-changing 'waiting list' for houses yet to be built. Once the people to 'receive' a new house are identified, the 'consultation process' begins. Rather than any involvement in the architectural process, such actual consultation is limited to taking into account wishes as to design and location in the following ways. Usually, the number of bedrooms has been predetermined by council finances, and so if a three-bedroom house is to be built, the new 'owner' (in fact the person receiving the house does not hold legal title to the property and is required to pay rent to the council)[2] is shown three models of three-bedroom houses that fall within the budget constraints of the council. I have not been able to undertake extensive research on this, but my impression is that Warlpiri people generally choose the biggest house, or, if they are all of equal size, the one most closely resembling a stereotypical 'suburban' style. Next, they have some control over where the house is to be built (within given building constraints, sewerage and power connections and so forth) and in some instances, the orientation in space of the house on the chosen block.[3] Lastly, and also of course within the financial constraints set by council, sometimes people get to choose the colour of 'their' house. However, generally the question is not 'what colour would you like?' but something along the lines of 'Would you prefer pink or blue?'.

There is, however, a building in Heidegger's sense that is performed by Yapa at Yuendumu. In and around the houses, every night, Yapa erect their *camps*. Getting the bedding out, arranging swags and people in *yunta*, although lacking permanent structures, is exactly a building in Heidegger's sense. In the *olden days*, Yapa set up *camp* wherever they were, structuring sleeping arrangements so that they spatially reflected the gender and marital distinctions of those people present. Today's *camps* differ on a number of accounts: they are within the settlement rather than being located in different places across the Tanami; today they are more varied and complex in social composition than they were likely to have been in the past; they are erected out of different materials: beds, swags and blankets rather than moulds in the sand; walls, cars or suitcases rather than windbreaks out of branches, and so forth. Yet, as in the *olden days*, *camps* are set up every night, and as in the *olden days*, they serve specific purposes and they reflect gender and marital distinctions as well as personal choice. *Camps* are *das Gewohnte*.

So what we find at Yuendumu is the simultaneous building of two types of structures, each reflective of the series it belongs to. Most importantly, these two types of building, *camps* and houses, do not only spatially coincide, but they interrelate through the social practices of the people living in them. *Camps* are adjusted to fit into new spaces (and times) and houses are appropriated to make *camps* fit into them.

The structures of houses are built for Yapa, who engage with them habitually, amongst other things by building their own structures within them. Such use of houses does not coincide with the way in which they are *meant* to be used, and consequently, it triggers a steady flow of criticism from the mainstream.

Dwelling

Dwelling, according to Heidegger, is intricately interlinked with building, but has some degree of primacy over it. He says that we 'do not dwell because we have built, but we build and have built because we dwell, that is because we are *dwellers*' (Heidegger 1993: 350, original emphasis). Dwelling, in Heidegger's sense, is the way we are in the world; it does not, and it cannot, arise solely out of the structures we dwell in but is reflected in them. What happens, though, if there are two series that intersect, where building is done both 'for' and 'by', as at Yuendumu?

Practices of dwelling, or ways of being in the world (which I have analysed throughout this book through the example of Warlpiri social practices of engaging with domestic space), are always formulated in dialogue with the world. As the world today is different from that of the *olden days*, so ways of dwelling today differ from ways of being in the world in the *olden days*. For example, living in settlements, in prolonged and close proximity to more people than ever before has meant, amongst many other things, that marriage practices changed as a result, which in turn has impacted on the ways in which jilimi have transformed into phenomena of novel social complexity, purpose, size and number. The jilimi I described in this book has certain commonalities with an *olden days* one, but is inherently different. Moreover, the jilimi is both a *camp* and a four-bedroom house. Warlpiri people dwell within this intersection; they live in both simultaneously, *camps* and houses; they speak English and Warlpiri, they know their country and how to hunt and gather, they watch television, go shopping, perform Warlpiri rituals, drive cars, work for the council or the childcare centre, go to church, know which firewood burns slowly or gives most heat, which one smokes. This does not, however, mean, as is often assumed in populist models, that Yapa live in between worlds — one (that of the hunting and gathering past) that is lost, and another (that of Western modernity) that is not yet reached — or that they negotiate two worlds (a Yapa one and a Kardiya one).

'Dwelling', Heidegger says, 'is the manner in which mortals are on earth' (Heidegger 2001: 146).[4] We experience the world through our bodies, through ways of knowing that are embodied, and we continually communicate with the world about this knowing and understand the world through it. There is only ever one way of being, as there is always only one body from which one experiences such being in the world. By their being in the world and through their bodies, Yapa accommodate the intersection of the two different series of building–dwelling–thinking that characterises their contemporary lives. Dwelling at contemporary Yuendumu thus means that people live in *camps* (and in houses), and that these *camps* are in a settlement — a spatial manifestation, if ever there was one, of sedentisation, and the myriad of other colonial and post-colonial processes flowing from it. Yapa continually deal with the reverberations of this intersection of two different series of building–dwelling–thinking, through transforming, adjusting and modifying ways of dwelling, and thus absorb and accommodate the contradictions posed by the intersection of the two different series, the contradictions inherent in being fourth world people in a first world nation state.

Thinking

The third part in each of the series, thinking, is a way of being in and understanding the world that is intricately linked to, arises out of, and feeds back into building and dwelling. As Heidegger puts it:

> Where the word *bauen* [building] still speaks in its original sense it also says *how far* the essence of dwelling reaches. That is, *bauen, buan, bhu, beo* are our word *bin* in the versions: *ich bin*, I am, *du bist*, you are, the imperative form *bis*, be. What then does *ich bin* [I am] mean? The old word *bauen*, to which the *bin* belongs, answers: *ich bin, du bist* mean I dwell, you dwell. (Heidegger 1993: 349, emphasis in original)

And where in Germanic languages 'to build' equates 'to be', in Warlpiri 'ngurra' equates *camp*, family, time and country. Each series, in its own way, summarises notions of being in the world and of being a person. Personhood, in the Warlpiri case, revolves around the tensions of autonomy and relatedness. To live, shape, create, form, transform and express personhood thus defined, mobility permeates everyday life, immediacy is the primary way of being in the world, and intimacy is expressed and learned in specific ways. These core values — mobility, immediacy and intimacy — underpin Warlpiri sociality, Yapa ways of being in the world, Yapa thinking in Heidegger's sense.

However, through the ever-presence of the intersection of the Western and the Warlpiri series at Yuendumu, the values underpinning the Western series — stability, privacy and future-orientation (through accumulation) — are there at Yuendumu as well. They may not be given precedence in the ways in which people relate to each other and the world on the level of everyday interaction, but these values certainly exist in Yuendumu, and are often communicated to Yapa through the criticisms by people who live within the Western series of building–dwelling–thinking.

To view the Warlpiri longing for houses as expressing a desire to live a Western lifestyle, a life revolving around the values of privacy, stability and future-orientation, values that conflict with Yapa ways of being in and thinking about the world, would be to interpret these wishes from within the Western series of building–dwelling–thinking. Instead, we need to remember that at Yuendumu houses are physical manifestations of the intersection of two opposing series of building–dwelling–thinking; and as such houses symbolise contradictory and incongruent expectations and desires. In other words, there are two readings — houses as symbolising the state's *expectations* and houses as symbolising Warlpiri people's *desires* — and while expressed through the same symbol, they are greatly at odds with each other.

Warlpiri people's desires for houses come out of a deep appreciation of the metaphoric potency of the house, learned through decades of interaction with wider Australia. The geographical location of Yuendumu may be described as 'remote'; however, this does not mean that Warlpiri people live in isolation. Yapa are citizens of the twenty-first century much as non-Indigenous Australians are, and are conscious, both through personal experience and through the media, of the dominant values. Warlpiri people are painfully aware of the low regard non-Indigenous people have of, for example, humpies, and read this, at least subconsciously, as low regard for Warlpiri dwelling and thinking — so much so that the Warlpiri Media Association which issues permits to take photographs at Yuendumu expressedly forbids the taking of photographs of humpies, as well as of people in domestic settings independent of physical structure.

In a socio-political climate intolerant of difference, the desire for houses is a desire for sanctuary from public, policy, and political disregard for alternative practices of dwelling and thinking. Wishing for a *house* is to use a metaphor that Westerners can understand. Wishing for a house expresses a desire for acceptance by the large and powerful encompassing society, as represented in the first instance by the state. This is not, I believe, a wish to *be* what is considered normal (live within the Western series of building–dwelling–thinking) but a desire to be *considered* normal. Furthermore, houses, because of their great metaphoric potency, also stand for those things that non-Indigenous Australians have and that Warlpiri people lack: good health, low mortality rates, good education, good incomes and so forth. Houses in this regard symbolise Warlpiri desires not to *be* like non-Indigenous Australians but to *have* what they have; the desire for a house here symbolises a desire for equality. And lastly, houses symbolise a wish for control expressed through a symbol readable by the Western majority.

I think it is fair to assume that Tamsin would not at all say 'no' to an actual house, but the house she describes is not a 'real' one. She described it as 'really really big, with lots of rooms, and every room has furniture in it. Sofas, and beds, new blankets, and tables and chairs. And every room has a stereo in it, and a television, and a video player and a playstation' and she would be the only person living in it. Nobody at Yuendumu, and hardly anybody anywhere else, actually lives like this. That is, she is not describing a way of 'dwelling' but something else. I believe what she wishes for is more than just 'a house'. As I have emphasised, houses are powerful symbols. At Yuendumu, houses are also symbols of power; they are provided by the state, and they are provided with an agenda. Houses are beacons signalling a way of life and a way of being that is different from Warlpiri everyday experience. Houses are built and granted with little Warlpiri involvement. Houses are taken away, the ways in which Yapa dwell in them are criticised, and there are numerous attempts forcing people to dwell in them in the expected way (including by such means as the withdrawal of welfare money and refusal to undertake repairs, for example). Read this way, houses mediate the idea of what people do *not* have: control.

What Tamsin wants is a house that is hers and hers alone, built to her specifications, where it is for her to decide how to live in it and with whom to share and whom to exclude. What she wants, if only such an impossible thing could be possible, is control over a house (a space, her life) that is her own. Considering that Yuendumu is built on Aboriginal land, what is also, I think, encapsulated in her dream, is a desire for control over that which she already considers belongs to her. This desired life includes the known: Yuendumu and all it stands for, and right there in Yuendumu the possibilities of the wider world, houses and all they stand for. Most importantly, it is a desire to live a life not controlled by others and from the outside, but one where she is in control, where *she* holds the keys.

Yuendumu infrastructure

This appendix lists Yuendumu's main institutions and organisations following their numbering in Figure 3 (page 24), which indicates their locations within the settlement (note that number 1 indicates the location of our *jilimi*). This list reflects the status quo during the most concentrated fieldwork effort for this book (1998–2000). The pace of change is reflected in the addition of new programs and institutions and the collapse of others since then. In 2005, for example, Adult Education was hardly used, whereas two new programs were prolific: an addition to the Youth Program, Jaru Pirrjiridi, and the federally funded WYN Health (Willowra, Yuendumu, Nyirrpi). By 2008, other programs have contracted or grown substantially: a solar farm has been built to supply additional power next to the old diesel generator, for example, and a reshuffling of established organisations is underway as part of the Commonwealth government's NT 'intervention'.

Yuendumu Clinic (2) has substantially grown since first set up. It employs a District Medical Officer, four Remote Nurses, two Trainee Nurses, and up to six Aboriginal Health Workers. It flies in a general practitioner and other medical specialists on a regular basis, and the Royal Flying Doctor Service is used in emergencies. It monitors the growth and well-being of infants and children, and is open to all residents of Yuendumu.

Warlpiri Media Association (WMA) (3) was incorporated in November 1984 as an organisation concerned with Warlpiri video production, and initially also to print books for the bilingual program at the school (see below). Since then it has grown far beyond its original purpose. Today, WMA is involved in the production of local videos, as well as films now broadcasted on national television (more recently, among others, *Bush Mechanics* and *Aboriginal Rules*). This development began with the original series of *Manyu-wana* videos in the 1980s, a locally produced Warlpiri version of *Sesame Street*. They have been highly successful, screening on national television as well as in Warlpiri settlements, and took up production again in the late 1990s. WMA handles television and radio broadcasting, and operates the Broadcasting for Aboriginal Remote Communities Scheme (BRACS) at Yuendumu and surrounding settlements.

WMA also has become a watchdog organisation for the handling of and access to Warlpiri film and photographic images. To film or take photographs at Yuendumu today requires a permit by WMA, providing Warlpiri people with a tool to regulate the use of these media.

Tanami Network is housed in the same building; this is the organisation that oversees the videoconferencing facility at Yuendumu. This is used for inter-settlement video-meetings, secondary and adult education, prison links, recruitment, legal hearings, international cultural exchanges and so forth.

Also housed in the same complex is **Adult Education**. The main institution through which adult education at Yuendumu is conducted is Batchelor Institute of Indigenous Tertiary Education (which has locations around the Northern Territory including at Batchelor itself, 100 kilometres south of Darwin). Instructors teach Warlpiri people periodically at Yuendumu, and Warlpiri people also regularly fly to Batchelor to attend courses.

The **Youth Centre** (3a) houses a disco, operated on up to four nights a week, has a game room with pool tables, videos, and Playstations, and employs a Youth Development Officer through the Commonwealth Department of Health as well as CDEP staff to organise activities, such as basketball nights, football, roller skating and so forth. It sometimes works closely with the **Yuendumu Substance Misuse Program**, locally called 'Mt Theo Program'. This is a highly successful program for petrol-sniffing children and teenagers, who are taken out of the settlement to Mt Theo, an outstation about 150 kilometres to the west, where they are looked after by senior Warlpiri people until their return to Yuendumu.

The **Baptist Church** (4) is staffed by a Kardiya Baptist Minister and is mainly run by Yuendumu residents. Sunday services are often conducted by residents, as are baptisms and funerals. The Minister and his wife also run a small second-hand clothes store from their house. There are also three Catholic Nuns, called 'Little Sisters', based at Yuendumu, who have prayer meetings at their house on Sundays; and when the Pastor from Balgo (a settlement 500 kilometres to the northwest) passes through, he conducts mass there. There are also a number of Pentecostals resident at Yuendumu; however, the main enclave of Pentecostal Warlpiri people is at Nyirrpi, a settlement 150 kilometres to the south of Yuendumu. The 1996 ABS census (ABS 1998) for Yuendumu gives the following numbers for religious affiliation: 445 Baptists, 54 Lutheran, 45 Catholic, 13 Pentecostal, 7 Anglican and 47 'no religion or not stated'.

The so-called '**Big Shop**' (5) is run by the Yuendumu Social Club, and is a self-serve supermarket-style store, selling food and essential items such as axes, brooms and billy cans, as well as some clothes and blankets. It operates petrol and diesel bowsers, and runs a take-away during lunchtime on weekdays. The shop operates an 'envelope system', in which the money from the pensions of a number of older people is held, as well as allocations for schoolchildren, from which they pick up $5 to buy lunch every weekday. The Yuendumu Social Club is community-owned, has an elected committee and the profits from the store are intended to flow back to the residents of Yuendumu. It makes donations to the school for annual 'country visits' (see below), as well as to the Youth Centre and often towards the expenses of mortuary rituals.

Warlukurlangu Aboriginal Artist Association (6) was founded in the mid-1980s. It provides Yuendumu artists with stretched canvas and paints and buys back the paintings, paying 50 per cent of the sale to the artist, with the other half going towards the running of the art centre. Much of the art sold through the art centre is internationally acclaimed. It is shown at many national and international exhibitions; 'large canvas' commissions involve the work of many artists; and performative installations of 'ground paintings' take place in national and international galleries.

The **Yuendumu Mining Co. Garage and Store** (7), locally called 'Mining', runs a small over-the-counter store, a petrol and a diesel bowser, and a garage. It undertakes occasional geological work, and also buys and sells bush foods.

The **CDEP Office** (8) is the administrative centre of the CDEP Program at Yuendumu. It administers the program, and also initiates projects and training, such as landscaping, occupational heath and safety training, welding courses and so forth. CDEP began at Yuendumu in March 1997 and has had a mixed history of success since.

The **Council Office** (9) houses **Yuendumu Council** as well as the **Yuendumu Post Office** and the **Yuendumu Centrelink Office**. The elected Council holds its meetings there, and it is the central administration of the settlement, dealing with issues such as housing and essential services. It is also the location for court sessions held at Yuendumu.

Yuendumu School (10) has grown substantially since its foundation by the first Baptist missionaries. Today there are more than 200 children enrolled for pre-school, primary, post-primary and secondary study to year

10 (the latter by correspondence). The school has thirty-nine staff including fifteen teachers, five of whom are Indigenous. It is run as a bilingual school, starting with Warlpiri as the classroom language and gradually introducing English. The bilingual program is supported by a teacher linguist and a printery which prepares teaching materials in Warlpiri. The school offers a bus pick-up service through the School Home Liaison Officer, occasional self-financed lunches are available to children, and there is an annual one-week long 'country visit', where children are taught by their elders in their own country about their Warlpiri heritage.

The **Yuendumu Central Land Council Office** (11) is the local branch of the Central Land Council, based in Alice Springs. It has one Indigenous employee whose main responsibility is to coordinate the provision of practical expertise in consultation, research and other tasks associated with the use of Aboriginal land under the *Aboriginal Land Rights Act (NT) 1976* and the *Native Title Act 1993*, and to liaise between the Warlpiri people in the region and the head office in Alice Springs.

Yuendumu's **Old People's Program** (12) operates a meals-on-wheels program and undertakes some home-care of old people. Its administrative centre is currently housed in the Old People's Respite Centre, a building designed by Kathy Keys in collaboration with a number of women from Yuendumu and completed in 2000, which has yet to begin operation.

The **Women's Centre** (13) facilitates a number of programs, including Night Patrol, which entails patrolling the settlement and surrounds at night, to keep alcohol from being smuggled into Yuendumu (which is a 'dry' zone, i.e. alcohol is not permitted). Night Patrol also intervenes in alcohol-related brawls, or alerts the police to do so. It also alerts the Substance Misuse Program Coordinator if children are found sniffing petrol (see Warlpiri Media Association 1998). Yuendumu Night Patrol is one of a very few Night Patrols around the country run exclusively by women. The Women's Centre also assists with other programs and courses, e.g. the Strong Women Strong Babies Program, sewing courses, and courses in tandem with CAT (Centre for Appropriate Technology). Both the Old People's Program and the Childcare Centre are now independent spin-offs from the Women's Centre.

The **Childcare Centre** (14) was the first licensed childcare centre in remote Central Australia and is currently fully subsidised. It is licensed for twenty-two children but usually has fewer to look after. It operates from 8.30 a.m. to 1 p.m. and sometimes also in the afternoon.

Yuendumu's **Police Station** (15) employs a sergeant and between two and three police, as well as one or two Indigenous police aides.

The **Council Garage** (16) looks after big machinery required for the grading of roads and constructions work, as well as other Council vehicles.

The **Powerhouse** (17) is where the generator is kept that provides Yuendumu with electricity.

GLOSSARY

bad news — message about a death

boss for oneself — autonomy

business — ceremonies, ritual

business woman — woman who engages in and takes responsibility for ritual and ceremonies

camp — domestic space consisting of windbreaks, rows of sleepers and fires

cruising — driving or walking around, checking out what is going on elsewhere, and visiting

divorced — the end of sexual relations in a marriage

dolla-wangu — without money, broke

grow up — to look after and nurture a child

early days — the period of initial settlement and strict institutional control

humpies — shelters of corrugated iron and bush materials

jangkayi — men's camp

jarnpa — a person who walks around at night in order to kill another person and make trouble, men with special powers to make themselves invisible who wear emu-feather foot covering to dissimulate tracks, who travel with harmful intentions, kurdaitcha, bogey-man

jilimi — women's camp

jinamardarni — to hold and to look after

jinta — one, alone, single, singly, single-handed, solitary, same, unique

jukurrpa — dream, Dreaming, ancestral beings and associated rituals, designs, songs, places, ceremonies time of the ancestral beings, story, ritual, song, law, custom

kala-rla — lunchtime

kapu — he/she/it will (do something)

kardirri — white, light in colour

Kardiya — non-Indigenous person, whitefella

karikurda — erratic wind that changes direction, 'upside-down' winds

karlarra — west

karlarra-wardingki — 'those belonging to the west', polite way of referring to women

karna — I am (doing something)

-ku — suffix: to, for

kulkurru — in the middle

kumparri — thunder

kunarlupu — storm clouds, hail

kurdaitcha — see *jarnpa*

kurdu-kurdu — children, storm clouds

kurdu-kurdu-pinyi — to form clouds, make offspring, generate, form, spawn, and procreate

kurlangu — belonging to

-kurra — towards

lawa — no

look after — to be in a relationship of responsibility towards (a child, a ceremony, country)

marlpa — company, companion, companionship

-mayi — turning a sentence into a question, 'isn't it?'

munga — night

mungalyurru — early morning

mungalyurru-rla — as the sun comes up

munga-ngka — night-time, at night, in the night

ngapa — water, rain

ngati — mother, kinship term

-ngka — on, in, at; suffixed onto words with one or two syllables

ngunaka — lie down!

ngunami — to be, to lie, lying down

ngurra — home, camp, shelter, nest, ancestral place, country

ngurra-jarra — two camps, two nights

ngurra-jinta — one camp, one place, one night

ngurra-kurlarni-nyarra — (lit. camp-southside) = patrimoiety of J/Nakamarra, Jupurrurla/Napurrurla, J/Nampijinpa, J/Nangala subsections *ngurra-ngajuku* — my home

ngurrara — country, fatherland, place, land, home

ngurrarntija, ngurra-wardingki — person belonging to a certain place, countryman, householder.

ngurra-yatuju-mparra — patrimoiety of J/Napanangka, J/Napangardi, J/Nungarrayi, J/Napaljarri subsections

ngurra-yuntuyuntu — place where many people lived for an extended period of time, large camp, long-term camp

nullahnullah —Aboriginal English term for fighting stick, also *kuturu*

olden days — pre-contact and early contact times, characterised by a nomadic lifestyle, a hunting and gathering economy and an elaborate ritual life

pipa —paper, bible, church service, funeral

-rla — on, in, at; suffixed to words with more than two syllables

run around — having transient sexual relationships

sorry, sorry business — vernacular term for mortuary rituals

sorry camp — camp people sleep in during mortuary rituals

sorry mob — group of people who have travelled from other settlements to participate in mortuary rituals

stopping — staying at, living with

story time — sitting around a fire with close friends and relatives and exchanging news and gossip, remembering events from the past, planning trips, and joking

visiting— coming and going from *camp* to *camp* for social interaction, daytime activity

visitor — 'strangers', people one does not know but who are in Yuendumu for some reason

wantimi —to fall

Warlpiri — name of people traditionally occupying northern part of the Ngalia Basin, the Tanami Desert, Lander River, Hansen River (see also *Yapa*), name of the language spoken by Warlpiri people

warlu — fire, firewood, hot, ashes, fireplace, hearth, cooking fire

warungka — deaf, forgetful, unable to understand or remember, stupid, retarded, foolish, mindless, uncaring, feeble-minded; also used for the very young and the very old: not fully knowledgeable social persons

wirnpa — lightning

wiyarrpa —poor bugger, poor thing, sympathetic exclamation *women's business* — women's ceremonies and rituals

wuraji — afternoon

wuraji-wuraji — around sunset, late afternoon, evening

yalka — space between windbreak and head of sleeper

yani — going, walking

yanirlipa — we go

yanirra — going away (from us)

yantarra —go away!

Yapa — person, Warlpiri person, Aboriginal person, people, Warlpiri people

yaparla — reciprocal kin term for a person's FM, FMZ and FMB, and SC

yarlu — space with nothing on or over it

yarlukuru — synonym for *jilimi,* women's camp

yarrkujuju — place where deceased person lived, where person died, camp of dead person, deceased person's camp

yatijarra — north

yitipi — outside, on the outside

yungka-ju! — give me!

yungkami — giving

yunta — windbreak, place where people sleep

yupukarra — married people's camp

yuwarli — house (physical structure)

yuwayi —yes

NOTES

Chapter 1

1. Today, with a change in the Australian political climate, Yuendumu and other places like it are no longer commonly referred to as 'settlements'; the new term of choice is 'community'. This new term, although widely used by both Indigenous and non-Indigenous people in everyday discourse, is problematic in the context of this book, combining as it does the spatial with a new ideology of 'identity' (see among others Hinkson 1999; Holcombe 1998; Rowse 1990, 1992; Trigger 1986, 1992). I retain use of the term 'settlement' to highlight Yuendumu's origin as a government-instigated endeavour concerned to bring about social transformation. This usage allows me to distinguish between Yuendumu's presence as a spatio-physical entity and the people who live in it.

2. The connection between dwelling and being, with more specific unidirectionality, is also found in Piaget (1951; 1954; 1956), who, in regard to child development, emphasises children's interaction with the spatiality of the house as significant in their social and intellectual development of motor, spatial, social and intellectual habitability.

3. The point about housing as a tool of social reform has also been made in non-colonial contexts, especially as an attempt to 'uplift' the 'lower classes' in Western European countries (see for example Loefgren 1984; Kemeny 1992; Attfield 1999; Dolan 1999).

4. For more detailed accounts of Aboriginal housing policy, see (among others) contributions in the volume edited by Heppell (1979a) and those in Read (2000). For Yuendumu especially see Keys (2000), and for an ethnography on Aboriginal perceptions of housing see Ross (1987).

5. This is not to say that the book stands in opposition to previous research with Warlpiri people; indeed it is anchored within and heavily dependent upon the large body of anthropological and other literature about Warlpiri people. While I draw more extensively on some parts of this literature

than on others, this literature as a whole underpins my analyses. I refer the interested reader to David Nash's websites collating and updating Warlpiri references: for non-linguistic references (in the main anthropological) see www.anu.edu.au/linguistics/nash/aust/wlp/wlp-eth-ref.html; and for linguistic references see www.anu.edu.au/linguistics/nash/aust/wlp/wlp-lx-ref.html.

6. The period of ancestral creation called *jukurrpa*, and its entanglements with the present, are not part of this account. For excellent discussions of Warlpiri time concepts in this regard see Dussart (2000) and Munn (1970, 1992).

7. Note that most Warlpiri nouns take the same form in the singular and the plural, i.e. one jilimi, five jilimi. At Yuendumu a shift seems to be occurring currently from the former term 'jilimi' to 'yarlukuru', which is imported from further south. I decided to retain the use of the term 'jilimi', as it is more prominent in the literature (on the two terms, see also Keys 1999: 16–18).

8. At Yuendumu, the term 'Toyota' designates any kind of four-wheel-drive vehicle, the favoured choice of transport. All roads connecting Yuendumu to surrounding settlements, outstations, hunting grounds and sacred sites are rough 'dirt' tracks, often badly corrugated, and are much more comfortably negotiated by large four-wheel-drive vehicles. Moreover, during heavy summer rains these tracks are frequently flooded and become inaccessible to normal vehicles. Equally important is the fact that Toyotas are roomier and allow more people to travel. Access to vehicle transportation was much coveted, and while having a Toyota was not exactly a condition of allowing me to do fieldwork, it was strongly encouraged.

9. In all cases pseudonyms are used.

10. Age also plays a role in the classification of kinship. For example, all other women of the same skinname of approximately the same age are considered sisters, while those much younger are brother's son's daughters, and those much older, father's father's sisters.

11. Others before me have discussed and described different aspects of the history of Yuendumu in detail; here I concentrate only on the developments central to the particular concerns of this book. For more on Yuendumu's history, see among others Hinkson (1999: 17–20), Keys (1999: 59–62), Meggitt (1962: 28–9), Middleton and Francis (1976: 10–15), Rowse (1998), Steer (1996) and Young (1981: 56–123). Historical accounts of pre-settlement events are included in, amongst others, Elias (2001) and Watts and Fisher (2000). Also pertinent in this context is Olive Pink's pre-settlement material. She was the first anthropologist to work with Warlpiri people, based for intermittent periods from 1933 to 1945 in the Tanami Desert, first at Yunmaji, then at Jila, and later close to the Granites goldfields and at Thompson's Rockhole. Unfortunately most of her Warlpiri material was never published (see Marcus 1993 for the underlying reasons for this, and Marcus 2001 for an evocative portrait of Olive Pink's relations with Warlpiri people).

12. The Yuendumu Cattle Company was transferred and became an Aboriginal corporation, called Ngarliyikirlangu Cattle Company in 1979, and by the mid-1990s had ceased operation.

13. The debate around welfare and Aboriginal entanglements with the state and consequent dependency is extensive and on-going (see among many others Altman and Sanders 1991; Altman and Smith 1992; Beckett 1985; Daly et al. 2002; Martin 2001; Pearson 2000; Peterson and Sanders 1998; Sackett 1990; Sanders 1986, 2001).

14. Census data for remote Aboriginal settlements are notoriously unreliable due to both high mobility and under-enumeration (see among others Martin and Taylor 1995; Taylor 1996a, 1996b; Taylor and Bell 1996). This is reflected in some of the Yuendumu population estimates made during the main fieldwork period:

    • The 1996 Australian Bureau of Statistics census gives 773 residents for Yuendumu and its outstations, 137 of whom identified as non-Indigenous (ABS 1998).

    • The Health Centre Population Screening List for October 1997 gives a total of 930 residents (Yuendumu Health Profile 1999).

    • ATSIC's *Community Housing and Infrastructure Need Survey* (CHINS) indicates 875 usual residents (ATSIC 1999).

    • The Territory Health Services surveys conducted in 1998 to 2000 found the following figures: In November 1998, of 818 persons living at Yuendumu, 745 were Indigenous, and 73 were non-Indigenous. In June 1999, of 721 persons living at Yuendumu, 640 were Indigenous, and 81 non-Indigenous. And in August 2000, of 901 persons living at Yuendumu, 795 were Indigenous and 106 were non-Indigenous.

15. The Warlpiri term 'Kardiya', supposedly from 'kardirri' for white or light in colour (Hale 1990: 31), means Whitefella, referring to people of non-Aboriginal origin generally (whether 'white' or not). The Warlpiri term 'Yapa' has a wide range of meanings. Its most general use centres on 'human being' or 'person'. Situationally, it carries more specific meanings. These range from referring to black people in general (e.g. a comment frequently made in connection with a World Vision ad filmed in Africa is: '*Wiyarrpa Yapa*' — 'dear Blackfella'), or to refer to all Australian Aboriginal peoples (in opposition to non-Indigenous Australians). In more localised contexts, it is used to differentiate Warlpiri people (Yapa) from, for example, Pitjantjatjara people (Anangu).

16. Reasons to move residence include: death-related taboos of former residences (see also Musharbash 2008b), marriage, fights in former residence, and availability of housing. Note that people may also have multiple residences across a number of Camps (see Musharbash 2000 for examples).

17. The only other anthropologist paying close attention to these changes in Camp composition is Dussart (1988, 2000: 41), who outlined six Camps, albeit slightly different from the ones I found ten years later. See also Young

(1981: 66–9) for a description and map of Yuendumu's Camps in the late 1970s, suggestive of future developments.

18. Other 'suburbs' where smaller numbers of non-Indigenous people reside are East Camp, South Camp, and Inner West Camp.

Chapter 2

1. For a small selection of the anthropological literature on the socio-cultural significance of dwellings, see Bourdier and Al Sayyad 1989; Burton 1997; Carsten and Hugh-Jones 1995; Cieraad 1999; Comaroff and Comaroff 1992; Cunningham 1973; Fox 1993; Kana 1980; Kuper 1980; Lawrence and Low 1990; Loefgren 1984; Low and Lawrence 2003; Oliver 1975; Pine 1996; Rapoport 1969; Rybczynski 1987; Tambiah 1969; Uhl 1989.

2. I do not want to imply that life before sedentisation was static and unchanging. What I am referring to is the period immediately preceding contact, a period about which Warlpiri people reflect frequently. Moreover, I believe that innovation took place in a number of domains, foremost perhaps the ritual, but may have been less significant in regard to residential arrangements, which are at issue here.

3. Another possible interpretation of east–west sleeping would link gender and associated cardinal directions to sleeping orientation, meaning that women, who are associated with the west, would be least accessible and, through the sleeping orientation, least visible to single men in the east.

4. On the significance of threshold in Western-style houses, see Rosselin (1999), who describes the complex social negotiations of entering Parisian apartments without entrance halls, and Dolan (1999) on the erection of porches and so forth upon purchase of previously rented houses in Thatcherite England.

5. In the ritual context, the concentric circles relay Warlpiri ideas of the creation of the cosmos through the deeds of ancestral beings (jukurrpa) during the creation period (jukurrpa), depicting their travels and the meanings associated with this. Munn (1970) has described and analysed these notions most elaborately in her paper on the transformation of subjects into objects (and see critiques and discussions thereof in Dubinskas and Traweek 1984; Morton 1987, 1989). Myers (esp. 1976; 1986a) has done excellent work outlining the spiritual links between camp, country and people as expressed by the term 'ngurra'.

6. There are instances where concentric circles are used in sand stories, in which case a number of concentric circles are connected by a line, with the latter depicting a journey and each set of circles standing for an overnight stop.

7. In the ensuing case studies of life in the *camps* of Yuendumu, I indicate the presence or absence of a house if relevant.

8. Keys (2000) argues that at Yuendumu houses are conceptually associated with yupukarra as this Warlpiri residential composition equates most closely the Western nuclear family with which in mind most houses were erected. I am not convinced this represents Warlpiri views and practice accurately.

9. The extent of outside living seems to be changing slowly. By 2007, there seemed to be fewer Yapa sleeping outside than, say, ten years ago, especially in winter. One main reason seems to be better maintenance and repair services, ensuring that heating is available inside houses and people rely less on fires for warmth in winter.

10. Yapa-occupied houses tend to have much less furniture in them than houses occupied by non-Indigenous people, as well as fewer decorative items, although this is slowly changing.

11. Typically, further storage space is found in trees and shade structures surrounding a *camp* and/or house; this is where axes, shovels, rakes, spears, boomerangs, and the like are kept. If there are shade structures with a roof, or the roof of the house itself is reachable, items are stored there as well, particularly kangaroo meat so that it is out of reach of the dogs. If there is a house, firewood is piled up on or next to the verandah, to keep it dry should it rain — otherwise it is left in a pile not too far from where people sleep.

    Food is hardly ever stored in kitchens, except for perishable goods, which may be stored in the fridge if there is one. Rather than storing food, people often go shopping for each meal and consume it immediately, or keep their food close to their person where they can see it, for example on a low wall, in the branches of a tree or on the roof of a shade structure. However, many people keep a small cache of 'emergency food' (mostly tinned items) hidden somewhere among their possessions.

12. Even if a house has a fence, the fact remains that for yarlu to be meaningful space, there actually needs to be people present (meaning, a *camp* needs to be in existence) as a fence surrounding a deserted house does *not* designate yarlu space.

13. On 'drunken fights', see among others Martin (1993) and Sackett (1977).

14. Today further private space is found in suitcases stored in rooms, lockable cupboards, and so forth.

15. I know of and have written about two exceptions (Musharbash n.d.), one being an old widower who established his own camp after his wife's death, where he sleeps alone. His choice to live on his own has powerful connotations. It is a statement about the loneliness he feels, and it constitutes a strong appeal to his kin to look after him and care for him. The other example is of an old woman without any immediate family. Her choice to sleep on her own is an expression of her 'loneliness' not only in Yuendumu but 'in the world'.

16. The Warlpiri dictionary translates 'marlpa' as 'company, companion, companionship, accompanying, jointly'. Dussart (2000: 115–16 and 2004)

uses the term 'marlpa' to denote more specifically 'friend'. In this book it carries the more general meaning of 'sociality' and 'company'. Translating 'marlpa' as 'friend' causes analytical difficulties, since there already exists an Aboriginal English term *friend* that at Yuendumu is reserved for relationships with non-Indigenous people.

17. There is some overlap between such two-directional relationality — seeking company for comfort and to provide comfort — and the responsibility of 'holding and looking after', which Myers (1986a) discussed in great depth based on the Pinupi concept 'kanyininpa'; see also Dussart (2000) for the Warlpiri equivalent *jinamardarni*. 'Holding and looking after' captures not only relations between people but also between people and country, and ritual and spiritual matters, and is imparted from a senior position.

Chapter 3

1. Jilimi are social structures for men minimally during the day, and under certain circumstances also at night.

2. Further, Meggitt says, 'The circumcision ceremony is, among other things, a public indication that a particular matriline will later provide the lad with a wife. Other men, by acting as the boy's *jualbiri*, those who decorate him before the circumcision, guarantee that they will ensure that this matriline honours its obligation'. (Meggitt 1962: 266).

   Bell (1980b: 266) makes two corrections to this view, (1) that women as well as men, are involved in these negotiations, and (2) that for women, promised marriages are not *ideal* marriages so much as their *first* marriages.

3. A number of Aboriginal English terms are used to describe different kinds of sexual relationships. (1) The terms *boyfriend* and *girlfriend* describe a relationship different to a marriage mainly through its lack of co-residentiality. *Boyfriend/girlfriend* relationships may be long-term and stable, or short-lived, but generally entail a flow of goods from the boyfriend to the girlfriend, continuing even after the relationship is over. (2) *Running around* has the connotation of promiscuously looking for sex, and as a term relates human sexual behaviour to that of dogs. Dogs, it is said at Yuendumu, fornicate indiscriminately. They belong to people and have subsection terms, or skinnames, but 'they do not know', i.e. they do not behave according to the rules governing social behaviour the way humans do/or should do. Thus, a person who is *running around* is somebody who is looking for sex, regardless of with whom and under which circumstance.

4. All three kinds of marriages began with the girl's or woman's walk through the *camp* to join the man.

5. Warlpiri people tend not to get married in civil or religious ceremonies (I know of two exceptions, both involving a Warlpiri and a non-Indigenous spouse, and living outside Warlpiri country). Living with each other in a yupukarra, and public acceptance of this arrangement as constituting a

marriage, fulfil these requirements, even in the eyes of the Australian state. When filling out forms, whether for welfare, taxation or other purposes, Warlpiri people do not seem to be required to prove their marital status. And it needs to be highlighted that a Warlpiri marriage substantially differs from both a certified Australian marriage and a de facto relationship. Warlpiri spouses are highly unlikely to share their financial arrangements, which is a prerequisite for de facto relationships; and Warlpiri divorces do not require courts and other administrative involvement.

6. Marriage is thus related to residentiality as well as to sexuality in particular ways. Consider for example that, in local parlance, when a marriage ends it is said to be *finished*, while the term to be *divorced* means to still have a spouse, to still live with them, but to have ceased sexual relations. As one woman put it: 'I am divorced. My husband does not sleep close to me, I left him, he drinks too much. He sleeps at home but we are not married. He used to be strong, he had shiny eyes, he was stockman, always riding on that horse, riding, riding, riding. Now, I don't like him talking to me, it makes me sick. He says: "Nungarrayi, how are you, I worry for you, sick woman, wiyarrpa". But I don't like listening to him. He does not worry for me, he just drinks.'

   To be *divorced* means that sexual relations have ceased, while other aspects of the marriage, such as co-residence, sharing of food, and care for children and grandchildren, continue. Not living together any more constitutes the end of a marriage.

7. The situation in regards to jangkayi is different. In the *olden days*, men moved into jangkayi after initiation and stayed in them until marriage, which they entered when significantly older then women. This means that most *olden days camps* had jangkayi attached to them, while jilimi only existed when women were widowed and until they re-married.

8. In the ideal case, in which children grow up in their parents' yupukarra, their mother provides the most immediate emotional support and, assisted by others, especially her close female relatives, looks after the children's nutritional needs, upbringing and early childhood education (see amongst others Hamilton 1981; Musharbash 2000). The father spends less time with his children, but ideally is loving and caring throughout their upbringing. Once children reach adolescence, their patriline becomes more involved in their education, particularly as it relates to rights and responsibilities to land, as expressed through ritual. Boys then are educated by their father, his brothers and other male members of the patriline, and girls by their father's sisters, father's mothers and other female members of the patriline.

9. If the children of a failed marriage have been weaned, then often their patriline insists on taking over childcare and child-raising responsibilities, meaning that such children often move in with their paternal grandmothers rather than with their mothers. I know of a few maternal grandmothers who

took up such responsibilities, but often in these cases there did not exist a 'proper' marriage — the child was the result of *running around*, in which case there were doubts about which patriline is his or hers.

10. To be able to observe all coming and going and other activity is a main requirement for a living space. The house visually blocked the south yard and thus hindered its usage. In fact, the only time I am aware of that a yunta was put up there was when one of the jilimi residents was expected to die. Surrounded by her sisters, this old woman spent her last days and nights in an *olden days*-style yunta in the south yard.

11. The use of rooms is slowly changing. In 2007, for example, in two *camps* I lived in the following occurred. In the first *camp* most rooms were allocated to couples, who did, indeed, use them as bedrooms. In the second *camp* most residents slept outside in summer (with the exception of a small number of young men who used one bedroom on and off as a jangkayi), while most nights in winter all residents slept inside, and two bedrooms were used as yupukarra, one as jangkayi, and the fourth bedroom (with the door open) and the living room as jilimi. Here I also came across an example of occasional sleeping alone in one bedroom. This happened when only one particular man was present in the jangkayi, however; on those nights that he slept alone, the bedroom door was always open.

Chapter 4

1. Warlpiri people do not differentiate rights and responsibilities in terms of the length of time a person stays in a *camp*, as do census takers for example, who distinguish between 'residents' and 'visitors'. The Australian Bureau of Statistics (ABS 1991; ABS 1996), for example, defines people who 'usually live in a particular dwelling' as residents and those who are staying in the same dwelling (overnight) but usually reside elsewhere as visitors (for an example of following this usage in ethnography see Moisseeff 1999). This distinction does not work at Yuendumu, where the boundaries between visitor and resident are blurred indeed if defined like this. Warlpiri people frequently change their 'usual residence' and/or often have a number of 'usual residences'. Accordingly, I call any person who sleeps in a *camp* (independent of the length of their stay) a resident, and reserve the term visiting for spending time in a *camp* during the day. This latter case is supported also by local terminology, in which *visiting* when used as a verb refers to daytime activities. Warlpiri people say, 'Let's go visit X in hospital', or 'I went visiting Y's *camp* for *story time*'. The noun *visitor*, on the other hand, in Aboriginal English at Yuendumu refers to 'strangers', people one does not know but who are in Yuendumu for some reason (e.g. people who have travelled from afar to Yuendumu for initiation rituals).

2. I elaborate on practices of demand sharing in Chapters 7 and 9, and see also Martin 1993; Myers 1982; Peterson 1993, 1997; Schwab 1995.

3. Sansom's (1978, 1980, 1982, 1988) work on this issue is expansive.

4. To provide one last example. The Centre for Aboriginal Economic Policy Research (CAEPR), which positions itself in between the public policy arena and the ethnographic domain, since its earliest publications in 1991 has been occupied with the term 'household' and its use in respect to Indigenous Australia. In particular, CAEPR has been concerned with and criticised the household definitions used by the Australian Bureau of Statistics (ABS) (see among others Finlayson and Auld 1999; Martin and Taylor 1995; Musharbash 2000, Smith 1991, 1992; Smith and Daly 1996).

The 1991 ABS definition reads: 'A household is a group of people who reside and eat together (in a single dwelling) [...] as a single unit in the sense that they have common housekeeping arrangements, i.e. they have some common provision for food and other essentials for living (ABS 1991: 60).

The 1996 ABS definition reads: 'A household is defined as a group of two or more related or unrelated people who usually reside in the same dwelling, who regard themselves as a household, and who make common provisions for food and other essentials' (ABS 1996: glossary).

CAEPR heavily criticised the ABS definitions for ignoring the realities of Aboriginal circumstances:

(1) High mobility creates enormous fluctuations in 'the people who reside and eat together', i.e. there is no stable social unit constituted by residing and eating together.

(2) 'Common housekeeping arrangements' exist across dwelling boundaries and may exclude people within one dwelling.

(3) 'Usual residence in the same dwelling' excludes the Aboriginal practice of having a number of 'home bases'.

CAEPR's criticism is focussed on the realities in Aboriginal Australia of the compositional complexity of residents within any one dwelling, on the sharing of resources across dwellings, and on the high mobility of residents through dwellings. Curiously, though, despite the problems perceived in relation to the concept, most CAEPR publications continued to use the term household as a basic unit for analysis and comparison (see Rowse 2002 for a similar critique).

5. Nevertheless, only five years later a landmark work on households was published. In this study Netting, Wilk, and Arnould strongly emphasise the term's usefulness for cross-cultural comparison. Households to them are 'task-oriented residence units' (1984: xx), and previous confusions associated with the term are to be dispersed by introducing 'morphology and activity' as subcategories of analysis. Morphology refers to the structural composition of household personnel, and activity to what household members do. They present five types of activities to be used in analysis: production, distribution, transmission, reproduction and co-residence. Needless to say, the renaming of 'function' into 'activity' did not solve any of

the previous problems. Neither did the casting of different household types within an evolutionary framework do anything to enhance the concept.

6. During the first few weeks of fieldwork I felt bewildered by the flow of people through the jilimi, and I was often not confident enough to ask for the names of people I did not know. By and by I got to know most people through the appropriate channels (asking in the morning when taking the census would *not* have been appropriate), and after a while worked out polite ways of inquiring about a person's name when I did not know it.

7. It is likely that some individuals whose names I did not know were counted several times if they stayed in the jilimi for more than one night or on a number of occasions.

8. Annie moved into Nora's room only a couple of months before I moved into another camp with Polly and Celeste. Since I am not as familiar with Annie as with the other four focal women, I focus more extensively on the latter.

9. Mt Theo is an outstation about 150 kilometres north-west of Yuendumu. It is used to house kids who were caught petrol-sniffing at Yuendumu (see Brady 1992 on petrol sniffing generally; Stojanowski n.d. on the Mt Theo Programme). Since Jenna and her husband often lapsed into petrol-sniffing, both spent substantial amounts of time there.

10. In the past, the newly-weds would have lived with the wife's parents first before moving to the husband's country later (see Peterson 1978).

11. For example, Annie has a large number of sisters and half-sisters; however, only two of them stay with her regularly, and much more often than do the others. Moreover, while a handful of her sisters stay with her frequently, a number of other sisters stay with her rarely or never. A similar point can be made about the individuals staying with Polly, Celeste, Joy and Nora. Each of these women has other people as closely related to them as the ones staying with them regularly, who however stay with them less frequently or not at all.

12. When I visited Yuendumu for the first time in 1994, as well as on subsequent trips I made, Greta was based at this particular jilimi, and had moved elsewhere fairly recently just before I began this census in 1998.

13. Joy, for example, was simultaneously a core resident in the jilimi and in her *divorced* husband's *camp*; Nora was a also regular resident at her close son Hector's *camp*, Celeste was an on-and-off resident Camilla's *camp*, and Polly a sporadic one in all sorts of *camps*.

14. Beckett (1988) and Birdsall (1988) comment on similar patterns among Aboriginal people in the 'settled' parts of New South Wales and Western Australia respectively. Beckett elaborates: 'An Aborigine may go 200 miles to a place where he is known, rather than 10 miles to a place where he is

not. Usually, being known means having kin who will receive him and act as sponsors in the local community. The area within which he moves — his 'beat' as I shall call it — is defined by the distribution of kin' (Beckett 1988: 119).

What Beckett calls 'beats' and Birdsall calls 'runs' and 'lines' are spatial representations of the patterns of mobility within personal networks as I have outlined them. Here, I have explored the same kind of mobility at a micro-level within a settlement. Despite the fact that Beckett and Birdsall are dealing with movement between towns, often many hundreds of kilometres apart, there are clear isomorphisms here.

15. I specifically examine mobility through the *camps* and the settlement of Yuendumu; of course this extends into and includes extensive inter-settlement mobility (see Young and Doohan, 1989).

16. While the household in the Aboriginal context is generally understood within a context of monetary budgeting, in other contexts it is more broadly defined by a number of activities performed by the people who share a dwelling, and here approaches substantial overlap with the 'residential group'.

Chapter 5

1. Literally: 'Water will fall, won't it?' 'No, northwards it is moving.'

2. 'Kurdu-kurdu', which literally means 'children', also builds the stem for the verb 'kurdu-kurdu-pinyi', which means to form clouds, make offspring, generate, form, spawn, and procreate — neatly alluding to the interconnections between water and fertility. The other word I was given for individual smaller storm clouds was 'kunarlupu', which the dictionary translates as 'hail'.

3. At Yuendumu, the term *bad news* is always and exclusively used as a euphemism for death. *Good news* on the other hand is used for descriptions of newly developed liaisons, especially in joking between cousins. 'I heard the good news', for example, said by one female cousin to another thus means that the first one has found out about a liaison the other is having. Note that *good news* does not, as in some other Indigenous communities, refer to the bible; this is called *pipa*, from 'paper', i.e. 'book'.

4. Greta, Nora and Joy are all bringing up/looking after (some of) their sons' children. The practice of children being *grown up* by their paternal grandmothers when their parents' marriage deteriorates does not only benefit the grandchildren, (currently) without parental carers, but often is an arrangement actively sought by older single women. They often form close bonds with one particular son's child (yaparla), replacing in care, physical and emotional closeness and all other regards the mother–child relationship.

Chapter 6

1. For more detail on the public–private distinction, see Myers (1976; 1979; 1986a; 1988b), who has elaborated, in great theoretical depth and with admirable ethnographic insight, the notion of autonomy and relatedness in everyday social relationships between people, and in an ontological sense between people and jukurrpa.

2. There are other ways of learning and other things to be learned. For example, the ability of telling who is walking behind you by the sound of their steps is not knowledge acquired by sleeping next to a person, and so forth.

3. I slept outside the jilimi as frequently as Nora, Polly, Joy and Celeste, and the 60 nights are thus not consecutive ones. Joy seemed absent less often than the others because during much of the census time I was travelling with her — i.e. when absent, we were both absent.

4. The table only registers those people who slept *immediately* next to any of the four women, not the entire range of people that made up their yunta. As yunta can be quite long, comprising up to ten or so people, to include all of them would have impacted on clarity. Note also that there may be either one or two immediate sleeping companions, depending on whether a woman slept on the inside or the outside of a yunta.

5. As Nora's yunta was often on the verandah (while mine was in the yard), and as Toby and Ray both slept under Nora's blankets, I was often unsure which one of the two was the one lying next to Nora. As it makes no difference in regards to my interpretation (nor did it matter to Nora, Ray and Toby), I use Toby and Ray somewhat interchangeably here.

6. On the concepts of being *boss for oneself* and caring for others, see among others Bell (1993), Dussart (2000), and Myers (1976, 1986a).

7. Meggitt somewhat dismissively called jilimi 'hotbeds of gossip' (1962: 236).

8. Nora's rallying against being associated with the elderly might have been so strong because that is exactly what happened. Soon after the move to 'her' house, Nora did start to be labelled warungka (see Musharbash forthcoming for details).

9. As Nangala was blind and senile, she was not able to use the bathroom on her own, or squat at the foot end of the yunta, and also frequently forgot to ask people to help her. Her yitipi position is thus purely practical and has nothing to do with seniority.

Chapter 7

1. Time zoning can also be used to analyse settlement space (as opposed to individual *camps*). Time zoning in the settlement of Yuendumu means that in certain spaces and during certain times different activities are performed, and it is particularly useful in analysing the respective Yapa and Kardiya uses

and presences in different places and at different times in the settlement (thus adding an important dimension to the analysis of what is often called 'the interface' or 'third space': see for example Hinkson 1999; Hinkson and Smith 2005; Holcombe 1998; Merlan 1998; Rowse 1992; Trigger 1992). Weekday business hours are distinctly marked by a concentrated visible presence of Kardiya, especially around the Park. It is during this time that resident Kardiya leave their houses, mainly for work. Moreover, this is the time when 'Government Kardiya' and contractors come into the settlement 'from Alice Springs and Canberra'. Between 9 a.m. and 5 p.m. the roads of Yuendumu are busy with 'Government Toyotas', each bearing the name of the organisation the driver works for on their sides: Central Land Council, Centrelink, Telecom, Territory Health Services (THS), NT Government, and whoever else has business to conduct in Yuendumu. The immediate end of the business day is marked by an even greater presence of Kardiya vehicles on the roads of Yuendumu, as they run their last errands and then drive home, or leave the settlement. A little while after that, the settlement has an entirely different feel to it: through Kardiya absence, Yapa become the prominent presence. Now *they* are visible walking and driving around, cruising, 'singing out' to people in a *camp* they drive by, stopping for a chat, congregating in groups discussing news. After 5 p.m. on weekdays, all day on weekends, and particularly during the long summer holidays when most Kardiya leave, Yuendumu is quite simply a different place.

2. For a comparative description of the daily cycle in houses and *camps* at Halls Creek, see Ross (1987, Chapter 4).

3. Most *camps* are attached to houses and these often have kitchens. However most are ill-equipped, stoves are more often than not broken, and cooking Warlpiri-style is more easily done on fires.

4. Men sometimes prepare their own meat, or have it cooked for them by their wives, mothers, or grandmothers — depending on where they are eating and who is present.

5. *Camps* are rarely empty of people. Empty *camps* are considered 'spooky', especially since nobody is present to watch over what is going on and people have no idea who or what entered the *camp* during their absence. *Camps* are only ever empty when all or most residents travel to another community, or when they are abandoned because a death occurred.

6. Damper is a simple flat bread made of self-raising flour and hot water, baked on hot ashes or on a wire over a small fire. On how to make damper, see White (1997).

7. Generally margarine is used; however it is called 'butter'.

8. Residents in the jilimi may also go elsewhere to request food, of course. For example, once when Polly and Celeste wanted jam and were not getting along with Joy who had some, they went to Camilla's *camp* to ask her for some.

9. Occasionally, all-male camping groups make so-called Johnny cakes, fried damper (personal communication N. Peterson).

10. In time, I entered into similar arrangements as Pearl and Bertha did, buying flour and receiving damper from the woman I gave the flour to.

11. The arrangements for Big Shop contributions to mortuary rituals change with different store managers and elected committees; sometimes they are 'donations' at other times 'loans'. Unfortunately, I was not able to obtain precise data on these transactions.

12. Sansom (1982) argues along similar lines for an emergent matrifocality as an element of the Aboriginal commonality. But see Finlayson (1991) for a critique of matrifocality and its commonly assumed implications based on ethnographic research at Kuranda, northern Queensland.

13. Damper production is of course also a reminder of colonialism and its effects and how some of these, such as houses and damper, have become central to daily life.

14. There is a second, interrelated, kind of *cruising* practiced at Yuendumu by children and teenagers at night. After dark, often until very late at night, they *cruise* around an area bordering on the western end of the Park, between the basketball court in the north and the Youth Centre in the south. Flocks of children and teenagers walk up and down that strip in groups of varying compositions, somewhat determined by age, gender, kin and co-residency, but fairly fluid. They stroll up and down, checking each other out, all the while imbuing that space at that time with their distinctive presence.

15. Gambling in Aboriginal settlements has been discussed in more detail by Harris (1991), Martin (1993: Chapter 3) and especially Altman (1987) among others. And on a comparative note see Riches (1975). Martin (1993: 129–34) lists the rules for some of the games most often played at Aurukun, which are similar to those of the games played at Yuendumu, although the names differ.

16. Wayililinynpa is an outstation and the country surrounding it about 60 kilometres south of Yuendumu (see Figure 1, Central Australia, for location).

17. *Warlu* is the Warlpiri word for both fire and firewood, and also encompasses a number of related meanings such as hot, ashes, fireplace, hearth, cooking fire and so on.

18. On generosity and 'demand sharing' see also Martin (1993) and Myers (1982, 1986a, 1986b,1988a).

19. It is not unusual for Yuendumu residents to receive welfare cheques in neighbouring settlements, I have described this practice in more detail elsewhere (Musharbash 2000: 59–60).

Chapter 8

1. For a while Tamsin and her husband shared the derelict house with Adrian and Stella.
2. It remains for future research to investigate the nature of the interrelationships between these highly fluid everyday personal networks and the much more enduring kin groups of the ritual domain (on the latter see Dussart 2000).
3. Due to the often short-lived nature of contemporary marriages, a child's main carers may be a close female relative other than their mother, most often a yaparla (FM), but often a MZ or MM and their close sisters.
4. There is a significant difference between Darwin fringe camps and Yuendumu in what this performance entails. In the former commensality is essential and couples who 'got no real kitchen anymore' (Sansom 1988: 171) are denied their marital status, whereas in Yuendumu co-residence in a yupukarra is crucial.
5. However, the violence of these outbursts, as well as the regularity with which they occur, hint towards Tamsin's frustrations about her biological mother's perceived lack of caring, which riles her so much precisely because she wants it. Thus these outbursts which deny motherhood in fact confirm it.
6. The Aboriginal English term *friend* is restricted in its use for Kardiya friends of Yapa, while Dussart (2004, 2000: 115–6) has also used the English term friend as a translation for marlpa. As marlpa (as company) can be given to anyone, and while there certainly is a difference between marlpa and good marlpa, it seems to me that neither *friend* nor marlpa adequately captures the reality of, for example, two sisters who are emotionally very close to each other. Firth, in the preface to *The Anthropology of Friendship* has called this phenomenon 'kin-friends, a real category to be distinguished from simple kin' (Firth 1999: xiii). However, none of the contributors to the book took up this issue, while all maintain that friendship is something qualitatively different to kinship, and, along the lines of Samson's quote, that kinship studies have tended to overshadow research into friendship (see contributions in Bell and Coleman 1999). I do not think that friendship covers the issue particularly well at all, as it in turn diverts attention from a second issue, namely that kin relations do not necessarily necessitate amicability.
7. This is not to say that Tamsin *actually* would enjoy time and space on her own; knowing her well I also know that she in fact hates being alone.
8. Personal communication, Andrew Murchin and Nancy Napurrurla Oldfield, May 1999.
9. Movement is also triggered by death, and people respond to it by moving out of *camps* that become yarrkujuju and by defining their paths through the settlement through places of avoidance (see also Musharbash 2008b).

Conclusion

1. It always struck me that one reason why Bourdieu's term 'habitus' in English just does not have the right ring to it (sounding stilted rather than 'obvious'), must be that in French *habiter* has the double meaning of 'to live in (a house)' and 'the familiar' or 'the habitual'; a connection which is mirrored in the German terms for living inside houses (*wohnen*) and the familiar (*das Gewohnte*, literally 'the lived in' but meaning normal, habitual, familiar, regular).

2. Technically, all Warlpiri people living at Yuendumu if they have an income (welfare or waged) are required to pay rent, independent of where they live. That is, rent is collected per head, not per house, and independent of whether a person lives in a house or a *humpy*, or how many people live in one house.

3. As there are only a certain number of sites available for new houses at Yuendumu, this choice is somewhat limited. Moreover, as there is often a substantial waiting period between choosing a site and moving into the completed house, problems may arise. For example, in 2004, Celeste chose a site for 'her' house in East Camp, opposite Nora's *camp* (ideally, she would have liked to live in West Camp but was told there were no sites available there). The house was built two years later, and in early 2007 she moved in. However, in the meantime Nora's *camp* had become deserted (yarrkujuju) because of the death of one of Nora's grandsons; and Celeste's new house is now surrounded by the houses of people she is not close to. This concerned her so much that she considered not moving in, even though she had been on the housing waiting list for more than eight years and it was highly unlikely she would ever get to the top of the list again.

4. This is the only instance where I have drawn on a different translation. In the 1993 edition it says, rather less clearly, 'That range reveals itself to us as soon as we recall that human being consists in dwelling and, indeed, dwelling in the sense of the stay of mortals on the earth' (Heidegger 1993: 351).

BIBLIOGRAPHY

ABS 1991, *1991 Census Dictionary. cat. no. 2901.0*, Australian Bureau of Statistics, Canberra.

—1996, *1996 Census Dictionary. cat. no. 2901.0*, Australian Bureau of Statistics, Canberra.

—1998, *1996 Census of Population and Housing, Yuendumu. Cat no. 2020.0*, Australian Bureau of Statistics, Canberra.

Altman, JC 1987, Hunter-Gatherers Today: An Aboriginal Economy in North Australia, AIAS, Canberra.

Altman, JC & M Hinkson (eds) 2007, *Coercive Reconciliation: Stabilise, Normalise, Exit Aboriginal Australia*, Arena Publications, Melbourne.

Altman, JC & W Sanders 1991, *From Exclusion to Dependence: Aborigines and the Welfare State in Australia*, CAEPR Discussion Paper no. 1, Centre for Aboriginal Economic Policy Research, Australian National University, Canberra.

Altman, JC & DE Smith 1992, *Estimating the Reliance of Aboriginal Australians on Welfare: Some Policy Implications*. CAEPR Discussion Paper no. 19, Centre for Aboriginal Economic Policy Research, Australian National University, Canberra.

Anderson, C & F Dussart 1988, 'Dreamings in Acrylic: Western Desert Art', in P Sutton (ed.), *Dreamings: The Art of Aboriginal Australia*, Viking, New York, pp. 89–142.

ATSIC 1999, *Community Housing and Infrastructure Need Survey (CHINS)*, Aboriginal and Torres Strait Islander Commission, Canberra.

Attfield, J 1999, 'Bringing Modernity Home: Open Plan in the British Domestic Interior', in I Cieraad (ed.), *At Home: An Anthropology of Domestic Space*, Syracuse University Press, Syracuse, pp. 73–82.

Aubert, V & H White 1959a, 'Sleep: A Sociological Interpretation I', *Acta Sociologica*, vol. 4, no. 2, pp. 48–54.

—1959b, 'Sleep: a sociological interpretation II', *Acta Sociologica*, vol. 4, no. 3, pp. 1–16.

Bachelard, G 1994 [1958], *The Poetics of Space*, Beacon Press, Boston.

Beckett, J 1985, 'Colonialism in a Welfare State: The Case of the Australian Aborigines', *Cultural Survival Quarterly*, vol. 18, pp. 7–24.

—1988, 'Kinship, Mobility and Community in Rural New South Wales', in I Keen (ed.), *Being Black. Aboriginal Cultures in 'Settled' Australia*, Aboriginal Studies Press, Canberra, pp. 117–36.

Bell, D 1980a, 'Daughters of the Dreaming', PhD Thesis, Australian National University, Canberra.

—1980b, 'Desert Politics: Choices in the 'Marriage Market', in M Etienne & E Leacock (eds), *Women and Colonization: Anthropological Perspectives*, Praeger, New York, pp. 239–69.

—1993, *Daughters of the Dreaming*. Second Edition, Allen & Unwin, St Leonards.

Bell, S & S Coleman (eds) 1999, *The Anthropology of Friendship*, Berg, Oxford.

Bird-David, N 1992, 'Beyond "The Original Affluent Society": A Culturalist Reformulation', *Current Anthropology*, vol. 33, no. 1, pp. 25–47.

—1994, 'Sociality and Immediacy: Or, Past and Present Conversations on Bands', *Man*, vol. 29, no. 3, pp. 583–603.

Birdsall, C 1988, 'All one Family', in I Keen (ed.), *Being Black. Aboriginal Cultures in 'Settled' Australia*, Aboriginal Studies Press, Canberra, pp. 137–58.

Bourdier, JP & N Al Sayyad (eds) 1989, *Dwellings, Settlements, and Tradition: Cross-cultural Perspectives*, University Press of America, Lanham.

Bourdieu, P 1977, *Outline of a Theory of Practice*, Cambridge University Press, Cambridge.

—1990 [1970], 'The Kabyle House or the World Reversed', in *The Logic of Practice*, Polity Press, Cambridge, pp. 271–83.

—2000, *The Logic of Practice*, Cambridge University Press, Cambridge.

Brady, M 1992, *Heavy Metal: The Social Meaning of Petrol Sniffing in Australia*, Aboriginal Studies Press, Canberra.

Burton, A 1997, 'House/Daughter/Nation: Interiority, Architecture, and Historical Imagination in Janaki Majumdar's "Family History"', *Journal of Asian Studies*, vol. 65, no. 4, pp. 921–46.

Carsten, J & S Hugh-Jones (eds) 1995, *About the House: Lévi-Strauss and Beyond*, Cambridge University Press, Cambridge.

Cieraad, I (ed.) 1999, *At Home: An Anthropology of Domestic Space*, Syracuse University Press, Syracuse.

Comaroff, J & J Comaroff 1992, 'Home-Made Hegemony', in KT Hansen (ed.), *African Encounters with Domesticity*, Rutgers University Press, New Brunswick, pp. 37–74.

Cunningham, CE 1973, 'Order in the Atoni House', in R Needham (ed.), *Right & Left: Essays on Dual Symbolic Classification*, University of Chicago Press, Chicago, pp. 204–38.

Daly, A, R Henry & DE Smith 2002, *Welfare and the Domestic Economy of Indigenous Families: Policy Implications from a Longitudinal Survey*, CAEPR Discussion Paper no. 239, Centre for Aboriginal Economic Policy Research, Australian National University, Canberra.

Dolan, JA 1999, '"I've Always Fancied Owning Me Own Lion": Ideological Motivations in External House Decoration', in I Cieraad (ed.), *At Home: An Anthropology of Domestic Space*, Syracuse University Press: Syracuse, pp. 60–72.

Dubinskas, FA & S Traweek 1984, 'Closer to the Ground: A Reinterpretation of Walbiri Iconography', *Man*, vol. 19, pp. 15–30.

Dussart, F 1988, 'Warlpiri Women's Yawulyu Ceremonies: A Forum for Socialization and Innovation', PhD Thesis, Australian National University, Canberra.

—1992, 'The Politics of Female Identity: Warlpiri Widows at Yuendumu', *Ethnology*, vol. 31, no. 4, pp. 337–50.

—2000, *The Politics of Ritual in an Aboriginal Settlement: Kinship, Gender, and the Currency of Knowledge*, Smithsonian Institution Press, Washington.

—2004, 'Shown but not Shared, Presented but not Proffered: Redefining Ritual Identity among Warlpiri Ritual Performers, 1990–2000', *Australian Journal of Anthropology*, vol. 15, no. 3, pp. 253–66.

Elias, DJ 2001, 'Golden Dreams: People, Place and Mining in the Tanami Desert', PhD Thesis, Australian National University, Canberra.

Finlayson, JD 1991, 'Don't Depend On Me: Autonomy and Independence in an Aboriginal Community in Northern Queensland', PhD Thesis, Australian National University, Canberra.

Finlayson, J, A Daly & DE Smith 2000, 'The Kuranda Community Case Study', in *Indigenous Families and the Welfare System: Two Community Case Studies*. CAEPR Research Monograph no. 17, DE Smith (ed.), Centre for Aboriginal Economic Policy Research, Australian National University, Canberra, pp. 25–51.

Finlayson, JD & AJ Auld 1999, *Shoe or Stew? Balancing Wants and Needs in Indigenous Households: A Study of Appropriate Income Support Payments and Policies for Families,* CAEPR Discussion Paper no. 182, Centre for Aboriginal Economic Policy Research, Australian National University, Canberra.

Firth, R 1999, 'Preface', in S Bell & S Coleman (eds), *The Anthropology of Friendship*, Berg, Oxford, pp. xiii–xvi.

Fox, JJ 1993, *Inside Austronesian Houses: Perspectives on Domestic Designs for Living*, Department of Anthropology in Association with the Comparative Austronesian Project, Research School of Pacific Studies, Australian National University, Canberra.

Goodale, JC 1996, '*Taramaguti* Today: Changing Roles of Senior Tiwi Wives as Household Managers', *Pacific Studies*, vol. 19, no. 4, pp. 131–54.

Hale, KL 1990, *Warlpiri to English Vocabulary,* Institute for Aboriginal Development, Alice Springs.

Hamilton, A 1981, *Nature and Nurture: Aboriginal Child-rearing in North-Central Arnhem Land,* AIAS, Canberra.

Harris, P 1991, *Mathematics in a Cultural Context: Aboriginal Perspectives on Space, Time, and Money,* Deakin University Press, Geelong.

Harris, SG 1987, 'Yolgnu Rules of Interpersonal Communication', in WH Edwards (ed.), *Traditional Aboriginal Society. A Reade*r, Macmillan, Melbourne, pp. 1–9.

Hawkes, K 1993, 'Why Hunter-Gatherers Work: An Ancient Version of the Problem of Public Goods', *Current Anthropology,* vol. 34, no. 4, pp. 341–61.

Heidegger, M 1993 [1951] 'Building Dwelling Thinking' [Bauen Wohnen Denken], in DF Krell (ed.), *Martin Heidegger: Basic Writings from Being and Time (1927) to The Task of Thinking (1964)*, Routledge, London, pp. 347–63.

—2001 'Building Dwelling Thinking', in *Poetry, Language, Thought: Martin Heidegger* (translated by Albert Hofstadter), Perennial Classics, New York, pp. 143–59.

Heppell, M (ed.) 1979a, *A Black Reality: Aboriginal Camps and Housing in Remote Australia*, AIAS, Canberra.

—1979b, 'Introduction: Past and Present Approaches and Future Trends in Aboriginal Housing', in M Heppell (ed.), *A Black Reality: Aboriginal Camps and Housing in Remote Australia*, AIAS, Canberra, pp. 1–64.

Hiatt, LR 1982, 'Traditional Attitudes to Land Resources', in RM Berndt (ed.), *Aboriginal Sites, Rites and Resource Development*, University of Western Australia Press, Perth, pp. 13–26.

Hinkson, MJ 1999, 'Warlpiri Connections: New Technology, New Enterprise and Emergent Social Forms at Yuendumu', PhD Thesis, La Trobe University, Melbourne.

Hinkson, M, G James & D Nelson 1997, *Yanardilyi – Cockatoo Creek*, CD-Rom, Tanami Network, Yuendumu.

Hinkson, M & B Smith (eds) 2005, *Figuring the intercultural in Aboriginal Australia,* special issue of *Oceania*, vol. 75, no. 3.

Holcombe, SE 1998, 'Amunturrngu: An Emergent Community in Central Australia', PhD Thesis, University of Newcastle, Newcastle.

Ingold, T, D Riches, & J Woodburn (eds) 1988, *Hunters and Gatherers: Property, Power and Ideology,* Berg, Oxford.

Jackson, M 1995, *At Home in the World,* Duke University Press, Durham.

Kana, NL 1980, 'The Order and Significance of the Suvanese House', in JJ Fox (ed.), *The Flow of Life*, Harvard University Press, Cambridge, pp. 221–30.

Kemeny, J 1992, *Housing and Social Theory,* Routledge, London.

Kendon, A 1988, *Sign Languages of Aboriginal Australia: Cultural, Semiotic and Communicative Perspectives,* Cambridge University Press, Cambridge.

Keys, C 1999, 'The Architectural Implications of Warlpiri Jilimi', PhD Thesis, University of Queensland, Brisbane.

—2000, 'The House and the *Yupukarra*: Yuendumu 1946–96', in P Read (ed.), *Settlement. A History of Australian Indigenous Housing,* Aboriginal Studies Press, Canberra, pp. 8–29.

Kuper, A 1980, 'Symbolic Dimensions of the Southern Bantu Homestead', *Africa,* vol. 50, no. 1, pp. 8–23.

Lawrence, DL & SM Low 1990, 'The Built Environment and Spatial Form', *Annual Review of Anthropology,* vol. 19, pp. 453–505.

Lee, RB & I DeVore (eds) 1968, *Man the Hunter,* Aldine, Chicago.

Liberman, K 1985, *Understanding Interaction in Central Australia: An Ethnomethodological Study of Australian Aboriginal People,* Routledge & Kegan Paul, Boston.

Loefgren, O 1984, 'The Sweetness of Home: Class, Culture and Family Life in Sweden', *Ethnologia Europaea,* vol. 14, no. 1, pp. 44–64.

Long, JPM 1970, *Aboriginal Settlements: A Survey of Institutional Communities in Eastern Australia,* Australian National University Press, Canberra.

Low S & D Lawrence (eds) 2003, *The Anthropology of Space and Place,* Blackwell, Oxford.

Marcus, J 1993, 'The Beauty, Simplicity and Honour of Truth: Olive Pink in the 1940s', in J Marcus (ed.), *First in Their Field. Women and Australian Anthropology,* Melbourne University Press, Melbourne, pp. 111–35.

—2001, *The Indomitable Miss Pink: A Life in Anthropology,* UNSW Press, Sydney.

Martin, DF 1993, 'Autonomy and Relatedness: An Ethnography of Wik People of Aurukun, Western Cape York Peninsula', PhD Thesis, Australian National University, Canberra.

—2001, *Is Welfare Dependency 'Welfare Poison'? An Assessment of Noel Pearson's Proposals for Aboriginal Welfare Reform.* CAEPR Discussion Paper no. 213, Centre for Aboriginal Economic Policy Research, Australian National University, Canberra.

Martin, DF & J Taylor 1995, *Enumerating the Aboriginal Population of Remote Australia: Methodological and Conceptual Issues,* CAEPR Discussion Paper no. 91, Centre for Aboriginal Economic Policy Research, Australian National University, Canberra.

Mauss, M 1979 [1934] *Sociology and Psychology. Marcel Mauss* (trans. B Brewster), Routledge & Kegan Paul, London.

Meggitt, MJ 1955, 'Djanba among the Walbiri, Central Australia', *Anthropos,* vol. 50, pp. 375–403.

—1962, *Desert People: A Study of the Walbiri Aborigines of Central Australia*, Angus & Robertson, Sydney.

—1965, 'Marriage among the Walbiri of Central Australia: A Statistical Examination, in RM Berndt (ed.), *Aboriginal Man in Australia*, Angus & Roberston, Sydney, pp. 146–66.

—1968 '"Marriage Classes" and Demography in Central Australia', in RB Lee and I DeVore (eds), *Man the Hunter*, Aldine, New York, pp. 176–81.

Merlan, F 1998, *Caging the Rainbow: Places, Politics, and Aborigines in a North Australian Town*, University of Hawai'i, Honolulu.

Michaels, E 1986, *The Aboriginal Invention of Television in Central Australia 1982–1986*, AIAS, Canberra.

—1987, *For a Cultural Future: Francis Jupurrurla makes TV at Yuendumu*, Artspace, Melbourne.

—1994, *Bad Aboriginal Art: Tradition, Media and Technological Horizons*, Allen & Unwin, St Leonards.

Middleton, MR & SH Francis 1976, *Yuendumu and its Children: Life and Health on an Aboriginal Settlement*, Australian Government Publishing Service, Canberra.

Moisseeff, M 1999, *An Aboriginal Village in South Australia: A Snapshot of Davenport*, Australian Institute of Aboriginal and Torres Strait Islander Studies, Canberra.

Moore, HL 1986, *Space, Text, and Gender: An Anthropological Study of the Marakwet of Kenya*, Guilford Press, New York.

Morgan, LH 1965 [1881], *Houses and House-life of the American Aborigines*, University of Chicago Press, Chicago.

Morphy, H 1983, '"Now you Understand": An Analysis of the Way Yolgnu have Used Sacred Knowledge to Retain Their Autonomy', in N Peterson & M Langton (eds) *Aborigines, Land and Landrights*, Aboriginal Studies Press, Canberra, pp. 110–33.

Morton, J 1987, 'Singing Subjects and Sacred Objects: More on Munn's "Transformation of Subjects into Objects" in Central Australian Myth', *Oceania*, vol. 58, pp. 100–18.

—1989, 'Singing Subjects and Sacred Objects: A Psychological Interpretation of the "Transformation of Subjects into Objects" in Central Australian Myth', *Oceania*, vol. 59, pp. 280–98.

Munn, ND 1963, 'The Walbiri Sand Story', *Australian Territories*, vol. 3, no. 6, pp. 37–44.

—1966, 'Visual Categories: An Approach to the Study of Representational Systems', *American Anthropologist*, vol. 68, no. 4, pp. 936–50.

—1970, 'The Transformation of Subjects into Objects in Walbiri and Pitjantjatjara Myth', in RM Berndt (ed.), *Australian Aboriginal Anthropology: Modern Studies in the Social Anthropology of Australian Aborigines*, University of Western Australia Press, Nedlands, pp. 141–63.

—1973, *Walbiri Iconography: Graphic Representation and Cultural Symbolism in a Central Australian Society*, Cornell University Press, Ithaca.

—1992, 'The Cultural Anthropology of Time: A Critical Essay', *Annual Review of Anthropology*, vol. 21, pp. 93–123.

Munro, M & R Madigan 1999, 'Negotiating Space in the Family Home', in I Cieraad (ed.), *At Home: An Anthropology of Domestic Space*, Syracuse University Press, Syracuse, pp. 107–17.

Musharbash, Y 2000, 'The Yuendumu Community Case Study', in DE Smith (ed.), *Indigenous Families and the Welfare System: Two Community Case Studies*. CAEPR Research Monograph no. 17, Centre for Aboriginal Economic Policy Research, Australian National University, Canberra, pp. 53–84.

—2001 *Indigenous Families and the Welfare System: The Yuendumu Case Study, Stage Two*, CAEPR Discussion Paper no. 217, Centre for Aboriginal Economic Policy Research, Australian National University, Canberra.

— 2004, 'Red Bucket for the Red Cordial, Green Bucket for the Green Cordial: On the Logic and Logistics of Warlpiri Birthday Parties', *Australian Journal of Anthropology*, vol. 15, no. 1, pp. 12–22.

—2007, 'Boredom, Time, and Modernity: An Example from Aboriginal Australia', *American Anthropologist*, vol. 109, no. 2, pp. 307–17.

— 2008a, 'Perilous Laughter: Examples from Yuendumu', *Anthropological Forum*, vol.18, no.3, in press.

—2008b 'Sorry Business is Yapa Way: Warlpiri Mortuary Rituals as Embodied Practice, in K Glaskin, VK Burbank, Y Musharbash & M Tonkinson (eds), *Mortality, Mortuary Practices and Mourning in Indigenous Australia*, Ashgate, Aldershot, pp. 21–36.

— forthcoming, 'Warungka: On Becoming and Unbecoming a Warlpiri Person', in U Eickelkamp & P Fietz (eds), *Growing Up in Central Australia: Indigenous Experiences of Childhood, Youth and Transformations*.

—n.d., 'Sleep, Emotions and the Body: Reading Warlpiri Sleeping Arrangements as Corporeal Expressions of Emotions', paper delivered at University of Melbourne, May 2007.

Myers, FR 1976, ' "To have and to hold": A Study of Persistence and Change in Pintupi Social Life', PhD Thesis, Bryn Mawr College, Philadelphia.

—1979, 'Emotions and the Self', *Ethos*, vol. 7, pp. 343–70.

—1982, 'Always Ask: Resource Use and Land Ownership Among Pintupi Aborigines of the Australian Western Desert', in NM Williams & ES Hunn (eds), *Resource Managers: North American and Australian Hunter-Gatherers*, AAAS Selected Symposia Series, Washington, pp. 173–95.

—1986a, *Pintupi Country, Pintupi Self: Sentiment, Place and Politics among Western Desert Aborigines*, Smithsonian Institution Press, Washington.

—1986b, 'Reflections on a Meeting: Structure, Language, and the Polity in a Small-Scale Society', *American Ethnologist*, vol. 13, no. 3, pp. 430–47.

—1988a, 'Burning the Truck and Holding the Country: Property, Time and the Negotiation of Identity among Pintupi Aborigines', in T Ingold, D Riches & J Woodburn (eds), *Hunters and Gatherers: Property, Power and Ideology*, Berg, Oxford, pp. 52–74.

—1988b, 'The Logic and Meaning of Anger Among Pintupi Aborigines', *Man*, vol. 23, no. 4, pp. 589–610.

Netting RM, RR Wilk & EJ Arnould (eds) 1984, *Households: Comparative and Historical Studies of the Domestic Group*, University of California Press, Berkeley.

Oliver, P (ed.) 1975, *Shelter, Sign, and Symbol*, Barrie & Jenkins, London.

Pearson, N 2000, *Our Right to Take Responsibility*, Noel Pearson and Associates, Cairns.

Peterson, N 1969, 'Secular and Ritual Links: Two Basic and Opposed Principles of Australian Social Organization as Illustrated by Walbiri Ethnography', *Mankind*, vol. 7, pp. 27–35.

—1978, 'The Importance of Women in Determining the Composition of residential Groups in Aboriginal Australia', in F Gale (ed.), *Women's Role in Aboriginal Society*, AIAS, Canberra, pp. 16–27.

—1981, 'Art of the Desert', in C Cooper (ed.), *Aboriginal Australia*, Australian Gallery Directors Council, Sydney, pp. 43–51.

—1986, *Australian Territorial Organization: A Band Perspective*, University of Sydney, Sydney.

—1993, 'Demand Sharing: Reciprocity and the Pressure for Generosity among Foragers', *American Anthropologist*, vol. 95, no. 4, pp. 860–74.

—1997, 'Demand Sharing: Sociobiology and the Pressure for Generosity among Foragers', in F Merlan, J Morton & A Rumsey (eds), *Scholar and Sceptic. Australian Aboriginal Studies in Honour of LR Hiatt*, Aboriginal Studies Press, Canberra, pp. 171–90.

Peterson, N & W Sanders (eds) 1998, *Citizenship and Indigenous Australians: Changing Conceptions and Possibilities*, Cambridge University Press, Cambridge.

Piaget, J 1951, *The Child's Conception of the World*, Routledge & Kegan Paul, London.

—1954, *The Construction of Reality in the Child*, Basic Books, New York.

—1956, *The Child's Conception of Space*, Routledge & Kegan Paul, London.

Pine, F 1996, 'Naming the House and Naming the Land: Kinship and Social Groups in Highland Poland', *Journal of the Royal Anthropological Institute*, vol. 2, no. 3, pp. 443–59.

Poirier, S 2005, *A World of Relationships: Itineraries, Dreams and Events in the Australian Western Desert*, University of Toronto Press, Toronto.

Povinelli, EA 1993, '"Might Be Something": The Language of Indeterminacy in Australian Aboriginal Land Use', *Man*, vol. 28, no. 4, pp. 671–704.

Rapoport, A 1969, *House Form and Culture*, Prentice-Hall, Englewood Cliffs.

Read, P (ed.) 2000, *Settlement: A History of Australian Indigenous Housing*, Aboriginal Studies Press, Canberra.

Riches, D 1975, 'Cash, Credit and Gambling in a Modern Eskimo Economy: Speculations on Origins of Spheres of Economic Exchange', *Man*, vol. 10, no. 1, pp. 21–33.

Robben, ACGM 1989, 'Habits of the Home: Spatial Hegemony and the Structuration of House and Society in Brazil', *American Anthropologist*, vol. 91, no. 3, 570–88.

Ross, H 1987, *Just for Living. Aboriginal Perceptions of Housing in Northwest Australia*, Aboriginal Studies Press, Canberra.

Rosselin, C 1999, 'The Ins and Outs of the Hall: A Parisian Example', in I Cieraad (ed.), *At Home: An Anthropology of Domestic Space*, Syracuse University Press, Syracuse, pp. 53–9.

Rowse, T 1990, 'Enlisting the Warlpiri', *Continuum*, vol. 3, no. 2, pp. 174–215.

—1992, *Remote Possibilities: The Aboriginal Domain and the Administrative Imagination*, North Australia Research Unit, Australian National University, Darwin.

—1998, *White Flour, White Power: From Rations to Citizenship in Central Australia*, Cambridge University Press, Cambridge.

—2002, *Indigenous Futures: Choice and Development for Aboriginal and Islander Australia*, UNSW Press, Sydney.

Rybczynski, W 1987, *Home: A Short History of an Idea*, Penguin Books, New York.

Sackett, L 1977, 'Liquor and the Law: Wiluna, Western Australia', in RM Berndt (ed.), *Aborigines and Change: Australia in the '70s*, AIAS, Canberra, Canberra, pp. 90–9.

—1990, 'Welfare Colonialism: Developing Divisions at Wiluna', in R Tonkinson & M Howard (eds), *Going it Alone? Prospects for Aboriginal Autonomy*, Aboriginal Studies Press, Canberra, pp. 201–17.

Sahlins, MD 1972, *Stone Age Economics*, Aldine-Atherton, Chicago.

Sanders, W 1986, 'Access, Administration and Politics: The Australian Social Security System and Aborigines', PhD Thesis, Australian National University, Canberra.

—1990, 'Reconstructing Aboriginal Housing Policy for Remote Areas: How much Room to Manoeuvre?' *Australian Journal of Public Administration*, vol. 49, no. 1, pp. 38–50.

—1994, 'Social Security', in *The Encyclopaedia of Aboriginal Australia*, vol. 2, M–Z, DH Horton (ed.), Aboriginal Studies Press, Canberra, pp. 1002–3.

—2001, *Indigenous Australians and the Rules of the Social Security System: Universalism, Appropriateness, and Justice.* CAEPR Discussion Paper No. 212, Centre for Aboriginal Economic Policy Research, Australian National University, Canberra.

Sansom, B 1978, 'Sex, Age and Social Control in Mobs of the Darwin Hinterland', in JS La Fontaine (ed.), *Sex and Age as Principles of Social Differentiation*, Academic Press, London, pp. 89–108.

—1980, *The Camp at Wallaby Cross: Aboriginal Fringe Dwellers in Darwin*, AIAS, Canberra.

—1982, 'The Aboriginal Commonality', in RM Berndt (ed.), *Aboriginal Sites, Rights and Resource Development*, University of Western Australia Press, Nedlands, pp. 117–38.

—1988, 'A Grammar of Exchange', in I Keen (ed.), *Being Black: Aboriginal Cultures in 'Settled' Australia*, Aboriginal Studies Press, Canberra, pp. 159–77.

Schwab, RG 1995 *The Calculus of Reciprocity: Principles and Implications of Aboriginal Sharing*, CAEPR Discussion Paper no. 100, Centre for Aboriginal Economic Policy Research, Australian National University, Canberra.

Schwartz, B 1970, 'Notes on the Sociology of Sleep', *Sociological Quarterly*, vol. 11, no. 4, pp. 485–99.

Smith, DE 1991, *Toward an Aboriginal Household Expenditure Survey: Conceptual, Methodological and Cultural Considerations*, CAEPR Discussion Paper no. 10, Centre for Aboriginal Economic Policy Research, Australian National University, Canberra.

—1992 'The Cultural Appropriateness of Existing Survey Questions and Concepts', in JC Altman (ed.), *A National Survey of Indigenous Australians: Options and Implications*, CAEPR Research Monograph no. 3, Centre for Aboriginal Economic Policy Research, Australian National University, Canberra. pp. 68–85.

Smith, DE & A Daly 1996, *The Economic Status of Indigenous Australian Households: A Statistical and Ethnographic Analysis*, CAEPR Discussion Paper no. 109, Centre for Aboriginal Economic Policy Research, Australian National University, Canberra.

Steer, PJ 1996, *It Happened at Yuendumu*, Philip J Steer, Baxter.

Stojanowski, A n.d., 'Mt Theo Story 1999: Tribal Elders Working with Petrol Sniffers', unpublished paper, Yuendumu.

Stoller, P 1989, *The Taste of Ethnographic Things: The Senses in Anthropology*, University of Pennsylvania Press, Philadelphia.

Tambiah, SJ 1969, 'Animals are Good to Think and Good to Prohibit', *Ethnology*, vol. 8, no. 4., pp. 423–59.

Taylor, J 1996a, *Short-term Indigenous Population Mobility and Service Delivery*, CAEPR Discussion Paper no. 118, Centre for Aboriginal Economic Policy Research, Australian National University, Canberra.

—1996b, 'Surveying Mobile Populations: Lost Opportunity and Future Needs', in J C Altman & J Taylor (eds), *The 1994 National Aboriginal and Torres Strait Islander Survey: Findings and Future Prospects*, CAEPR Research Monograph no. 11, Centre for Aboriginal Economic Policy Research, Australian National University, Canberra, pp. 40–52.

Taylor, J & M Bell 1996, 'Population Mobility and Indigenous Peoples: The View from Australia', *International Journal of Population Geography*, vol. 2, no. 2, pp. 153–71.

Testart, A 1987 'Game Sharing Systems and Kinship Systems among Hunter-Gatherers', *Man*, vol. 22, no. 2, pp. 287–304.

Trigger, DS 1986, 'Blackfella and Whitefellas: The Conepts of Domain and Social Closure in the Analysis of Race-relations', *Mankind*, vol. 16, no. 2, pp. 99–117.

—1992, *'Whitefella Comin': Aboriginal Responses to Colonialism in Northern Australia*, Cambridge University Press, Cambridge.

Uhl, S 1989, 'Making the Bed: Creating the Home in Escalona, Andalusia', *Ethnology*, vol. 28, no. 2, pp. 151–66.

Verdon, M 1979, 'Sleeping Together: The Dynamics of Residence Among the Abutia Ewe', *Journal of Anthropological Research*, vol. 35, pp. 401–25.

Warlpiri Media Association 1998. 'Night Patrol' (Munga Wardingki-patu). video, 30 minutes. WMA, Yuendumu.

Watson, C 1997, 'Re-embodying Sand Drawing and Re-evaluating the Status of the Camp: The Practice and Iconography of Women's Public Sand Drawing' in Balgo, WA, *Australian Journal of Anthropology*, vol. 8, no.1, pp. 104–24.

Watts, L & SJ Fisher 2000, 'Pikilyi: Water Rights, Human Rights', MA Thesis, Charles Darwin University, Darwin.

White, I 1997, 'The Natives Live Well', in J Kuper (ed.), *The Anthropologist's Cookbook*, Kegan Paul, London, pp. 216–20.

Williams, NM & ES Hunn (eds) 1981, *Resource Managers: North American and Australian Hunter-Gatherers*, Westview Press for the American Association for the Advancement of Science, Boulder.

Woodburn, J 1982, 'Egalitarian Societies', *Man*, vol. 17, no. 3, pp. 431–51.

Yanagisako, SJ 1979, 'Family and Household: The Analysis of Domestic Groups', *Annual Review of Anthropology*, vol. 8, pp. 161–205.

Young, EA 1981, *Tribal Communities in Rural Areas*, Australian National University, Canberra.

Young, EA & K Doohan, 1989, *Mobility for Survival: A Process Analysis of Aboriginal Population Movement in Central Australia*, North Australia Research Unit, Australian National University, Darwin.

Yuendumu Health Profile 1999, 'Health Profile Database', unpublished community-based document, updated periodically, Yuendumu Clinic, Yuendumu.

INDEX